All books are subject to recall after two weeks

DATE DUE

GAYLORD   PRINTED IN U.S.A.

CHILDREN IN SOCIETY

This reader forms part of The Open University course *Working with children and families* and the selection of chapters is related to other materials available to students. The course aims to develop skills, values and knowledge for work with young children and families in a range of settings across health, education and social care. If you are interested in studying this course, or related courses, please write to the Information Officer, School of Health and Social Welfare, The Open University, Walton Hall, Milton Keynes, MK7 6AA, UK. Details can also be viewed on our web page http://www.open.ac.uk.

Opinions expressed in the reader are not necessarily those of the Course Team or of The Open University.

Also published in association with The Open University:

SOCIAL WORK: THEMES, ISSUES AND CRITICAL DEBATES
Edited by Robert Adams, Lena Dominelli and Malcolm Payne

COMMUNITY CARE: A READER Second Edition
Edited by Joanna Bornat, Julia Johnson, Charmaine Pereira, David Pilgrim and Fiona Williams

THE CHALLENGE OF PROMOTING HEALTH
Edited by Linda Jones and Moyra Sidell

DEBATES AND DILEMMAS IN PROMOTING HEALTH
Edited by Moyra Sidell, Linda Jones, Alyson Peberdy and Jeanne Katz

MENTAL HEALTH MATTERS
Edited by Tom Heller, Jill Reynolds, Roger Gomm, Rosemary Muston and Stephen Pattison

PROMOTING HEALTH
Edited by Jeanne Katz and Alyson Peberdy

SPEAKING OUR MINDS
Edited by Jim Read and Jill Reynolds

HEALTH PROMOTION
Angela Scriven and Judy Orme

HEALTH AND WELLBEING
Edited by Alan Beattie, Marjorie Gott, Linda Jones and Moyra Sidell

THE LAW AND SOCIAL WORK: CONTEMPORARY ISSUES FOR PRACTICE
Edited by Lesley-Anne Cull and Jeremy Roche

Children in Society

Contemporary Theory, Policy and Practice

Edited by

Pam Foley, Jeremy Roche and Stanley Tucker

at The Open University

palgrave in association with TheOpen University

Compilation, original and editorial material
© The Open University 2001

First published 2001 by
PALGRAVE
Houndmills, Basingstoke, Hampshire RG21 6XS and
175 Fifth Avenue, New York, N.Y. 10010
Companies and representatives throughout the world

PALGRAVE is the new global academic imprint of
St. Martin's Press LLC Scholarly and Reference Division and
Palgrave Publishers Ltd (formerly Macmillan Press Ltd).

ISBN 0–333–94588–3 hardcover
ISBN 0–333–94589–1 paperback

This book is printed on paper suitable for recycling and
made from fully managed and sustained forest sources.

A catalogue record for this book is available
from the British Library.

Library of Congress Cataloging-in-Publication Data

Children in society : contemporary theory, policy and practice /
edited by Pam Foley, Jeremy Roche, and Stanley Tucker.
    p. cm.
  Includes bibliographical references and index.
  ISBN 0–333–94588–3
  1. Child welfare. 2. Children—Services for. 3. Social work with
children. 4. Family social work. I. Foley, Pam. II. Roche, Jeremy.
III. Tucker, Stanley.

HV713 .C3965 2000
362.7—dc21   00–048344

Editing and origination by
Aardvark Editorial, Mendham, Suffolk

10 9   8   7   6   5   4   3   2   1
10 09 08 07 06 05 04 03 02 01

Printed and bound in Great Britain by
Creative Print & Design (Wales), Ebbw Vale

Contents

List of Contributors

David Berridge is Professor of Child and Family Welfare at the University of Luton and was previously Research Director of the National Children's Bureau. His main research interests include children in need, children living away from home (especially in residential and foster care) and services for minority ethnic groups. His most recent book, written with Isabelle Brodie, is *Children's Homes Revisited* (1998).

Dorit Braun is Chief Executive of Parentline Plus. Her career has spanned adult and community education, family education, child protection and work with health professionals. Parentline Plus works to shape and expand services and support to families. Parentline Plus, Unit 520 Highgate Studios, 53–57 Highgate Road, London NW5 1TL. Telephone: 020 7284 5500; 0808 800 2222 (helpline only).

Donald Christie is Senior Lecturer and coordinates Professional Studies in the Department of Educational Studies at the University of Strathclyde. A former primary teacher and a chartered psychologist, his research interests lie in children's social competence and in the processes of professional development.

Jenny Church is a Senior Lecturer in the Childhood Studies Division of the School of Community, Health and Social Studies at Anglia Polytechnic University. Her main interest is the nursing care of children and young people. Her MA research study and special interest area is partnership care with children and families.

Lesley-Anne Cull is a Lecturer in the School of Health and Social Welfare at The Open University. She is a practising barrister and has researched and written widely in the areas of child and family law.

Ronny Flynn is a black woman Lecturer in the School of Health and Social Welfare at The Open University. She previously worked at the University of Luton on 'Making Research Count', a national initiative to develop the promotion and use of research in social work practice.

Pam Foley is a Lecturer in the School of Health and Social Welfare at The Open University. Her doctorate focused on the medical discourses of childbirth, and her continuing research interests involve children's health and health care, and the sociology of the body.

Barry Goldson is a Lecturer in the Department of Sociology, Social Policy and Social Work Studies at the University of Liverpool. He has researched and published widely, and has recently edited two books on youth crime and youth justice: *Youth Justice: Contemporary Policy and Practice* (1999) and *The New Youth Justice* (2000).

Lorraine Green is a researcher and Lecturer in the School of Human and Health Sciences at the University of Huddersfield. Her research interests centre on children and childhood, power, gender, the body, sexual abuse, and sexuality and organizations.

Anne Griffiths is a Reader in the Faculty of Law at Edinburgh University. She is co-author of a book on Scots *Family Law* (1997) with Lilian Edwards. Her research on the Scottish children's hearing system in Glasgow forms part of a comparative research project on 'The Child's Voice in Legal Proceedings' funded by the Annenberg Foundation in the USA. She has done extensive research on family law in Botswana. Her current research interests revolve around gender, culture, and socio-legal approaches to working with families.

Catherine Humphreys is a Senior Lecturer in the Department of Social Policy and Social Work at the University of Warwick. Her research, writing and practice interests have been in the area of violence against women and children, and in the links between the abuse of women and the abuse of children. She has pursued these issues as a social work practitioner and researcher in both Australia and the UK.

Gordon Jack is Lecturer in Social Work and Head of the Department of Social Work and Probation Studies at The University of Exeter. Before joining the university in 1991 he had worked for fifteen years as a social worker and manager in child care services, with three local authority social services departments in the north of England.

Randy Frances Kandel is an Adjunct Associate Professor in the Department of Anthropology at John Jay College of Criminal Justice, City University of New York. She is also an attorney in private practice and Co-Director of Smart Decision, a mediation firm. Her present research interests lie at the intersection of family, law, and culture at the local, international and global level. Her most recent book is *Family Law: Essential Terms and Concepts*.

Gerison Lansdown was until June 2000 the director of the Children's Rights Alliance for England. She has written and lectured in the field of children's rights both nationally and internationally. She now works as an independent researcher and writer on children's rights. Children's Rights Alliance, Chancery House, 319 City Road, London, EC1V 1LJ. Telephone: 020 7278 8222.

Ruth Marchant works directly with disabled children and in service development and design. Ruth co-directs Triangle, which provides training and consultancy in relation to disabled children and child protection, communication and children's rights. Triangle also provides specialist outreach support for disabled children presenting severely challenging behaviour. Triangle Services for Children, Unit 310, 91 Western Road, Brighton, East Sussex, BN1 2NW. Telephone: 01273 241015 email: info@triangle-services.co.uk

Berry Mayall is Reader in Childhood Studies at the Social Science Research Unit, Institute of Education, London University. She has worked as a researcher on studies exploring parents' and children's everyday lives and their experiences and views of education, health and welfare services. Her current work is funded through an ESRC Research Fellowship. Recent publications include *Children's Childhoods* (1994), *Children, Health and the Social Order* (1996) and, edited with Leena Alanen, *Conceptualizing Child–Adult Relations* (2001).

Kwame Owusu-Bempah is Lecturer in Psychology at Leicester University School of Social Work. He has researched and published extensively in the areas of race, anti-discrimination and equal opportunities, and psycho-social development. His recent publications include *Psychology: Beyond Western Perspectives* (with Dennis Howitt; in press). His current research interests include the psycho-social development of separated children.

John Pinkerton is Senior Research Fellow at the Centre for Child Care Research, Queen's University Belfast. His areas of interest are care-leaving and family support. In a voluntary capacity he was a founder member of, and for over 10 years case work adviser to, a mutual support group for the families of children in care.

Martin Robb is a Lecturer in the School of Health and Social Welfare at The Open University. He previously worked in adult and community education, and his interests include parenting, gender and childcare, and children's cultural experience. He is co-editor of *Understanding Health and Social Care* (1998).

Marcus Roberts works in the Children's Legal Centre at the University of Essex. He is the co-editor of *Childright*, a journal dealing with law and policy affecting children and young people. He has written on a range of issues including child poverty, the division between parental and state responsibility for children, New Labour childcare policy and racism in schools. Children's Legal Centre, University of Essex, Wivenhoe Park, Colchester, C04 3SQ. Telephone: 01206 872466; 01206 873820 (advice line).

Jeremy Roche is a Lecturer in the School of Health and Social Welfare at The Open University. He writes and researches in the field of children's rights and the law, and is co-editor of *Youth in Society* (1997) and *Changing Experiences of Youth* (1997).

Sandy Ruxton is an independent policy researcher, specializing in children's rights. His work is well known at European level and includes *A Children's Policy for 21st Century Europe: First Steps* (1999) and *Children in Europe* (1996). His other policy and research interests include men and masculinities, asylum and migration, and economic, social and cultural rights. He lives and works in Oxford.

Wendy Stainton Rogers is a Senior Lecturer in the School of Health and Social Welfare at The Open University. Her work combines writing, research and teaching in the area of child welfare and children's rights with writing and research in the fields of theoretical and critical psychology.

Nigel Thomas is a Lecturer in Applied Social Studies at the University of Wales, Swansea. He was previously a social work practitioner and manager. His main research interests lie in the care of children and in children's participation in decision-making. He is the author of *Children, Family and the State; Decision Making and Participation* (2000).

Chris Thurston is a Senior Lecturer in the Childhood Studies Division of the School of Community, Health and Social Studies at Anglia Polytechnic University. Her interests as a qualified children's nurse include caring for children, sick and well, both in hospital and in the community. She has recently completed research exploring how different professional groups can learn from each other.

Stanley Tucker lectures in the School of Health and Social Welfare at The Open University. His interests include social policy, education and social care. He is co-editor of *Youth in Society* (1997) and *Changing Experiences of Youth* (1997).

Children in Society: Contemporary Theory, Policy and Practice

Pam Foley, Jeremy Roche and Stanley Tucker

In bringing together the collection of writings for this reader, we have been struck by the range and intensity of the changes impacting on children. These changes operate at the theoretical, political and practice levels, but the significance of these changes is deeply contested. There is a sense of a 'loss of childhood', children being denied their right to childhood. Children, it is suggested, are being exposed to the vagaries of the adult world too soon, and not only they, but all of 'us' – parents, other relatives and the wider society – are the losers (Miles, 1994). Childhood is seen as increasingly vulnerable to new forms of exploitation, particularly to an intense commercialization with children as consumers of technical goods, toys and leisure services, the mass media playing a crucial role (Kline, 1993) although others see the potential for positive developments in the new technologies (Buckingham, 2000). Some commentators refer to a 'crisis' in childhood, childhood being not so much celebrated (if it ever was) but perceived as a source of disruption, if not an actual threat. This 'crisis in childhood' is linked with a parallel 'crisis in the family' – the family is in decline, as is the experience and condition of childhood (Wyness, 2000); here the imagery is one of disintegration, or even disappearance, rather than change.

There are, however, other voices to be heard among the popular and academic debates surrounding contemporary childhood. For many, the condition of childhood is one of change, and change for the better. There has been an idealization of the past and nostalgia for a 'golden age' of childhood that gets in the way of how we think about children in society today. It gets in the way in three senses. First, it operates as an unreal standard against which certain aspects of modern childhood are measured. How can we evaluate what is going on today when the conventional history is one which denies the scale of the individual and institutional abuse of power that children faced on a daily basis? This is not to subscribe to de Mause's thesis that childhood is a 'nightmare from which we have only recently begun to awaken' (de Mause, 1976, p. 1). Rather it is to argue that the idealization of a past phase of childhood (and its corollary 'happy family life') very often leads to expressions of regret concerning the present.

Second, and somewhat paradoxically, despite the above comments we need to remind ourselves of what went on in relation to children: floggings at school and in the penal system, sustained pressure on unmarried mothers to separate them from their newborn babies, the forced emigration of children, the enforced isolation of hospitalized children, the discriminatory ethos of schools and the repression of girls' educational achievement. Third, the 'golden age' viewpoint obscures the plurality of childhoods in an unreal haze of uniformity. Children have always experienced very different childhoods according to their social and parental backgrounds.

Blowing away the mist of nostalgia that envelops childhoods of the past allows us to reflect upon why children were treated in these ways and why they appeared so uncontroversial at the time. Some things stand out – children have not been seen as people possessing rights, and the lives of adults and children have become more deeply demarcated, allowing adults to draw upon and act upon both old and new adult concepts of what children are and what childhood is. Children, separated into the social institution of childhood, have found adults deaf to their unhappiness, confusion and sense of loss.

This is the context within which we have brought together the contributions for this collection. Many commentators (and indeed many parents and others) have very different sets of ideas about children, childhood, family life and the direction in which society seems to be going. Here we wish to explore in more detail three interconnected aspects of the contemporary social positioning of children.

Welfare

Many of the changes over the past two decades have been based on a desire to promote and safeguard the welfare of children in society. In this sense there is a positive and well-meaning agenda. The welfare of children is of long-standing concern and continues to give rise to a range of policy and legislative innovation. However, the 'politics of childhood' are fluid, and action taken in the best interests of children can be controversial and contested.

In its second report on the United Nations Convention on the Rights of the Child (UNCRC) in 1999, the UK government pointed to a series of pieces of legislation and initiatives that had positively affected the lives of children. These included Quality Protects (a three-year programme to transform the public care system), Sure Start (a programme to support children aged 0–3 years old and their families in deprived areas), a National Childcare Strategy to ensure good-quality, affordable childcare for children aged 0–14, the allocation of money from the National Lottery funds for out-of-school clubs for children, and extra resources to reduce infant class sizes. Children living in poverty have also become a central focus of governmental concern and action. Yet what the listing of these initiatives does not capture is the difficulty of developing and delivering non-stigmatizing services for children and families. This entails strategies for both combating social exclusion and promoting social inclusion. The demand for social justice and the ending of all forms of discrimination is central. If all children are to have a sense of belonging and being valued, there needs to be a radical revision of service design and provision. So it is not just a question of new services, but also a matter of who played a role in the design and delivery of these services, how they are received, and whether all sections of the community experience a relevant and good-quality service.

Running alongside this fashioning of a new agenda for children is a demand for greater accountability from both government and service users. Government is concerned that new policy initiatives are delivered. Anxiety surrounding the care and education of children has resulted in a questioning of existing professional practice with children as well as the development of new policy initiatives. Anxieties about educational standards have led to radical changes in early years provision and an intensification of assessing standards of teaching and learning in schools. This is practically and symbolically marked by the role of OFSTED, which now plays a major inspection role in relation to primary and pre-school provision. The emphasis on regulation and inspection is in part fuelled by a revised view of the social and educational needs of children, by the desire to monitor and verify changes in policy as well as a mistrust of the practices of some who work with children (Tucker, 1999).

As noted above not all childhoods are the same: children are differently positioned in society. Race, class, religion, gender and disability shape their lives. These factors have an impact on their health, life chances and educational experience. Positive and proactive action to combat the prejudice and disrespectful treatment of all children, whether by adults or other children, is an integral part of the commitment to promote children's quality of life. For children in care, for whom the state is the parent, the consequences can be very negative; Quality Protects is concerned to improve the experience of being in care. In 1997 the Utting Report *People Like Us* (DoH/Welsh Office, 1997) made a number of recommendations to improve the procedures for the recruitment of personnel in the childcare field. The resulting legislation, such as the Protection of Children Act 1999, raises serious civil liberties issues, for example how people end up on the list of persons whom it will be a criminal offence to employ as a carer. This legislation is justified on the basis of the widespread and legitimate concern about organized child abuse. The Waterhouse Report (DoH/Welsh Office, 2000) has served to confirm the view that such legislative action is needed. Running through much of this concern about the welfare of children is, however, another persistent 'story': children in situations of vulnerability were neither listened to nor believed when they tried to tell adults about the abuse being perpetrated. This links with the second aspect of the changing world of childhood – the emergence of children's rights. Are children's rights the antidote for the 'culture of disrespect' surrounding children?

Children's rights

The children's rights movement may be seen as a positive sign, a sign of progress rather than evidence of the decline of childhood and family life. The children's rights movement received a boost with the UK government's signing and ratification of the UNCRC in 1991 despite continued parental nervousness about the idea of children's rights. It came into force in the UK in January 1992. All the rights contained in the UNCRC are to be enjoyed without discrimination of any kind. Many organizations that work with children now routinely refer to the UNCRC in their campaigning and draw on particular provisions of the UNCRC to support their claims. Others, for example Children's Express and Article 12, have as their central aim the increased participation of children and young people in society. The UNCRC is a wide-ranging document that straddles conventional concerns about the welfare of children and child protection as well as giving voice to citizenship claims on behalf of children. In this reader a number of chapters refer to Article 12 of the UNCRC. This provides that:

1   States Parties shall assure to the child who is capable of forming his or her own views the right to express those views freely in all matters affecting the child, the views of the child being given due weight in accordance with the age and maturity of the child.

2   For this purpose, the child shall in particular be provided the opportunity to be heard in any judicial and administrative proceedings affecting the child, either directly, or through a representative or an appropriate body, in a manner consistent with the procedural rules of national law.

Yet children have more and fewer rights than adults. Unlike adults they do not have the right to vote, to make contracts and to see certain categories of film. This is justified on the basis that children either do not yet have the competence to make certain kinds of decision or, because of their vulnerability, need to be protected from particular images and knowledge. The special rights they enjoy are geared towards their protection rather than their social participation. The impact of the UNCRC, with its emphasis on participation rights, coinciding with the persistent message from practice that children in the main have not been listened to or taken seriously could be very substantial. So while many of the rights contained in the UNCRC are not controversial as they are based on traditional concerns with the welfare and protection of children, the participation or citizenship rights of the UNCRC are qualitatively different. Action supposedly taken in the child's best interests that has no regard for what that child thinks or feels will be contrary to the UNCRC. So will action that breaches the child's right to information and privacy. It is these rights which challenge the traditional conceptions of what it is to be a child.

Children in social context

Third, the social positioning of children is inextricably linked with wider social changes associated with the roles of men and women, families and the state. Major changes to the form and composition of families in Western Europe and the US, notably their decreasing size and the increasing involvement of women in the workforce, necessarily impact upon the lives of children. Children, however, remain largely understood as dependent individuals who should develop primarily within a family structure. Families, themselves structured by external material and cultural forces, both subtlety and directly shape children's lives. Similarly childcare and health care settings, schools and courts can all influence the lives of children. Each setting draws upon wider political, philosophical, pedagogical and psychological debates and ideas about children and works to produce outcomes largely decided upon by adults.

Woven through adult ideas about children and childhood are children's own ideas, needs, resources and interests (which may or may not be compatible with those of other recognizable social groups). Children, like other social groups, categories and classes, are exposed to societal forces. At the same time children and childhood are influenced in particular ways, exactly as other social groups, in accordance with the group's status, the extent to which the group is valued and the relative strengths of other social groupings (Qvortrup *et al.,* 1994). Children participate in the changing social world, both within and outside the family; while some babies and very young children now spend large amounts of their time in an extra-familial setting, older children may now find their public spaces (for example, streets) shrinking. In the variety of social settings children experience, they may find their competence unacknowledged and their viewpoints overlooked or ignored; they are understood to be unreliable commentators on their own lives. Contemporary children move through their childhoods, working with and against ingrained expectations, to create their own personal and collective social space within the confines of adult culture.

In this introduction we have not been concerned to review each chapter or summarize the arguments contained therein. Rather, we have focused on the key policy developments and debates surrounding childhood. This has entailed reflecting on the contested nature of childhood and the increasing regulation of children's lives. The questions that we hope we have succeeded in raising here concern the place of children and childhood in our society, the boundary between adulthood and childhood, and what we and children want now and in the future. To enable us, and you the reader, to reflect upon these questions, we have drawn together contributions that reflect a diversity of perspectives and fields of work connected with ways of thinking about and working with children.

Part I

Contemporary Childhoods

1

The Development of Child Health and Welfare Services in England (1900–1948)

Pam Foley

Children's health and welfare services were among the earliest health and welfare provision in England and were widespread before the National Health Service was established in 1948. Health and welfare services are an integral part of human societies and cultures. As such, health and welfare professions and services both shape and are shaped by re-visionings, theories and understandings of children and childhood as they emerge. Historical analysis reveals how social, cultural and economic circumstances make possible the emergence and reception of certain ideas about children and childhoods. This may lead us to see our current services as being similarly constructed. It may also lead to a recognition of how ideas prevalent in the past remain rooted and alive in our health and welfare services today. This chapter aims to provide a brief historical overview of the foundations and development of health and welfare services for children during the first half of the twentieth century and suggests how they made a major contribution to the social identity of the child.

A national resource

Early breaches of the previously private world of the home and family had been accomplished by key agencies in child protection such as the National Society for the Prevention of Cruelty to Children (NSPCC) in the late nineteenth century. As the twentieth century opened, however, political and social preoccupations in the countries of Western Europe were dominated by concerns for the quality of their respective populations. In England, the extent of poor health among adult men, brought to light by

Boer War (1899–1902) recruitment, was identified both as an urgent national problem and as being rooted in their poor health as children (Hendrick, 1994). Widespread ill-health, disability and early deaths among babies and children were in evidence from both the perinatal and the infant mortality rate, which remained high while the birth rate and adult death rate were falling (Dwork, 1987). The question of the physical state of the nation, including that of the infant and child population, was first analysed by the Interdepartmental Committee on Physical Deterioration in 1904, and a deluge of government reports were to follow – five further reports between 1910 and 1916 (Lewis, 1984).

While women of all classes were encouraged to see their duty and reward in bearing and raising healthy children, it was particularly working class mothers who now became identified as being responsible for the social problem of weak and sickly children (Lewis, 1984). Highly influential reports by George Newman, the Chief Medical Officer to the Board of Education (and subsequently Chief Medical Officer to the Ministry of Health when it was set up in 1920) blamed women for the bad management of their households, their ignorance concerning care of children and their lack of a proper sense of maternal obligation, particularly lacking, he thought, in women working outside the home (Hendrick, 1994). During his long period of influence, Newman was repeatedly to recommend the education of working class women to raise the standard of domestic competence and to install the proper ideals of motherhood and home life in British girls and women. In reiterating these convictions he, and others, ignored statistical evidence available at the time showing infant mortality to be primarily a feature of inner city slums (Lewis, 1984). The education of mothers as a solution to the problem of children's ill-health became a firmly rooted idea.

The socialization of girls into particular class and gender roles through Edwardian elementary schools was well underway by the early decades of the twentieth century (Dyhouse, 1981). For small girls the curriculum was heavily weighted towards needlework, laundry, cookery and housewifery. The ideas of service and self-sacrifice common to concepts of both middle and working class girlhood and womanhood had become a central tenet of their state education. Domestic training posing as education was now extended further to alleviate the problem seemingly posed by working class mothers. For adult women the first 'Schools for Mothers' appeared, opening in St Pancras in 1907, and by 1913 150 such schools were in operation, teaching 'mothercraft' to mothers (Dwork, 1987). The response to these education schemes from those at whom they were aimed, working class women, appears to have been positive. Women saw themselves as the key to child health and welfare, and expressed their appreciation of any and all information that the clinics could provide (Llewellyn Davies, 1915).

Charitable work – visiting the poor – had been a powerful tradition for women of the Victorian and Edwardian period. The plethora of parish and charity organizations, as well as individual charitable work, framed much of middle class women's experience of their local community. Such activities conformed to the prevailing social convention that women and girls of all classes should serve others. Middle class visitors to working class homes gave sanitary and moral advice, advice likely to be framed in terms of individual family responsibility and the appropriate economic and social roles of men and women (Lewis, 1984). One such organization, the Ladies' Sanitary Reform Association, later renamed the Ladies' Health Society, had started in 1862 and was an early forerunner of what was to become health visiting (Hendrick, 1994).

The newly emerging idea of babies and children as a national resource – the nation's future, a national investment – led to a marked change in the level of influence the government was now prepared to try to exert upon families. Before the traditional network of charity visiting could become a regulated, locally coordinated system of clinics and health visitors, certain key pieces of legislation and reorganization had to be put into place. By 1905 there were around 50 towns in which the local authorities had appointed women as paid health visitors in addition to voluntary visitors. The Notification of Births Act (1907) (subsequently made compulsory in 1915) required that the local Medical Officer of Health be informed of every birth within 36 hours of the baby being born (Dwork, 1987). Midwives were also to be regulated, brought under the supervision of local authorities by the Midwives Act 1902 (their training, registration and supervision being further extended through successive Acts between 1902 and 1936). The names and addresses of all families with newborn babies could now be accessed and formed the basis for the system of both clinics (known as Infant Welfare Centres) where children could be weighed and examined, and of home visiting, where young children could be supervised until they went to school.

The need to hire women to carry out infant welfare work created the health visitor as a new category of specialized worker, drawing women from the voluntary sector to become paid professionals working as part of the public health system. In 1914 the Local Government Board offered grants to local authorities to cover expenditure for maternity and child welfare work, including salaries for health visitors (Dwork, 1987). The number of local authority health visitors increased from 600 in 1914 to 2,577 in 1918, and that of the maternity and child welfare centres from 650 in 1915 to 1,278 in 1918 (Hendrick, 1994). The Maternity and Child Welfare Act of 1918 consolidated this rapid growth in infant welfare work, and it became compulsory for local authorities to establish maternity and child welfare centres. These changes to the procedures surrounding childbirth made possible the official and medical surveillance of childbirth and infant care on a national scale. Throughout the 1920s and 30s local authorities assumed a patchy but sustained role in the provision of maternity services and health examinations for pre-school-children. However, widespread though clinics were, treatment, as opposed to examination, was much less accessible as most women and children, unlike insured working men, were still unable to get access to free medical care.

Meals, milk and medicine at school

By the beginning of the twentieth century universal compulsory education had begun to have a transformative effect on ways in which childhood was perceived and experienced. Schools meant children becoming increasingly economically inactive members of their families, spending most of their days in a world separate from adults. And in the elementary schools of late Victorian and Edwardian England, the ill-fed, poorly clothed, mentally and physically disabled children of the working class had become conspicuous. Children had become visible and accessible in new ways.

While schools separated the child's world from that of the adult's, they were also required to form a bridge between those two worlds by instructing children in the knowledge and competencies they were seen to lack. Educating sick and hungry children was, however, proving to be extremely difficult, if not impossible, as teachers repeatedly pointed out (Horn, 1989). The Education (Provision of Meals) Act 1906 gave permission to local authorities to feed some of their school-age children if they saw fit (a further Parliamentary Act in 1914 made this compulsory, subject to a means test) (Morton, 1997).

In the following decades the issue of free school meals for malnourished children continued to be fiercely debated. Children's malnutrition could be attributed to either unemployment or low wages, or, as was repeatedly claimed by official reports, the poor organization of household budgets and maternal ignorance of the nutritional value of certain foods (Hendrick, 1994). Subsidized milk for schoolchildren, introduced by the Milk in Schools Act of 1934 (Morton, 1997), appeared to be an attractive (especially to dairy farmers) if partial solution to the continuing problem of schoolchildren who showed signs of malnutrition. Ultimately, the school meals and milk services were used not as a measure to tackle the poor general level of child health but more prosaically to enable children to be educated (Hendrick, 1994). Not until the Education Act of 1944 did it become a statutory duty for LEAs to provide school meals for all primary and secondary schoolchildren who wanted them, and milk became free for schoolchildren from 1946 onwards (Morton, 1997).

The School Medical Service was established by the Education (Administrative Provisions) Act 1907 and was placed under the responsibility of the medical branch of the Board of Education, alongside the provision of special education for handicapped children and the Maternity and Infant welfare service (until all were transferred to the Ministry of Health when it was set up in 1919) (Morton, 1997). School Medical Officers carried out an examination of all children on entry into school and re-inspected children at regular intervals. They also examined school surroundings, visited during outbreaks of infectious diseases and followed up absentees said to be ill (Hendrick, 1994). Like the Infant Welfare Clinics, school medical inspections did not automatically lead to free treatment, but children and their families were referred to private practitioners, voluntary hospitals or charities. Free treatment was occasionally available, for example at the Deptford Children's Health Centre set up in 1910 by the educational pioneer Margaret McMillan and her sister, which received a grant from the London County Council (Horn, 1989).

In the inter-war period school environments deteriorated, rural schools already being particularly dilapidated with poorly lit, poorly heated and ventilated classrooms and primitive sanitary arrangements (Horn, 1989). Spending on children through their schools or through direct state aid remained restricted by financial retrenchment associated with the inter-war economic depression. Campaigners such as Eleanor Rathbone argued that a state financial contribution to the family would give recognition to women as mothers and pave the way for equal pay for women workers, but the British trade union movement, suspicious of undermining the 'family wage' for the male wage earner, did not support direct financial aid for children (Macnicol, 1992). Family allowances were eventually introduced in 1945 as part of the reorganization of Britain's social security system.

Like the Infant Welfare Clinics, the School Medical Service was quite different in nature from anything that had gone before. It examined and monitored all children in the public elementary schools, the healthy and the unhealthy alike. As such, this new form of health care could, as the first annual report of the Chief Medical Officer made clear, collect and report information about children. It undertook to provide educational authorities with information. In the Chief Medical Officer to the Board of Education's words in 1908, this information 'would guide education authorities in relation to physical and mental development of children during school life' (Van der Eyken, 1973, p. 148). How children's lives were lived, within the school context, would contribute to a body of knowledge about their physical and mental development. Measuring, weighing and examining children in clinics enabled the collection of mass records and measurements against which an individual child could be judged. As clinics diverged from the treatment of the sick to the monitoring of the entire child population, children could be more closely identified with clinical descriptions of their bodies (Armstrong, 1995). Clinical descriptions are understood as 'scientific', and the 'scientific' process is likely to present itself as uncovering 'natural' and 'universal' processes by which a child becomes an adult (Burman, 1994). Clinics thus represented children as universal and timeless expressions of certain biological selves rather than as people whose abilities are constructed in particular ways in accordance with particular times and particular cultures.

Without a corresponding growth in free health care, the impact of community and school clinics on child health would have remained limited, but these early clinics provided the foundation of the children's health and welfare services – a description of the 'normal' child. The clinics, the people who worked there, gathered information on what a normal child looked like, did and said, and thereby detected deviations from the norm. Clinics, examining, measuring, weighing and recording children, enabled the development of systems of regulation and intervention on which the health and welfare services could be built. And once clinics had begun to describe the 'normal' body of a child, it was not too difficult to begin also to describe the 'normal' mind of a child. If the nation needed children with healthy bodies, it also needed children with healthy minds; and this again was a function clinics could evolve to address.

Medicine for minds

Psychology, establishing itself in post-First World War universities, had, as one of its primary investigations the mind of the child. The 'new psychology' movement began with the opening of the Tavistock Clinic in 1920. Other clinics included Margaret Lowenfield's Children's Clinic in West London, which became the Institute of Child Psychology. A steady growth of 'child guidance clinics' followed, and their central coordinating body, the Child Guidance Council, was established in 1927. The number of clinics grew steadily through the 1920s and 30s to reach 54 by 1938 (Hendrick, 1994). Children were referred by parents, teachers, probation officers, social agencies, School Medical Officers or the courts, most referrals being for forms of behaviour that brought the child into conflict with adults (Hendrick, 1994). These clinics enabled the evolution of key workers such as psychiatrists, psychiatric social workers and educational psychologists.

Although differing in some aspects, psychological clinics for children shared an approach that visualized behavioural problems in terms of deeper aspects of children's mentality and emotion, the treatment of the child lying primarily in the investigation of the family and the relationships within it (Hendrick, 1994). By envisaging certain behaviours as 'maladjustments', child guidance not only offered to readjust children, but also emphasized that children's 'abnormal' or antisocial behaviour, as well as maladjustments of all forms, could be seen as a predictor of problems to come (Rose, 1985). As children became drawn into and defined by the psycho-medical world, the mind of the child came to be mapped into 'natural' developmental stages, just as its body had been. As development became defined through observation and measurement, such statements become normative rather than descriptive. In addition, as the focus shifted from the body of the child to the mind, the classificatory and regulatory framework of clinics expanded. The psycho-medical 'gaze' that now fell upon child and her or his family had broadened considerably.

Although the number of children treated in these clinics was small, psychological ideas about children and childhood, especially claims to understand the nature of mental development, took root in education, health and welfare, and seeped out to influence the wider cultural understandings of children and 'childhood'. During the 1930s the Child Guidance Council gave lectures to teacher training colleges and children's agencies such as the National Children's Homes and Barnardo's, wrote pamphlets for health and social care workers, published articles in popular magazines and gave talks on the radio (Hendrick, 1994). It offered advice on children in hospital, emotional growth and development, play and leisure, the causation of difficult behaviour, physical health and development and the re-education of young offenders. Individuals such as the prominent educationalist and psychologist Susan Isaacs gave their views on the healthy mental and moral growth of young children to government bodies (Van der Eyken, 1973). Isaacs became head of the London Institute for Education, and her book for parents, *The Nursery Years*, was so widely read that it was reprinted four times in the inter-war period (Urwin and Sharland, 1992).

Also during the 1930s local education authorities appointed psychologists and others with psychological training to work in teacher training colleges and educational administration. Mental tests devised by psychologists were used not only to determine the intelligence of schoolchildren and thereby decide whether they needed special schooling, but also to enable the selection of children moving from primary to either academic or non-academic secondary schools. The development of psychological theories also had a major impact on inter-war education theory and practice. Progressive educational ideas on child-centred learning were given intellectual weight by psychological theories and challenged established educational practices. Pioneers of psychoanalytic education of the times included Homer Lane, at whose co-educational school (the Little Commonwealth) for 'delinquent' adolescents, rules and codes of behaviour were self-regulated and A.S. Neill's Summerhill school, where learning was entirely self-directed (Van der Eyken, 1973).

At the end of the 1930s another experience linked to another war, the evacuation of children, was again to influence social policy. Press coverage of the physical and emotional state of many evacuees reflected the horrified public reaction to these underfed, sickly and lice-ridden urban children (Lowe, 1992). This national experience may have contributed to the growing pressure for the wider provision of help for deprived children after the war, but the evacuation experience was perhaps less the beginning of shared adversity leading to a greater open-ness to ideas of collectivism than an uncomfortable confirmation of the social divide (Lowe, 1992) – and less a question of the pricking of the middle class conscience than a further politicization of the working class families whose children experienced evacuation.

Post-war educational, social and health care legislation (the Education Act 1944, the Children Act 1948 and the NHS Act 1948) were evidence of the change to social policy regarding children that had taken place in the previous few decades. With the Education Act of 1944, school meals became universally available, medical and dental inspections led to free treatment, and other therapies such as speech therapy, audiometry, child guidance clinics and 'special education' became fully available. The Children Act 1948 set up children's departments in local authorities for the first time. Welfare principles of surveillance, prevention, intervention and treatment of the physical and psychological child within both the family and the school had been established. A new understanding of the needs of particular children and families had become widely accepted in government departments, among professionals working with children and in British culture generally. The role adopted by the post-war state was not an assumption of direct responsibility for child health and welfare but its support within families, through education, housing, health and social services.

Conclusion

Between 1900 and 1948 health and welfare services for children steadily propelled themselves up the social and political agenda. Particular social and historical conditions made possible the emergence and reception of certain ideas. The child health and welfare movement of the first half of the twentieth century acted as a means of expressing concern for the welfare of other people's children, a way of expressing the concept that children are valuable not simply to their parents, but also to the wider society. And what began with the need to improve the nation's physical health fed into a much more ambitious aim to assist social progress through focusing on the physical, emotional and mental health of children. Clinics directed at the child population appeared to offer an opportunity to deal with physical and mental ill-health before it reached adult proportions with a greater potential seriously to damage the wider community. By offering a means of targeting limited intervention by identifying particular children and particular families that needed help, clinics positioned themselves as an essential part of policies that had to address the health aspects of poverty and deprivation. Such an approach offered a manageable solution, focused on individual families, to social and economic problems. Just as importantly, clinics simultaneously provided information about children, contributing to what became widely understood of what constitutes a 'normal' child and a 'normal' childhood, and what could and should be done for an atypical child.

2

The Changing Experience of Childhood

Martin Robb

The aim of this chapter is to look behind the media headlines and popular assumptions, and to examine the evidence for change in the experience of childhood.

Four key areas of change in childhood experience are examined: material circumstances, health, education, and play and leisure. These areas have been selected partly because they illustrate some of the important debates about children's changing experience and partly because other aspects, albeit just as important, are covered in other chapters in this book.

Material circumstances

There is a popular assumption that children's lives are better in material terms than they were a generation or two ago. There is a general sense that most children today are better housed, clothed and fed, live in warmer and more comfortable homes, have more material possessions and enjoy greater access to opportunities for leisure and entertainment than in the past. The existence of specialist toy and clothing stores for children and the enormous investment in marketing goods specifically aimed at children would seem to provide evidence for these popular beliefs.

While living standards for a significant section of the population have risen in the past 30 years, there is, however, also evidence that a large number of children are not benefiting from these changes. A number of research studies have shown an *increase* in child poverty in recent decades. Bradshaw (1990), for example, found that child poverty more than doubled during the 1980s, resulting in more than one in four children living below the poverty line.

Other studies have drawn attention to the increasing link between social class and infant mortality during this period, as well as to the significantly higher number of children from minority ethnic groups living in poverty (e.g. Kumar, 1993). Similarly, Oppenheim and Lister draw on the Department of Social Security (DSS) figures to show that 'children from black and minority ethnic groups are at greater risk of poverty than white children' (Oppenheim and Lister, 1996, p. 127). At the time of writing the Labour government has pledged to introduce measures that will eliminate child poverty in the UK. It remains to be seen how far any measures taken will reverse the dramatic growth in inequality since the 1970s.

What the studies summarized here demonstrate is that the *experience* of material change has been different (and unequal) for children from different social groups. All children are, however, exposed to the rise in material expectations that has run alongside these changes. Research has shown that there is some truth in the commonplace story that children in the UK now have higher material expectations than in the past (Ashworth *et al.*, 1994). Children today are under an increased peer pressure to display their ownership of consumer goods, including the latest fashions in clothing.

Change of this nature has led to a stereotyped picture of modern children as spoilt and over-materialistic. Ashworth and his fellow researchers argue, however, that it would be wrong to blame children themselves for this state of affairs:

> As adults we surround ourselves with possessions. Ownership of the latest car, washing machine and compact disc player seem for many of us to be badges of social acceptability which we display to the outside world and by which we judge others. In 1990s Britain we are what we own. At the same time, however, we criticize children for displaying the same acquisitive tendencies. Their demands for the latest computer game, designer training shoes and video machines (VCRs) are said to indicate an unhealthy materialism which, in turn, is blamed for the supposed failings of the younger generation. (Ashworth and Walker, 1994, p. 23)

If as adults we use possessions to define our sense of identity, we can hardly blame children for doing the same. At the same time we need to acknowledge the part played by the retail and entertainment industries in creating these pressures on children and families.

Health

Another common assumption about the change in childhood experience is that children today are healthier than children in the past. After 50 years of the National Health Service and major advances in medicine and patient care, there is a general belief that children have a better chance of survival and of living a healthy life than their parents and grandparents.

Surveying trends in children's health in the 30 years from 1963 to 1993, Woodroffe and Glickmann found that infant mortality had fallen by 65 per cent in this period and that there had been a major reduction in neonatal mortality. There had also been a steep decline in the number of children born with congenital abnormalities such as spina bifida, largely because of improvements in antenatal screening and improved nutrition (Woodroffe and Glickmann, 1993).

Once again, however, these improvements have not affected all groups equally. The same researchers cite a catalogue of examples to show that the experience of poverty increases the risks to a child's health. Children in poorer families are four times more likely to die from injuries, the most common cause of death in later childhood, than are children from professional families. The difference is even greater for deaths in traffic accidents and fires: poorer families are less likely to have a car, a safe play area or safe heating (Woodroffe and Glickmann, 1993). There are also indications that some aspects of children's health may have worsened in recent years. A generation ago childhood asthma was relatively rare: now the sight of children bringing inhalers to school or nursery is commonplace. As Rosenbaum reports, the number of hospital admissions for childhood asthma increased fivefold from 1979 to 1989: 'it is the most common chronic disease of childhood' (Rosenbaum, 1993, p. 32). There is also a concern that children's health may be at risk from a deterioration in their diet, despite greater economic prosperity and the availability of a wider variety of food than a generation ago.

It is, however, important to see these apparent changes in context. Mayall speculates on the impact on nutritional standards of such political measures as devolving responsibility for school meals to local authorities, which in turn often subcontract to outside contractors (Mayall, 1996). As Church and Doyle state, the food industry spends £500 million per year marketing food and soft drinks (100 times more than the government-funded Health Education Authority has to spend on healthy eating advice). In an increasingly sophisticated and cut-throat marketplace, some food manufacturers are now producing classroom materials that Church and Doyle claim are 'often no more than plugs for products' (Church and Doyle, 1997, p. 3).

Education

Children in the UK spend most of their waking hours in formal education. In the words of one commentator, 'Compulsory education is one of the defining characteristics of modern childhood' (Wagg, 1996, p. 8). Today more children continue their formal education after 16 years of age than ever before, and at the other end of the age spectrum there are moves to encourage an earlier entry into formal education, with an expansion of nursery education and a wider range of pre-school provision. In many ways access to educational opportunities has increased for most children in this period. In theory, there is now free, universal schooling available to all children between the ages of 5 and 16. The abolition of selection at 11 in many parts of the UK means that there is something approaching formal equality of provision at secondary level. The number of students in higher education expanded rapidly during the 1980s and 90s, so that going to university has ceased to be seen as the privilege of an elite and has become an expectation for a substantial number of children.

At the same time there have been growing concerns about aspects of schooling in Britain, from different points of view. Wagg charts the development since the 1970s of a discourse about a supposed decline in educational standards, often blamed on a move away from formal methods and the dominance of child-centred approaches rooted in the 1960s (Wagg, 1996). A succession of reports has claimed that a large number of children are leaving school without adequate skills in literacy and numeracy, unprepared for employment and adult life. Conservative governments in the 1980s responded to these concerns by introducing a range of educational reforms, including a national curriculum, increased testing, the publication of league tables and greater parental choice. Under the Labour government elected in 1997, the emphasis on standards and accountability has continued with the introduction of compulsory literacy and numeracy hours in primary schools.

Although there is some evidence that such reforms have improved standards, there have also been criticisms that they reduce children's opportunities to develop personal, social and creative abilities. There is also a concern that increased testing and a greater emphasis on homework have placed new pressures on children at the same time as squeezing out time for play and other out-of-school activities. The number of school exclusions has increased, largely as a result of greater competition between schools over performance tables, and there is evidence that particular groups, such as African-Caribbean children, are suffering disproportionately.

Although girls' performance has improved, there are still concerns about inequalities of achievement. There are newer fears that boys are becoming increasingly alienated from formal education, while there is evidence of persistent underachievement by children from some minority ethnic groups, gypsy and traveller children and children who are in care.

Play and leisure

There is some evidence that children's independent mobility outside the home has decreased in recent years. In 1993 Rosenbaum claimed there was a link between increasing traffic volume and children's ability to get around by themselves:

> In the past 20 years, a period during which traffic levels have nearly doubled, children's independent mobility has declined dramatically... Whereas in 1971 86 per cent of primary school pupils aged seven to eleven went to school by themselves, in 1990 this only applied to 29 per cent. Similarly in 1971 63 per cent of these pupils were allowed to go to other places by themselves, but in 1990 this had dropped to 37 per cent... The main reason given by parents for restricting their children's freedom of movement was danger from traffic. In the light of these figures it is not surprising that 77 per cent of parents stated that they had more opportunity to go out alone as children compared to children today. (Rosenbaum, 1993, p. 59)

Ironically, an increase in children being taken to school and elsewhere by their parents itself leads to an increase in traffic on the road, which in turn increases fears for children's safety. Although there is no hard evidence, it would be reasonable to assume that fear of crime and the tide of panic caused by paedophile scandals has also increased parents' concerns about allowing their children to go out unaccompanied. It is difficult to determine whether the risk of traffic accidents and violent crime towards children has increased or whether it is simply the fear of these things, fuelled by media coverage, that has intensified. Either way, the result is the same: parents who are too afraid to let their children out alone and children who are increasingly confined to their own homes and the immediate surrounding area.

Davis and Jones carried out a study of children's access to the local environment in one urban area. They found a rather higher level of independent mobility than that reported by Rosenbaum, particularly among older children. On the basis of their research, however, they conclude that children have effectively been marginalized in many urban environments:

> The conceptualisation of children in transport and environmental planning as 'a problem' has resulted in an urban environment which is extremely hostile to their needs and aspirations. As problems children are tidied away behind railings, in parks, in gardens and – best of all – indoors. Outdoors, road safety advice is that children should be accompanied by responsible adults, should learn about traffic and stranger danger and should be restricted in their independent access and mobility. (Davis and Jones, 1997, pp. 350–1)

Particular groups of children may be more affected than others by the 'fear of crime'. Children from minority ethnic groups, for example, may be inhibited from wandering far from home by their own or their parents' fears of racial harassment.

If children are less free to play outside the home than before, there are also claims that they do not have adequate access to play facilities. Claiming to draw on evidence from a number of surveys, Lubelska asserts that there is:

> plenty of evidence of increasing numbers of children with nowhere to go after school; unacceptably high levels of child pedestrian road accidents; rising levels of juvenile crime and unhealthy children. Evidence too, of many children with nowhere to play including children in flats with no gardens and children living by busy roads, children restricted by the dangers in the countryside and by unsafe playgrounds and neighbourhoods. (Lubelska, 1993, p. 9)

Set against this background it is hardly surprising that children should be spending more time making use of home-based entertainment such as television and computers.

At the same time we need to consider the change in children's experience in the context of a change in the life of the population as a whole. For adults as well as children, the family home has become much more of a focus for leisure and entertainment than it was 30 years ago. Most homes are now warmer, more comfortable and more inviting places than they were in the past. Technological advances and the expansion of the consumer society have led to the almost universal ownership of a television, many families owning a second or third set, and figures for the ownership of video recorders, audio equipment and computers increasing all the time. Just as importantly, cultural changes mean that the mass media have become much more central to the way in which we live our lives. Increasingly, our access to news and opinion, sport and entertainment is mediated by television in particular. It is more and more difficult to shut out the mass media and at the same time remain an active participant in a fast-changing social world.

Children are not excluded from this process. Ashworth and Walker asked children in their sample about their own personal ownership of electrical goods:

> Sixty-eight per cent said they had some audio equipment, 62 per cent a computer or games machine of some kind, 52 per cent a television and 21 per cent a video… children's access to electrical consumer goods differed little between the more affluent and less affluent areas. (Ashworth and Walker, 1994, p. 25)

Once again it seems unfair to condemn children as acquisitive or media obsessed if they see adults' lives increasingly dominated by these forms of entertainment and if participation in a wider social world depends on access to the media. Nevertheless, children's use of television and more recently of computer games has been the focus of much fevered debate, amounting at times to a full-scale moral panic, in recent years. As one researcher says:

> All kinds of claims are made daily about the 'effects' of television on children, most usually deleterious effects. Many writings call on 'research evidence' to declare, variously, that watching television makes children fat, strains their eyes, or stops them reading. At best, research gives us half-truths, or generalized approximations of what happens in children's lives, particularly those elements of children's lives which remain elusive and unmeasurable. (Lealand, 1998, p. 13)

Although some research has appeared to show a link between watching certain kinds of programme and violent behaviour, other researchers have claimed that there is no simple correlation. The evidence is by no means clear cut. Buckingham (1996) argues that this is a complex issue and that many accounts overlook the ways in which children themselves talk about and actively make sense of television violence.

Gunter (1998) argues that, as with television, it is difficult to find hard evidence of antisocial effects deriving from video games. In fact he claims that playing such games may actually have a positive effect, for example in dealing with emotional and behavioural problems and in developing important new cognitive skills. Claims can also be made about the positive effects of television viewing on children. Through television, children have access to a wider world of information and a wider variety of viewpoints than their parents did as children. As with video games they may be acquiring skills in processing complex media messages that will be vital to them in a future that will be much less based on print media. Increasingly, children interact with television – sending email messages to children's channels, taking part in competitions and charity appeals, for example. Holland describes the way in which children's television in Britain has often created spaces for children's voices to be heard (Holland, 1996). There is also evidence that children are perfectly able to reject media messages that they do not like. Sensationalized accounts, however, tend to underplay this active role and often construe children as passively soaking up everything they watch.

Conclusion

This brief survey of some of the evidence for a change in children's experience should dispel any notion of straightforward, linear change, either for better or worse, in the quality of children's lives. The evidence that exists presents a much more complex and multi-layered picture. It also reminds us of the sheer diversity of children's experience and the danger of making sweeping generalizations. One aspect of that diversity is the continuing inequality between children from different social groups and the disadvantages that still face children on the basis of class, gender and ethnic background. This chapter has also demonstrated the importance of placing the children's experiences in the context of broader social and economic change, and therefore of resisting the temptation to 'blame' children for aspects of their lives that are largely beyond their control. At the same time it is vital to see children not as passive victims of events but as social actors, able to shape and influence the changing circumstances in which they are growing up.

3

Constructing Childhood, Constructing Child Concern

Wendy Stainton Rogers

> Now, children have become dangerous to us. We are scared of their sexual precocity and their violent instincts, and we have made them into society's scapegoats. ...We sentimentalize them... and abhor them... and are hopelessly confused about them. We want to protect them and want to be protected from them. We think they are sweet and we think they are terrifying. We love them while... they are charmingly playing at being adults, but when they take a few steps towards adulthood, we get scared and angry and morally censorious. (Gerrard, 1997, p. 5)

Our ideas about children are paradoxical. At one and the same time we see them as 'innocent' and want to protect them from adult exploitation and coercion, while also seeing them as menacing and dangerous, it being ourselves who need protection from them. This paradox shows up in the way that the media portray children. Consider, for example, the way in which the two 10-year-old boys who killed Jamie Bulger have been treated in the press – as monsters who should be locked away for life (see Davis and Bourhill, 1997, for a more detailed examination of this issue). Now compare this with the images of children used each year to raise money for Children in Need – they are portrayed as engaging little tots into whose lives a little sunshine can be brought if we raise enough money.

The social construction of childhood

One way to begin to make sense of our confusion about children is to recognize that our attitudes towards children – like all of our attitudes, expectations, understandings and so on – are *socially constructed*. By this what is meant is that the 'realities' that we take for granted – the things we 'know' about our world and how it works – are not things-out-there-in-the-world that we merely observe. Rather, they are constructed by human meaning-making.

Applying this to childhood, this says that there is no *natural* distinction that marks off children as a certain category of person. Rather, the category of 'a child' is just that – a category. Moreover, there is no benchmark of undisputed 'truth' that tells us what children are; there are merely different categories, each of which tells a different 'truth' about what children are. These categories 'work' for us in the way they do – they make sense to us – only within the context of the society and culture in which we live. We in Britain live in a world in which parents are obliged to send their children to school, in which the law distinguishes between adults and children, in which we have created children's television, children's books and children's toys, and in which food, sweets and other consumer products are marketed for children. In another place or at another time the concept of 'childhood' – which seems so self-evidently real to us – would mean something different. Or it might even be quite meaningless.

The disputed history of childhood

The above argument has indeed been made by the historian Aries. He claimed that, in the Western Europe of the Middle Ages, children were seen merely as miniature adults, with the same thinking capacities and personal qualities as adults, although, because of their small size, not quite the same physical abilities (such as strength). His evidence for this was a scrutiny of the letters, diaries and other documents, and pictures of children painted at the time. These showed children sharing in adult recreation and work activities, wearing the same clothes, eating and drinking the same things. But, Aries pointed out:

> This is not to suggest that children were neglected, foresaken or despised. The idea of childhood is not to be confused with affection for children; it corresponds with an awareness of a particular nature of childhood, that particular nature which distinguishes the child from the adult, even the young adult. In medieval society this awareness was lacking. That is why, as soon as the child could live without the constant solicitude of his [sic] mother, his nanny or his cradle rocker, he belonged to adult society. (Aries, 1962, p. 125)

According to Aries, from about the fifteenth century onwards, the images of children in paintings and documents began to change. This happened, he suggests, because a new understanding emerged, an understanding of 'childhood' as a category distinct and different from adulthood. Children came to be seen as different from adults, with particular needs *as children*. One manifestation of this was the rise in formal education, initially only for those children who came from wealthy families but gradually extending to all children.

Childhood innocence versus original sin

Other historians (for example, Shahar, 1990) have challenged Aries' views, arguing that the sources he used as evidence were limited to those arising from literate, aristocratic households. Shahar argues that the perception of the child as different from the adult goes much further back into history. Within Christianity, for example, she suggests that there have long been two opposing concepts of the child: as born either 'innocent' or sullied by 'original sin'.

The image of the child as born in a state of original sin, which drew upon Aristotelian notions overlaid with the Judaeo-Christian 'Adam and Eve' story, pervaded the middle ages. It was particularly potent within puritanism and later evangelical perceptions of the child. In this children were seen as naturally wicked and hence needing redemption. A good illustration of this is provided by Susannah Wesley, mother of the religious leader John Wesley, who recommended that parents must discipline their children in order to instil in them the moral character they need to be 'saved' from their innate sinfulness:

> Break their will betimes: begin this great work before they can run alone, before they can speak plain, or perhaps speak at all... make him [sic] do as he is bid, if you whip him ten times running to effect it... Break his will now and his soul will live, and he will probably bless you to all eternity. (Wesley, 1872, quoted in Jobling, 1978, p. 24)

Moving into the nineteenth century children tended to be portrayed more as 'naughty' than evil. Nineteenth- and twentieth-century literature abounds with tales of 'naughty boys', from *Tom Sawyer* to *Dennis the Menace* and particularly so in school stories from *Tom Brown's School-days*. Such images continue today – one just needs to look at the titles of books written for children, such as *My Naughty Little Sister*. Portrayals of children as inherently evil, though, persist too – in William Golding's *Lord of the Flies*, for example.

In contrast the 'romanticization' of childhood (see Hendrick, 1990) – the depiction of the child as charmingly pure and innocent – came to be particularly important within the eighteenth-century historical period often referred to as the Enlightenment. The best known romantic portrayal of the child of this time is probably Rousseau's *Emile*, but it was later widely propagated by such poets as Blake, Coleridge and Wordsworth in the nineteenth century. It persisted in much Victorian sentimentalist writing and can be seen in writing of the early twentieth century, such as J.M. Barrie's *Peter Pan* and Arthur Ransome's *Swallows and Amazons*. Today we can see it in how, for example, Disney movies portray children – as charming, inventive, cuddly and inherently 'nice' (even if sometimes a bit naughty).

Postmodernism and discourse

Social constructionism has more recently been augmented by another theory – that of postmodernism. Postmodernism accepts the tenets of social constructionism but also offers an extensive body of theorization about the processes of making, maintaining and using knowledge. It is also deployed across a much broader range of disciplines, including, for example, film theory and cultural studies.

One of its most important contributions is possibly the concept of 'discourse'. Within postmodernism 'discourse' is taken to mean a whole set of interconnected ideas that work together in a self-contained way, ideas that are held together by a particular ideology or view of the world. Thus we can talk, for example, about a 'feminist discourse' or a 'biomedical discourse', each of which has its own knowledge base, works from a particular set of assumptions, offers its own explanation of 'how the world works' and incorporates its own set of values and ethics.

The term 'discourse' is also used to specify a particular 'take' on some phenomenon. The two images of children set out in the previous section – the image of the 'innocent and wholesome child' and the image of the 'wicked and sinful child' – can be seen as based upon two different 'discourses of childhood'.

The first is a discourse based upon romanticizing childhood. It assumes that children are inherently good and that childhood is (or at least should be) a time of happiness and innocence, a protected time when children are to be allowed to enjoy their childhood before having to face the trials, tribulations and responsibilities of adulthood. Gerrard again encapsulates this well: the child who is 'lispy, thumb-sucking, winsome, adorable, nostalgic and wholesome', which, she says, is the image 'of a picture-book childhood' (Gerrard, 1997, p. 5). The second is a discourse based upon the puritan notion of 'original sin'. It assumes that children are inherently lacking in morality and that childhood is a time in which children need to be civilized – need to be taught right from wrong and how to overcome their 'base, animal nature' through socialization.

By using discourse as an analytic tool we can begin to see how adopting a particular *image* of childhood implies that we need to act towards children in a particular way. Adopting a *romanticization of childhood discourse* suggests that we should, as far as we can, protect children's innocence. We should take measures to separate them from all that is nasty in the adult world, from sex, from violence, from the worries and concerns of adults. We should do our best to make their childhood happy and carefree. In contrast, adopting a *puritan discourse of childhood* (based on the notion of 'original sin') suggests that children should be carefully controlled, regulated and disciplined. It implies that adults should have authority over children and should use this authority to act in the child's long-term interests, even if this makes the child unhappy or causes him or her short-term pain and distress.

The social construction of child concern

What is common between these two discourses is a 'concern' about children, a powerful implication that the adult world has a responsibility towards them, to *do* things for them. Each implies a different kind of action, but both agree that action needs to be taken. We can make sense of this by recasting the two discourses in a new terminology, calling them the *discourse of welfare* and the *discourse of control*.

The *discourse of welfare* rests on two main assumptions about children: that they are entitled to 'a good childhood' and that they need protection. This discourse informs current UK social policy towards children – especially very young children – and the law about children's care and upbringing. The England and Wales Children Act 1989, for example, has as its core principle that: 'When a court determines any question with respect to the upbringing of a child... the child's welfare shall be the court's paramount consideration' (s1(1)). It also allows intervention where the child is at risk of 'significant harm'.

The *discourse of control* rests on the assumption that children lack self-control and hence need to be regulated. This discourse informs education policy towards children, obliging them to be educated and imposing extensive regulation over the manner and content of their education.

These two discourses mostly co-exist pretty comfortably since they operate in different spheres of children's lives and inform different agencies and professional groups. But they can come into conflict. A good example is the heated debate going on at the time of writing this chapter about a parent's right to 'smack' a child. It is easy to see where the two sides are coming from: the pro-smacking lobby is drawing on the discourse of control, the anti-smacking lobby primarily on the discourse of welfare (albeit also informed by a children's rights discourse). Both argue that they have 'the best interests of the child' at heart, but they fundamentally disagree about what constitutes those 'best interests'.

Implications for practice

All this debate about social constructionism, postmodernism and discourse may seem very interesting at a theoretical level, but, you may be asking yourself, what *use* is it all? Do these ideas and theories have anything interesting to offer to those who work with children and their families?

Social constructionism now in fact constitutes a major critical paradigm in theorizing in applied fields such as health care and social work. Payne, for example, in a highly influential textbook on social work theory, introduces it by saying 'The major principle of this book is that *social work is a socially constructed activity*' (Payne, 1991, p. 7, emphasis in the original). Howe goes further, arguing that 'a child of modernity, social work now finds itself in a postmodern world, uncertain whether or not there are any deep and unwavering principles which define the essence of its character and hold it together as a coherent enterprise' (Howe, 1994, p. 513).

Writing specifically about child protection, Parton *et al.* suggest two reasons why a shift to a social constructionist approach is necessary. First, the present system, they say, is not working, at least in part because there is no moral consensus about what child abuse is or what should be done about it. It is hardly surprising, then, that the work itself is becoming highly stressful and practitioners feel under siege: they are being expected to do the impossible, to practise in the context of confusing and paradoxical tensions between competing discourses of child concern. When they fail – as they are bound to do in such circumstances – they are publicly pilloried for it. At the same time government is also under pressure, taken to task each time a new child abuse scandal hits the headlines. It has responded by creating an ever-more complex system of statutory regulation. It too is trying to do the impossible – devising policy against a backcloth of irreconcilable disputes over the best strategy to adopt.

Parton *et al.*'s second reason why change is needed is that the current approach fails to address in any adequate way the moral issues at stake:

> What is considered child abuse for the purposes of child protection policy and practice is much better characterized as a product of social negotiation between different values and beliefs, different social norms and professional knowledges and perspectives about children, child development and parenting. Far from being a medico-scientific reality, it is a phenomenon where moral reasoning and moral judgement are central. (Parton *et al.*, 1997, p. 67)

The point Parton *et al.* make is that the difficulties being faced will not be solved by 'finding better checklists or new models of psychopathology' (Dingwall *et al.*, 1983, p. 244). What is needed is a willingness to recognize that child protection is a moral and political endeavour (Parton, 1985), as well as a preparedness to examine the implications.

How can constructionism be applied to practice?

It may at first sight seem that all social constructionism has to offer is an explanation for the conflicts and confusions that beset attempts to act 'in the best interests of the child', but it does not help to resolve them. Howe (1994), however, suggests four principles for how social constructionism can be applied to practice: pluralism, participation, power and performance.

Pluralism

Adopting a pluralist position involves not trying to find comfortable compromises but accepting that there will always be a conflict between competing interests, perspectives and standpoints, about, for example, what is best for children and where their interests lie. Crucially, it is about accepting that no one of these is *inherently* better than another. We must not assume that professionals know best nor that any one agency or group has a monopoly on 'the truth'. Pluralism is about encouraging these different positions to be expressed, and finding ways of managing conflicting views in a constructive manner that shows respect for diversity. It is also about tolerating uncertainty and recognizing that it is often impossible to find neat or comfortable resolutions between competing interests.

Participation

Working from the assumption that as all truths are simply 'working truths', it is clear that decisions and actions need to be taken inclusively, enabling the participation of all those involved or affected by them. If conflict can be seen as potentially positive and managed effectively, it can then lead to innovative solutions. Inclusiveness has another benefit too. If people feel that they have been genuinely involved in making decisions and taking action, that their views have been listened to and treated with respect, they are much more likely to try to make solutions work, even when the one chosen is not the one they would prefer.

Power

Crucially, constructionism demands a sensitivity to issues of *power*, and a willingness to acknowledge how it is deployed and by whom. Taking constructionism seriously means not being naïve about power by, for example, ignoring the extent to which professionals are just as capable of protecting their own self-interest as are the family members with whom they work. It also involves recognizing that everybody has some avenues to power. Even the weakest have the power to resist and to undermine the 'best-laid plans'.

Performance

Performance is also about power but looks at how it is managed, especially through institutional and bureaucratic means. This includes both professional expertise and the knowledge-mongering of academics. It encourages us to look not just at what people say but also, crucially, at what they *do* and what the consequences of their actions are. It reminds us, for example, to consider whether professionals are engaging in 'defensive practice', designed more to protect themselves from censure than to achieve the ostensible aims of the action being taken.

I would like to add to this that social constructionism has another important thing going for it – *positivity*. It is an optimistic approach since it appreciates that revolutions (in social policy and professional practice at least) are not won with bullets and barricades but by 'changing hearts and minds'. I would like to make my last words those written by Rex Stainton Rogers more than 10 years ago, which I have always found inspirational:

> the real power of social constructionism ... lies not in its ability to deconstruct our present world as a less than perfect one to grow up in, nor in any specific utopia it may open up to examination, but in the idea of multiple realities itself. ...That we no longer hang children, burn them as witches or brand them as vagrants is not the victory of a few reformers, it is the victory of a whole society which has overcome the constructions that made such action possible. The killings and maimings of children that our society still generates can also be consigned to the history book – by the same processes that have made possible the worlds in which we now live. (R. Stainton Rogers, 1989, p. 29)

If we are to work towards achieving a better quality of life for children, constructionism suggests that we need the vision to imagine what better childhoods might be and the determination to achieve the conditions that will make those better childhoods possible. This is not just about finding ways of stopping treating children badly, but about finding positive ways to treat them well. If we can find the imagination to do that, there is a real possibility of taking our concern for children and using it to make a real difference to their lives and life opportunities.

4

The Demonization of Children: from the Symbolic to the Institutional

Barry Goldson

Children and childhood: tensions and contradictions

In populist discourse childhood is conceived as 'routine' and 'natural', yet childhood is also a site of adult anxiety and mobilizes extraordinary symbolic purchase (Jenks, 1996). In this sense childhood is often regarded as a barometer of the 'state of the nation'. Are children naturally 'pure', 'innocent' and 'untarnished' (the sentimentalist vision), or are they innately 'corrupt', 'sinful' and 'morally blemished' (thus being the legitimate source of adult anxiety)? Therefore, even the most cursory probing in relation to the meaning of children and childhood begins to raise complex questions, tensions and even contradictions.

Hendrick (1994) identifies a paradoxical 'victim-threat dualism' that helps us to understand both ambivalent responses to children, and the conceptual problematics of defining childhood. By engaging with a detailed historical analysis Hendrick develops the compelling argument that, since the early nineteenth century, children have been perceived both as vulnerable and in need of adult protection (the child as *victim*), and as impulsive/unsocialized and in need of adult correction and control (the child as *threat*). This connects with a developing recognition in social science that 'totalizing' definitions of children and childhood are simplistic and inadequate: they conceal the need to theorize childhood, they obfuscate the complexities of children's lives and, perhaps most problematically, they fail to recognize, and thus account for, adult ambivalence.

Adult anxiety with regard to children and childhood has rumbled uncomfortably in recent years in tandem with the emergence, development and consolidation of a 'widespread belief' that children and young people 'are in some way turning feral' (Jeffs and Smith, 1996). Haines and Drakeford (1999, p. 1) go further than this. They identify a 'pervasive negativity' that envelops perceptions of and responses to children, and they starkly suggest that 'our society does not like young people'. Indeed, the populist notion that a 'crisis' is beseting contemporary childhood, necessitating firm action, is not uncommon (Scraton, 1997). This chapter will develop a line of critical analysis and will aim to situate and contextualize such phenomena by placing particular emphasis on the means by which certain children have been ascribed 'demon' status and particularised childhoods have been 'demonized'.

Theorizing childhood: the social constructionist paradigm

There is a developing sociological literature on childhood that is rooted in the seminal work of the French historian Philippe Aries (1959). Aries' central conviction was that childhood is socially constructed and temporally, spatially and culturally determined. Although Aries is not beyond critique (Goldson, 1997a), his work has become increasingly influential in informing the theorization of children and childhood (James and Prout, 1997; Jenks, 1996; Corsaro, 1997). What is now known as the social constructionist paradigm poses a fundamental challenge to 'natural' and/or 'universalistic' conceptualizations of childhood. Instead, the means by which childhood is 'discovered' (Scarre, 1989) or 'invented' (Suransky, 1982) is central to contemporary debates. This is not to deny the significance of biological relations but to shift the focus from notions of naturalistic determinism to a critical analysis of the conceptual relativity of childhood within history. This approach is both interesting and important, but it is also complex and contested (Lavalette, 1999).

Much social constructionist analysis assesses the extent to which (what we call) 'childhood' is, or should be, differentiated from that which we call 'adulthood', as well as exploring the origin, legitimacy (or otherwise), purpose and consequence of such *intergenerational differentiation*. Equally important to intergenerational analyses, however, is the question of *intragenerational* distinction. Here the theoretical priorities engage with the concept of 'childhoods' and demand the deconstruction of a rather crude and monolithic concept of 'childhood'. This perspective introduces the multi-faceted and structurally influenced experience of 'childhood' within all of its heterogeneous variance, the primary determining contexts of class, 'race' and gender being particularly significant (Goldson, 1997a, pp. 20–1). It is at the level of intragenerational analysis therefore that children's experiences of disadvantaged childhoods are of interest, together with the means by which such childhoods are structurally produced and reproduced (both materially and conceptually). The processes whereby particular conceptualizations are manufactured in populist consciousness, and consolidated by state policy, are of primary significance. This is the terrain across which particular children can become 'demons' and particularized childhoods can be 'demonized', and such processes are not without a history.

Folk devils, demons and moral panics

The modern history of demonization is found in the work of Stanley Cohen (1972), Stuart Hall and his colleagues (1978), Geoffrey Pearson (1983) and Jock Young (1971), having since been revised and developed by many other commentators (see for example, Muncie, 1984; Muncie and McLaughlin, 1996; Thompson, 1998). Cohen (1972, pp. 9–11) writes:

> Societies appear to be subject, every now and then, to periods of moral panic. A condition, episode, person or group of persons emerges to become defined as a threat to societal values and interests; its nature is presented in a stylised and stereotypical fashion by the mass media... [it can have] serious and long-lasting repercussions and might produce such changes as those in legal and social policy... these groups have occupied a constant position as folk devils: visible reminders of what we should not be... public concern about a particular condition is generated, a 'symbolic crusade' mounted.

The significance here rests on two levels: the *symbolic* ('symbolic crusade') and the *institutional* (legal and social policy). Whether the 'demons' are mods and rockers (Cohen, 1972), black young people (Hall *et al.*, 1978), 'hooligans' (Pearson, 1983) or drug-users (Young, 1971), the effect of the 'moral panic', and the associated 'folk-devilling' and 'demonizing' processes, are essentially the same: social problems are 'created', public concern rapidly mounts, and those who are held responsible are subjected to withering criticism. More significantly, public disquiet, moral indignation and political anxiety are such that 'something must be done about it'. This is not to suggest that there is complete consensus and analytical uniformity in comprehending and contextualising moral panics and demonizing processes. Indeed, Thompson (1998, p. 9) rightly observes that 'different theorists may emphasise different characteristics of moral panics'. Notwithstanding this, two constituent elements underpin the demonising processes: first, concern and anxiety, and second, hostility and contempt. When the 'panic' is 'amplified' in the media and elsewhere, when it is represented as signifying a wider and deeper moral malaise, when the *anxiety* is explicitly connected with the *hostility* and each of the critical 'elements' interacts, it is then that both the symbolic and the institutional responses are legitimized and consolidated. When all of this hooks-up to even wider and more common anxieties, and is bolstered by the intrinsic ambivalence that lies deep within the adult psyche, as in the case of children and childhood, the 'demonizing' conditions simply await activation.

Demonization as symbolic: a crescendo of contempt

At the outset of this chapter I referred to a burgeoning sense of adult anxiety in relation to childhood. Such concern reached boiling point in the early 1990s, juvenile crime and the disorderly behaviour of children being located at its very kernel (Goldson, 1997b, 1999). Media coverage of car crime, outbreaks of civil unrest within which children and young people appeared to be prominent players (Brown, 1998; Campbell, 1993; Muncie, 1999a) and the construction of the 'bail bandit' and 'persistent young offender' (children apparently beyond the reach of the law) (Hagell and Newburn, 1994; Newburn, 1996), fuelled a new moral panic and the 'folk devilling of children and young people' (Carlen, 1996, p. 48). The media was active in stoking the coals of adult anxiety and 'amplifying' the construction of the child as threat. As Newburn (1996, p. 70) observes 'it was open season in the press':

Mini-gangster is beyond control (*Daily Express*, 9 September 1992)

One Boy Crime Wave. He was only eleven when his life of crime began with the theft of chocolate bars from a corner shop… within two years he had become a one boy crime wave (*Daily Mail*, 10 September 1992)

We've got too soft. Children are supposed to be little innocents not crooks in short trousers. But much of Britain is now facing a truly frightening explosion of kiddie crime. As we reveal today too many youngsters are turning into hardened hoods almost as soon as they've climbed out of their pram. (*Daily Star*, 30 November 1992)

Children, some children at least, were no longer 'little innocents' but 'mini-gangsters', 'crime waves', 'crooks in short trousers' and 'hardened hoods': the processes of demonization were underway. If further 'evidence' was required it was to come in the form of the most 'demonic' act of all – child murder.

In February 1993 a two-year-old child, James Bulger, was murdered on a railway siding in north Liverpool by two 10-year-old boys. The two boys were sentenced in November of the same year, and in passing sentence at Preston Crown Court, Judge Morland commented that the boys' 'cunning and very wicked' behaviour had resulted in 'an act of unparalleled evil and barbarity' (Goldson, 1998, p. 21). The judge's references to 'cunning', 'wickedness', 'evil' and 'barbarity' cut deep into the adult anxiety, echoing everywhere, and despite the atypicality of this tragic case, it set child demonization in symbolic concrete. The preferred 'explanation' for such tragedy was rooted in conceptualizations of 'evil'. A particularized demonic childhood was constructed:

> We will never be able to look at our children in the same way again... parents everywhere are asking themselves and their friends if the Mark of the Beast might not also be imprinted on their offspring. (*Sunday Times*, 28 November 1993)

Indeed, the extent of media coverage – nationally and internationally, tabloid and broadsheet alike – was unprecedented (Davis and Bourhill, 1997; Franklin and Petley, 1996; Hay, 1995; Morrison, 1997), and self-appointed 'moral entrepreneurs' and 'moral crusaders' (Becker, 1963), fervent and righteous, had a field-day.

The tragic case of child murder was crudely conjoined with the broader perceptions of juvenile crime and youth disorder. Indeed, the former was presented as the ultimate expression of the latter. Moreover, the atypicality of the Bulger case was ignored, and the material context within which juvenile crime was located was peripheralized. The significance of such 'dematerialising and decontextualizing' processes (Goldson, 1997b, pp. 136–138) has been explained elsewhere:

> Essentialism provides a cultural basis for conflict and is the necessary *pre-requisite* for demonization of parts of society. Demonization is important in that it allows the problems of society to be blamed upon 'others'... Here the customary inversion of causal reality occurs: instead of acknowledging that we have problems in society because of basic core contradictions in the social order, it is claimed that all the problems of society are because of the problems themselves. Get rid of the problems and society would be, *ipso facto*, problem free! (Young, 1999, p. 110, emphasis in the original)

Children thus became the problems, and they were conceptualized as both the *cause* and the *product* of wider social disorder and moral malaise. In this sense the moribund state of childhood was said to represent a wider immorality and irresponsibility steeped in permissiveness and rooted in the 1960s: the 'disintegration' of the nuclear family, inadequate parenting, fatherless families, fuddled professional purveyors of a corrosive 'excuse culture', indiscipline in schools, 'softness' in the courts, the clamour for rights without associated responsibilities, anomie and the emergence and consolidation of an amoral and utterly dysfunctional 'underclass'.

Equally, the demonization of children on the symbolic level was not limited to those in conflict with the law. It was more than this: it was a whole generation, a 'lost generation'. As Marina Warner asserted in her 1994 Reith Lectures:

> The child has never been seen as such a menacing enemy as today. Never before have children been so saturated with all the power of projected monstrousness to excite repulsion – and even terror. (cited in Franklin and Petley, 1996, p. 134)

Children everywhere were 'described in terms reserved for hated enemies' (Stern, 1998, pp. 169–170); they were subjected to a relentless 'outpouring of rage and hatred' (Davis and Bourhill, 1997, p. 56); the air was saturated with what Scraton (1999, unpublished paper) has recently termed the 'ideological whiff of child-hate'. The cumulative impact of child contempt had reached its crescendo. The demonization of children was symbolically established, 'modes and models of explanation' followed, and 'reaction' in the form of 'rescue and remedy' (Cohen, 1972) beckoned. Such 'rescue' and 'remedy' has taken a harsh form as the demonization of children has passed through a metamorphosis from the symbolic to the institutional.

Demonization as institutional: 'responsibilizing' children and 'adulterizing' childhood

Cohen (1985, p. 1), in his definitive work on social control, explains:

> social control, that is the organised ways in which society responds to behaviour and people it regards as deviant, problematic, worrying, threatening, troublesome or undesirable in some way or another. This response appears under many terms: punishment, deterrence, treatment, prevention, segregation... it is accompanied by other ideas and emotions: hatred, revenge, retaliation, disgust... The behaviour in question is classified under many headings: crime, delinquency, deviance, immorality, perversity, wickedness, deficiency... The people to whom the response is directed, are seen variously as monsters, fools, villains...

The symbolic demonization of children raised anxieties about childhood *per se* and in so doing provided the legitimacy for a correctional emphasis in law and policy. It is at this juncture that the symbolic meets the institutional. Institutional demonization is more sharply focused. Specific children and particularized childhoods, the 'problematic', 'worrying', 'threatening', 'troublesome' or 'undesirable', the 'monsters' and the 'villains', become the primary subjects of the adult-state gaze. These are the children who not only offend the law, but also offend adult sensibilities. These are the children who, according to Jenks (1996, p. 128), have been subjected to 'conceptual eviction' and 'removed from the category of "child" altogether'. These are the children who have been ascribed with levels and forms of responsibility hitherto reserved for adults. These are indeed the children who have been 'responsibilized' as their childhoods have been 'adulterized'. These are the children who have been institutionally demonized, a process seemingly driven by the 'hatred', 'revenge', 'retaliation' and 'disgust' to which Cohen (1985) refers.

Institutional demonization rests upon spurious domain assumptions. Individual agency is profiled, personal responsibility is piously ascribed, and structural context is just as emphatically denied. The emphasis is unequivocally located at the micro-level of individual responsibility and children's behaviour (with its attendant juxtapositions of decency–indecency, morality–immorality, right and wrong), as distinct from the macro material context and socio-economic conditions within which life is lived. The demonizing discourse takes no account of child poverty and youth exclusion; it negates the concerns relating to children's (physical and mental) health and well-being; it denies the profound deficits in state educational provision; and it disregards fundamental questions of social stability/instability as they relate to children and childhood, despite all of the evidence providing the detail, significance and meaning of such phenomena (Howarth *et al.*, 1999). Instead, decontextualized concerns regarding morality and responsibility are emphasized. Here the notion of the 'responsibilized' child shifts from the level of *symbolic* representation (political rhetoric and newspaper headline) to the very core of state policy as childhood, the childhood, that is of child 'offenders', has been *institutionally* 'adulterized'.

The Bulger trial was not an aberration. Holding children (as young as 10 years, and in certain cases younger) to be as responsible as adults is now endemic throughout the 'justice' process in England and Wales (Goldson, 1999; Muncie, 1999a, 1999b). Expanded forms of child incarceration, longer sentences, curfews for children under the age of 10, the 'naming and shaming' of children, the erosion of legal safeguards for the youngest children, 'fast-track' punishment, pervasive 'toughness', the abolition of cautioning and the introduction of new increasingly interventionist measures all add up to institutionalised demonization and criminalization (Goldson, 2000). Identifiable children, and particularized childhoods, have been systematically targeted in this way. To borrow the words of Hewlett (1993, p. 2), 'there is an anti-child spirit loose in these lands'.

Conclusion

I have argued that a curious ambivalence underpins adult conceptualizations of children and childhood. Sentimentality and anxiety are polarized. Constructions of innocence and vulnerability necessitating protection contrast sharply with conceptualizations of a threatening and dangerous childhood demanding correction. The social constructionist paradigm helps us to understand such tensions and contradictions. In recent years such ambivalence and definitional relativity have connected with other forms of anxiety and uncertainty. This has in turn been exploited and distorted, and has provided fertile ground upon which children and childhood, or more specifically identifiable children and particularized childhoods, have been demonised. A symbolic essentialism has legitimised an institutional back-lash that has especially targeted children in trouble.

Indeed, children who are thought to transgress the limits of what it is to be a child are classified as 'threats' and 'problems', being demonized and 'othered'. For the purposes of ascribing personal responsibility to such children, their childhood is, in essence, 'adulterized' and 'adulterated'. Little of this is rational; indeed quite the opposite is true (Goldson, 1999).

Brown (1998, p. 116) observes:

> [Children] have been constructed through policy not as citizens, but as objects of increasingly repressive modes of governance. As adult anxiety and punitive desire escalate, the (metaphorical) body of the delinquent is carved up to serve popular appetites, and effectiveness and rationality are increasingly subsumed under ideological imperative.

Thompson (1998, p. 18), however, leaves us with the core questions, 'What forces stand to benefit from it?, What role has the state played in its construction?, What real fears is it mobilising?'

5

Racism: an Important Factor in Practice with Ethnic Minority Children and Families

Kwame Owusu-Bempah

Professional practice in today's Britain must reflect the diversity of the populations it serves not only in terms of 'race' or ethnicity, but also in terms of culture and cultural practices, including language and religion. Responding to diverse communities is, however, no easy task for practitioners. While it may be relatively easy for social workers and health care personnel, for example, to learn something of other cultures, it is in the nature of every culture to be complex, dynamic and in a state of flux. That is, practitioners need to be responsive and dynamic in their approach to work with culturally or ethnically diverse populations.

This chapter discusses some of the areas of society as a whole in which racial discrimination impacts negatively upon the lives of black and ethnic minority communities. It explores also some of the ways in which progress can be made when working with these communities. To this end it examines the influence of beliefs and assumptions about race on practice with black and ethnic minority clients, the emphasis being on children and families. The discussion starts with brief definitions of racism, the rationale being that understanding racism and its effects will motivate childcare professionals seriously to consider racial discrimination as an important factor impinging upon the lives of black and ethnic minority children and their families in British society. As well as highlighting the major sectors of society in which these families are particularly disadvantaged, it also outlines strategies for developing practices that not only seek to be fair to all service users, but also actually endeavour to counteract racism and other social disadvantages facing them.

Racism: definitions

Jones (1972) has described three distinct, but mutually reinforcing, forms of racism: *individual racism, institutional racism*, and *cultural racism*. Briefly, *individual racism* relates to the personal beliefs, attitudes, prejudices and behaviours that individuals use to prejudge 'racial' groups negatively (or positively). Without the power invested in them by society and its institutions, many people are unable to express these feelings in direct action against minorities. *Institutional racism* involves the policies and practices of organizations that deny black and ethnic minority groups access to power and resources, often by construing them as being deficient in some way or holding them to blame for their low social and economic status or lack of power. These institutional policies and practices, actions and inactions, maintain the victims in socially, economically and politically disadvantaged positions in society. *Cultural racism* consists of the values, beliefs and ideas, usually embedded in our social representation or 'common sense' that endorse or sanction the belief in the superiority of one 'racial' group (white) and its culture or way of life over those of other groups.

  Intractably linked, these three forms of racism ensure that it is ubiquitous. Combined they enable racism to penetrate into the daily routines and lives of institutions and the individuals within them. In other words racism is not about attitudes alone but also about institutionally generated inequality, often manifest in employment and service provision. Hence, although others describe racism as the differential treatment of individuals considered to belong to a particular 'racial' group, it must be stressed that racial discrimination may occur without the accompanying feeling of prejudice (Howitt and Owusu-Bempah, 1990; Owusu-Bempah, 1994a). Consequently, despite the Race Relations Act 1976, research continues to show that racial discrimination prevails and pervades virtually every important sphere of British society, including education, employment, housing, health care and criminal justice (Brown, 1984; Esmail and Everington, 1993; Macpherson, 1999; Modood *et al.*, 1997; NAHA, 1988).

  In modern Britain it is extremely rare to witness crude racist bigotry, either in words or in deed. Racism is mutable so there are differences in the way in which it is conceptualized and articulated or manifested. The Race Relations Act 1976 distinguishes between two broad forms of racism: direct racial discrimination and indirect racial discrimination, including segregation and victimization. The terms 'individual racism' and 'institutional racism' are commonly used to refer to the former and the latter respectively. Each, however, involves an over-generalization of the characteristics of people on the basis of skin colour, anatomical features or culture, and using such stereotypes to justify their exclusion from power and resources or to provide second-rate services to those perceived to be different from one's own group.

The report of the Stephen Lawrence Enquiry offers a pragmatic definition of racism:

'Racism' in general terms consists of conduct or words or practices which advantage or disadvantage people because of their colour, culture or ethnic origin. In its... subtle form it is as damaging as in its overt form. (Macpherson, 1999, p. 6.34)

The report proceeds to delineate subtle racism:

'Institutional racism' consists of the collective failure of an organization to provide an appropriate and professional service to people because of their colour, culture, or ethnic origin. It can be seen or demonstrated in processes, attitudes and behaviour... and racist stereotyping which disadvantage minority ethnic people. (Macpherson, 1999, p. 47.12)

The prevalence of racism

In 1984 a large-scale survey, conducted under the auspices of the Policy Studies Institute, that involved both black and ethnic minority adults and white adults concluded:

As we systematically compared the jobs, incomes, unemployment rates, private housing, local authority housing, local environments and other aspects of the lives of people with different ethnic origins... the circumstances of black people came to be and continue to be worse than those of white people. (Brown, 1984, pp. 315–16)

This section highlights those important sectors of society – education, employment, housing, health and social welfare – in which collective failures, as described above, continue to have a lasting impact upon the lives of black and ethnic minority children and families.

Education

Research shows that black and ethnic minority children, especially African-Caribbean children, are (even at nursery level) treated less favourably than other children (e.g., Ogilvy *et al.*, 1990). Such treatment takes various forms, but exclusion, teachers' negative attitudes and, of course, racial violence and harassment have received special attention from investigators and concerned bodies as well as individuals.

Regarding exclusion as a manifestation of racism in the school system, the following report is presented as a case in point. Lyle *et al.* (1996) carried out research involving schools in Leicestershire, reporting *inter alia*:

- 7.1 per cent of permanently excluded pupils in the county were African-Caribbeans; this was *over five times* higher than their proportion (1.4 per cent); African-Caribbean pupils were also over-represented (by a factor of four) among those pupils who were excluded for a fixed period.

- African-Caribbean pupils were *five times* more likely to be permanently excluded than white children and over *43 times* more likely to be so than Asian children.

- For fixed periods, the rate for African-Caribbean children was *3.6 times* higher than for white children and over *eight times* higher than for Asian children.

These findings reflect a national trend; other investigators have also found an over-representation of African-Caribbean pupils in school exclusion; they have also reported a relationship between exclusion and under-achievement (CRE, 1995). In spite of this, school authorities favour explanations attributing this state of affairs to the children's lack of ability or motivation, or a lack of parental support for, or interest in, the children's education over those which locate the causes of the problem in the school system itself (Howitt and Owusu-Bempah, 1999). That the school system is a large part of the problem rather than its solution is, however, in no doubt as far as African-Caribbean people are concerned. Of those people who told the Leicestershire African-Caribbean survey that the education system was failing their children, nearly 70 per cent attributed the cause to racial discrimination.

Besides exclusion and teachers' negative attitudes and behaviour towards black pupils (see, for example, Connolly, 1998; Wright, 1992), such factors as racial violence and harassment, both within and outside school, have an equally detrimental effect on their emotional and physical well-being as well as their academic performance (CRE, 1987, 1988; Macpherson, 1999; Skellington and Morris, 1992).

Social services

In Britain, for historical and economic reasons, black people's contact with the social services antedates their contact with the school system. Hence, it may be argued that misconceptions, assumptions and stereotypes relating to black people and ethnic minority groups have had a longer (and perhaps greater) influence on social work than on education. Their family structures, especially childrearing practices, have been, and continue to be, negatively viewed by childcare professionals (Dwivedi and Varma, 1996; Lobo, 1987). Writing in 1987, for example, Lobo averred:

the 'maternal deprivation' effects of the West Indian child *living at home* is matched only by... children brought up in old-fashioned orphanage-institutions. (emphasis added)

It is impossible to assess the extent to which such damaging portrayals of the African-Caribbean family have influenced the decisions of child-care professionals – teachers, social workers, school psychologists, child psychiatrists and therapists – relating to African-Caribbean families and their children. The evidence nonetheless seems to indicate that they have contributed substantially to practitioners' perceptions and assessments of black children and their families, and that such portrayals have in some way contributed to the often-reported over-representation of black children in the public childcare system (Barn, 1993). Nor are such negative views directed at African-Caribbean families alone. South Asian children (especially girls) are often seen by professionals as being oppressed by their socialization (Howitt, 1992).

Housing and employment

As in 1984 and prior to that period, members of ethnic minority groups today face constraints with which the white majority do not have to contend, for example racial discrimination in the allocation of housing. They are concentrated in the inner city and other less desirable areas of the communities in which they find themselves (see, for example CRE, 1989, 1990; Lakey, 1997). They have no choice but to live in these circumstances with their children, with all the concomitant paucity of services and facilities.

Racial discrimination in the labour market is as prevalent as ever, although it may not be as overt as it was before the 1976 Race Relations Act. Research comparing the employment status of black and ethnic minorities and white people confirms that ethnic minorities have a much higher level of unemployment than white people (e.g. Brown, 1984; Wrench and Solomos, 1993). An obvious consequence of this is either poverty among ethnic minority families or their struggling to make ends meet on a low income. Pakistanis and Bangladeshis are reported to be especially disadvantaged in the labour market. Modood (1997) reports that the males of these groups continue to be disproportionately represented in manual work, having in terms of wages only two-thirds of the pay packet of white men. He reports that, in 1994, more than 80 per cent of Pakistani and Bangladeshi households – four times as many as white households – had an equivalent income below the national average.

Health care

The National Health Service, given its humanitarian values, might be expected to be an institution free from discrimination on any grounds. Until 1988 the National Health Service continued to deny its endemic racism, even to its victims – both employees (including doctors and nurses) and patients. The publication of a report by the National Association of Health Authorities (NAHA), *Action not Words*, changed this stance. The report conceded the prevalence and pervasiveness of racial discrimination in the health services:

> Such discrimination can be seen in access to and delivery of services as well as in employment practice... In providing health care, staff may apply racial stereo-typing when making assessment about black and minority ethnic individuals. (NAHA, 1988, p. 8)

It revealed failings particularly in the following areas of the National Health Service:

1 *The standard of care:* black and ethnic minority patients generally receive substandard care.

2 *Mental health:* black and ethnic minority members with mental health needs generally receive inadequate, and sometimes potentially harmful, treatment. Specifically, ethnic minority patients are frequently misdiagnosed, also often being recommended for stronger medication than the equivalent white patient. Mental health personnel's tendency to use physical treatments, including electric shock treatment, more readily on ethnic minority patients is well documented (Fernando, 1989; Howitt and Owusu-Bempah, 1994; Littlewood and Lipsedge, 1989; Mercer, 1984).

3 *Infant mortality:* infant mortality is higher in the black than in the white community as a result of unequal access to health services.

To summarize this section, the racial injustice experienced even by black and ethnic minority children's significant others is directly and vicariously experienced by them too. It is quite easy to see the mechanisms of the transgenerational effects of racial disadvantage. Parents who were discriminated against in education, for example, are very likely to transmit negative feelings about schooling to their offspring; bad child-care decisions made by professionals may cause both the parents and the children to suffer a lasting sense of injustice; a child whose mother received inadequate or inappropriate antenatal care because of the racism within the health care system may carry the effect for life; parents who have been allocated poor housing on racial grounds have little choice but to live in deleterious circumstances with their children; and parents who experience chronic unemployment or whose income is low are unlikely to afford to provide adequately for their children's developmental needs, including their emotional, intellectual, social and behavioural needs. Indeed, defined broadly, many of these children would fall into the category of 'children in need'. Amin and Oppenheim (1992) capture the combined and long-term adverse effects of these factors on black and ethnic minority children in the following terms:

> To be born into an ethnic minority in Britain – particularly [one]… whose origins are in Bangladesh, Caribbean or Pakistan – is to face a higher risk of leading a life marked by low income, repeated unemployment, poor health and housing… than someone who is white. (p. 63)

Principles of good practice

Both the UNCRC, and childcare legislation in the UK place a duty upon childcare agencies and practitioners to alleviate negative early experiences and structural disadvantages in order to improve the circumstances of *all* children, and thereby facilitate their healthy physical, emotional, mental and social development. Practices needed to achieve this important goal should go beyond the philosophy of child-centredness. They must have a broad enough approach to include not just the individual child, but also the family (nuclear or extended) and the wider environment (for example, the school). An eco-system perspective, for example, would be appropriate. Such an approach would seek to understand the structural factors that either facilitate or impede the family's functioning and consequently the child's well-being. It would have as one of its major aims the removal of the structural barriers hindering the child's healthy development. In short, appropriate childcare practices must be based upon appropriate principles. In the case of black and ethnic minority children the following, by no means exhaustive, are offered for consideration.

1 *Empowerment:* professional practices likely to eradicate, or at least reduce, racial discrimination and other social disadvantages must be guided not just by humanitarian or liberal principles but by a principle of 'genuine empowerment'. According to Owusu-Bempah (1994b) such practices seek not only to provide fair or non-discriminatory services (services that do not discriminate against users on any grounds) to service users but also actually to counteract or break down the structural barriers facing them, barriers to full growth and development.

2 *Early intervention:* given the nature of the effects of the early life experiences of children whose families experience multiple social disadvantage, intervention in the lives of the children and their families should be undertaken as early as possible. Any measure that tackles racial discrimination is likely to reduce many of the difficulties it causes in the children, such as emotional problems, behavioural difficulties and school failure. Such measures are likely also to promote the general well-being of their families.

3 *Positive experiences:* the UNCRC stresses that, in order to promote the well-being, growth and development of children, *all children*, regardless of their social position, race, colour, sex or ethnicity, must be provided with the appropriate resources, support and wherewithal. The UNCRC also advocates the provision of positive life experiences for all children as a strategy for reducing the psychological and social risks that some of them face.

4 *Rights for children:* related to the principle of positive early experiences is the recognition and acknowledgement that all children have the right to experience those conditions and circumstances which can best contribute to their healthy growth and development. This requires that life chances and opportunities are provided for every child irrespective of 'race', colour, ethnicity and so forth.

Putting principles into practice

Research points to the need for strategies that improve the life chances of children who may be at risk and that may involve supporting families who are under stress arising from poverty, disadvantage or other structural factors. This is a recognition that it is not only black and ethnic minority children and families who experience social and economic disadvantage and other social stressors. Notwithstanding, we must acknowledge that, in their case, racism or racial discrimination is a major factor compounding whatever problems they may share with other groups, such as the white working class. In other words strategies to combat the disadvantages facing them must take cognisance of this fact; they must, of necessity, incorporate policies and methods for tackling racial discrimination.

None of the principles outlined above can be realized without the political will, sanction, support and encouragement of the organization for which the individual practitioner is an agent. Strategies for supplying adequate professional care for all service users have to begin by developing an awareness and recognition of the potential difficulties that this endeavour entails at all levels of the organization. The following would be a minimal list of recommendations:

1 Professional bodies involved in any sense with the care of black and ethnic minority communities need an anti-racism/anti-discrimination policy and its effective implementation. This should cover all sectors of the organization's activities.

2 Individual practitioners must recognize that anti-racism/anti-discrimination is a process that may change and develop as the needs of the community change and develop. Furthermore, emphases continually alter over time, so what may seem to be a state-of-the-art practice today may become rather inadequate and dated tomorrow. It also has to be accepted that the issues and ways of dealing with them may change rapidly and unpredictably. The task, therefore, includes being aware of these changes and prepared to accommodate them.

3 Practitioners must understand the impact of racism on its victims, the aim of the endeavour being to find ways of helping others more effectively. In tandem with this, however, is the possibility of a two-way process in which the practitioner learns not only to practise better with clients or in different cultural milieus, but also more about themselves in their search for personal development. This is integral to the notion of continuing learning and professional development.

4 Following Pollard (1989), Owusu-Bempah (1997) has suggested an 'enabling' approach to work with black and ethnic minority children and families, one equally applicable to other disadvantaged families. The approach distinguishes between 'alterable' and 'static' variables. 'Alterable' variables relate to factors in a person or the environment that can be somehow manipulated to enhance their functioning. 'Static' variables represent factors that are not easily changed but only classify or label people. In the case of children in care, for example, the 'alterable variables' approach: (a) seeks to identify those children who seem to be thriving in the system and determine what factors are associated with their resilience; (b) also seeks to identity those factors within the system or environment which deleteriously affect, as well as those which enhance, their functioning. This framework requires a positive attitude towards black and ethnic minority families, identifying, fostering and encouraging their strengths. It is different from the problem family model, which tends to pathologize even the strengths of these families, such as the extended family structure and adoption/fostering within the community, as noted by various observers (Hylton, 1997; Owusu-Bempah, 1999a, b).

Conclusion: closing gaps

It is incumbent upon childcare professionals to monitor critically, and where necessary rectify, those aspects of their practice which may jeopardize the future of ethnic minority children and families. Owusu-Bempah (1994b) has argued that helping children entails a recognition and better understanding of their circumstances, including the psychological, social and material aspects. This demands the helper's preparedness to investigate and consider seriously and objectively the many factors that may cause or at least contribute to their difficulties. In the case of black and ethnic minority children these factors obviously include their daily experience of racism.

As the UNCRC emphasizes, the ultimate aim of childcare practice should ideally be one of achieving equality for all children, whoever, whatever and wherever they may be. Working to close gaps would be a good start. An important goal of childcare practice must be to reduce social inequality; it must have as its aim the removal of discrimination, especially normative discrimination that is covertly or invisibly institutionalized. Racial discrimination epitomises such discrimination.

6

Childcare Policy

Marcus Roberts

The aim of this chapter is to provide an overview of the recent development of childcare policy in the UK. Childcare is here interpreted broadly to include the variety of settings in which children depend upon adults for protection, care and support. It begins by looking at the challenges that confronted New Labour on its election to office in May 1997 and proceeds by considering what progress has been made in meeting these challenges. A conclusion highlights some more general points about childcare policy and children's rights. The First and Second UK Reports to the UN Committee on the Rights of the Child (hereafter referred to as the Convention) provide a framework for the discussion.

UK policy and the UN Committee on the Rights of the Child

Under the Convention, the UK government is required to submit a report to the UN Committee on the Rights of the Child (referred to here as the Committee) every five years. These reports deal with the development of law and policy over the relevant period. The Committee publishes a response in which positive developments are noted, areas of concern identified and suggestions and recommendations made.

The First Report

The UK submitted its First Report in February 1994 (DoH, 1994), the Committee responding in January 1995 (CRC, 1995). It welcomed some positive developments – notably steps to address sexual abuse – but was critical of policy in a number of areas. In particular it expressed concern about the number of children living in poverty, the administration of the juvenile justice system and the use of corporal punishment in independent schools and the home. The Committee was concerned about: 'insufficient expenditure... allocated to the social sector' (Childright, 1995, p. 3); inadequate support for asylum-seeking children; the disproportionate representation of children from certain minority groups in the care system; health inequalities between children of different socio-economic (and ethnic) groups; and the rate of divorce.

Recent research has confirmed that the UK's performance in many of these areas has been significantly worse than that of other European countries. The Institute of Fiscal Studies, for example, recently found that over four million children were living in poverty in the UK in 1995–96: one third of everyone below the age of 18 (Gregg *et al.*, 1999).

The Second Report

In the Second Report, the government can claim to have made progress in addressing child poverty and social exclusion (DoH, 1999c). The Prime Minister's historic pledge to eliminate child poverty within 20 years, made in his Beveridge lecture in March 1999, has been backed up by significant changes in law and policy, which, it is estimated, will lift around 1.2 million children out of poverty. New Labour has also done much to improve the position of looked-after children. It has introduced policies in a range of other areas – including protection against sexual exploitation and abuse, parenting education and health – that have been welcomed by organizations concerned with children's rights. This does not mean of course that New Labour is above criticism in these areas. For example, while it has made a start on child poverty, millions of British children continue to live below the poverty line.

It is argued that the government has not introduced adequate structures and mechanisms for the monitoring and implementation of the Convention (see, for example, Newell, 2000). In particular it has failed to support a campaign for the establishment of a statutory Children's Rights Commissioner at Westminster. Furthermore, the government continues to place less emphasis than it might on measures to promote consultation with children (see, for example, the recent report of the young person's organization Article 12, 1999). This is by no means unique to the UK and is still reflected in the attitudes of many people working in the childcare professions. Children are regarded as objects of adult concern, benevolence and instruction. There is nothing wrong with this view in itself: children – especially young children – are dependent on adults in these ways. However, what is without historical precedent in the development of the notion of children's rights is the idea of children as subjects who should be empowered to assert their rights against social workers, carers, teachers and even parents.

It would be wrong to give the impression that the New Labour government has done nothing to promote the rights of children as participants in decision-making processes. Responding to concerns expressed in response to the First Report, for example, government guidance on the conduct of hearings to consider the exclusion of a pupil from school makes clear that he or she should be allowed to speak on his or her behalf unless there is a good reason to refuse a request to do so (DfEE, 1999a). It is, however, fair to say that too little attention is paid, in the UK as elsewhere, to the right of children to challenge adult agendas, raise concerns with policy-makers and professionals and shape those institutions which most closely affect their lives.

Between the reports: key developments

Social exclusion and poverty

The concept of social exclusion has been central to policies addressed to the problems of the most disadvantaged children. The Social Exclusion Unit defines social exclusion as 'a shorthand term for what can happen when people or areas suffer from a combination of linked problems such as unemployment, poor skills, low incomes, poor housing, high crime environments, bad health, poverty and family breakdown' (Social Exclusion Unit website, p. 69). These problems, it argues, tend to reinforce each other, creating 'cycles of disadvantage' that pass from generation to generation, disadvantaging a substantial number of children from the earliest years of their lives. Much has also been made of the relationship between deprivation and delinquency, disadvantaged children being more likely to run into trouble at school and with the law.

A recognition of the interconnectedness of these problems explains the government's insistence on the need for 'joined up solutions to joined up problems'. The idea is a simple one. If a child is underperforming or misbehaving at school, for example, it is natural to ask whether this problem is related to other difficulties that the child is facing. What is the child's home life like? Are the parents struggling financially? Is the child adequately housed? To address difficulties at school, then, it is necessary to tackle a range of other difficulties. The 'problems' are 'joined up' and therefore so too are the solutions.

'Cycles of disadvantage' tend to perpetuate themselves from the earliest years of a child's life. In January 1999, in recognition of this, the government identified 60 'trailblazers' for a new initiative targeted at 0–3-year-olds in deprived areas, promising a total of 250 programmes within three years. This initiative is called Sure Start, and the government has allocated a total of £540 million to it. It guarantees a home visit to each family with a newborn baby to provide information about available services, 'joined up' action on the part of local health, education and childcare services to improve provision for young children and parents, and better access to early support (for example, childcare services, toddler groups and toy libraries).

This is one of a number of government programmes targeted at particular areas of the country. Other initiatives of this kind include the establishment of Health Action Zones and Education Action Zones (which came into operation in April 1998 and May 1998 respectively). These channel substantial investment into the health and education problems of the most deprived regions of the UK.

Child poverty is, of course, at the very heart of the problem of social exclusion, and the government has pledged to eliminate it. So what is distinctive about New Labour's approach to child poverty? It has abandoned the redistributive approach to poverty of the 1950s and 60s in favour of an *enabling* approach. This places the emphasis on the responsibilities of parents and other carers to provide for their families where they are able to do so. The government's role is to provide people with opportunities to take their families out of poverty and to improve the rewards for people taking lower-paid jobs (for the government's approach to poverty and social exclusion, see, in particular, DoH, 1999a).

This approach has profound implications for the development of policy affecting children. For example, parents – particularly lone parents – have often been prevented from working by lack of childcare provision. Childcare has therefore been central to the government's programme to tackle poverty. In July 1997, for example, it launched the New Deal for Lone Parents, intended to help lone parents back to work. Central to this 'New Deal' was a National Childcare Strategy. The number of people working in childcare is being increased by encouraging voluntary organizations to train childcare assistants, after-school activities have been extended, and childcare has been made more affordable. Changes to the tax and benefit system have been introduced to help with childcare costs. In the budget for March 1999, which was billed as a 'budget for children', the Chancellor announced the introduction of a childcare tax credit and a Sure Start Maternity Grant to help parents on benefits with the costs of a newborn child.

The government has also introduced changes to the tax and benefit system designed to 'make work pay' for those in less well-paid jobs. The national minimum wage is an obvious example. In addition, a Working Families Tax Credit (WFTC) came into operation in October 1999 to improve the financial position of parents in low-paid jobs. While introducing measures to improve the position of low-paid workers, the government has made much of the responsibilities of parents to take advantage of available opportunities to work.

The most significant measure to assist lone parents on income support financially also stressed the responsibility of parents, rather than the state, to provide for children. This time the emphasis was on the responsibilities of *absent* parents. The Child Support Agency was established by the previous Conservative administration, its role being to calculate the child maintenance payments due from absent parents (usually men) and ensure that they are paid to the parent caring for the child. Up until now lone parents on income support have not gained anything financially from this: any money received is deducted from Income Support on a pound for pound basis. Under the new system, which will be introduced by the Child Support, Pensions and Social Security Bill, currently going through Parliament, a Child Support Premium will be introduced: lone parents on income support will be allowed to keep the first £10 of their weekly child support maintenance payments. Even measures to improve the income of parents on Income Support emphasize parental responsibility – in this case the responsibilities of absent parents – rather than any obligation on the state or wider community to intervene directly to help the poorest children (by, for example, raising social security benefits).

Parents and families

Primary responsibility for the welfare and care of the majority of children rests with their parents. The government has therefore been centrally concerned with family and parenting issues.

The key document here is the Green Paper *Supporting Families*, published in November 1998 (Home Office, 1998). It places children's interests at the heart of a modern family policy and sets out the government's proposals for 'strengthening family life' (for the debate on the family and family policy, see Silva and Smart, 1999).

The government insists that marriage and the traditional family provide 'the most reliable framework for raising children' (Home Office, 1998, p. 30). Concern is therefore expressed about the sharp rise in the divorce rate and the increase in the number of children being brought up in single parent households (a concern shared by the UN Committee, judging by its response to the First Report).

The government's insistence on championing marriage is controversial. Many children flourish in non-traditional families and following the divorce and separation of their parents. Indeed, some research suggests that it is how well a family functions, and the extent of conflict within the family, rather than its structure as such, that is most significant for the welfare of children (MacFarlane *et al.*, 1995). Moreover, in insisting on the importance of marriage, the government is in danger of having a negative impact on the development of children growing up in non-traditional families by conveying the impression that these are second best.

One related issue that has been the subject of some recent controversy is adoption by gay or lesbian couples. There is growing acceptance of the benefits of this. In October 1999 the President of the Family Division of the High Court, Dame Elizabeth Butler-Sloss, spoke in favour of adoption by gay couples and unmarried single parents. Research had persuaded her that this was the best option for some children. 'It would be quite wrong', she concluded, 'when looking at the welfare of the child not to recognize that different children will need different kinds of parents. We should not close our minds to suitable families who are clearly not within the old fashioned approach' (Childright, 1999, p. 21). Apparently reaching the same conclusion, the Children's Society recently lifted its ban on considering applications from gay and lesbian couples seeking to foster or adopt children; a number of churches withheld donations in protest. The issue of family structure and its impact on children's interests thus remains controversial. However, there is a greater acceptance of the fact that children can and do flourish in a range of non-traditional family environments.

The government has set up a National Family and Parenting Institute to raise awareness of parenting issues, develop parenting support programmes, support research, advise government on family policy, and disseminate information. A new National Parenting Helpline (Parentline Plus) has also been established, providing the first point of contact for parents with concerns and problems, and directing them to more specialised services (for further information, see Chapter 26). An enhanced role for health visitors is also contemplated, which would extend their involvement through the pre-school years and even into the later stages of the child's development.

There is also a recognition from government that the pressures of the modern world, not least the demands of the workplace, can make it difficult for parents to provide adequate support for their children at crucial stages of their development. The government has introduced measures to ease these difficulties, although it has been widely criticized for failing to do enough. As of 14 December 1999, under the Employment Relations Act 1999, parents have the right to take up to 13 weeks parental leave, and to take time off work for a family crisis. Parental leave will, however, be unpaid, and it is doubtful that many parents will be able to afford to take it. In addition only parents whose children were born after midnight on 14 December 1999 are entitled to leave. This means an estimated 3.3 million working parents of children under five have no entitlement.

The government has, then, introduced a range of policies aimed at improving the support available to parents. At the same time it has made much of the responsibility of parents for the behaviour of their children. For example, the School Standards and Framework Act 1998 requires schools to 'adopt a home-school agreement (HSA) for the school, together with a parental declaration to be used in connection with the agreement'. The HSA sets forth 'the parental responsibilities, namely the responsibilities which the parents of such pupils are expected to discharge

in connection with the education of their children while they are registered pupils at the school'. HSAs do not have the force of law, and
schools cannot require parents to sign or penalize those who do not. Their
introduction, however, shows that the government is determined to insist
on the responsibilities of parents and other carers with respect to
children's education (Childright, 1998).

More controversial is the introduction of the Parenting Order under the
Crime and Disorder Act 1998. This new court order can be imposed on
the parents of children (including children under 10) involved in antisocial and offending behaviour or persistent truancy. Parents or guardians
may be required to attend counselling or guidance sessions and fined if
they do not comply. This approach is controversial: two objections to this
order were made by young offenders themselves interviewed by the
Children's Society (Children's Society, 1999). They did not think it fair to
hold parents responsible for crimes committed by children and feared that
parenting orders would increase the tensions in already difficult family
environments and expose children to a greater risk of parental violence. It
is also unclear whether the emphasis that the government is placing on
parental responsibility can be reconciled with its recognition, in
discussing social exclusion, of the complex relationships between disadvantage and delinquency, and the wide range of problems that make
young people more likely to offend.

Looked-after children

'Looked-after' children are disproportionately represented on virtually
every indicator of social exclusion in adult life. To take one example, a
Social Exclusion Unit report found that the permanent exclusion rate
among children in care was 10 times higher than average 'with perhaps as
many as 30% of children in care... out of mainstream education, either
excluded or truanting' (Social Exclusion Unit, 1998, p. 39). Abuse and
instability are areas of particular concern.

Regarding instability, a recent survey by the Who Cares? Trust found
that, among those children contacted who had been in care for five years
or more, a quarter had been in 11 or more different homes (Who Cares?
Trust, 1998). Regarding abuse, the key document is the Utting Report
(DoH/Welsh Office, 1997). It was commissioned by the Conservative
government at the time following a catalogue of revelations over a 20-
year period of widespread sexual, physical and emotional abuse of
children living in children's homes and other residential settings. The
report recommended the implementation of a comprehensive strategy for
residential childcare as well as legislation to regulate private foster care
and boarding schools. Further recommendations included ensuring that

there were sufficient residential and foster care placements and focusing on the health and educational needs of looked-after children.

More recently, on 15 February 2000, the Waterhouse Report on the abuse of children in care in North Wales was published. It found that there had been a widespread and systematic abuse, both physical and sexual, in many of the children's homes investigated and that in all the homes, whether or not there was abuse, the quality of care was below (often well below) an adequate standard (DoH/Welsh Office, 2000).

It should, however, be said that the government has done a great deal to improve the position of children unable to live with their parents. Some key initiatives are briefly discussed below.

Quality Protects

In September 1998, the government launched Quality Protects, to transform services for children in need (see, in particular, DoH, 1999a). This is a major three-year initiative to address problems in local authority services. Social services were also promised substantial additional resources in the form of a £375 million Children's Services Grant.

At the core of Quality Protects are eight objectives for local authority children's services. These include a shortening of the period of time children remain in care before being placed for adoption or long-term foster care, and a reduction of significant harm to children in the form of abuse and neglect. Local authorities must also develop strategies to improve the educational performance and health of children in care and to reduce the rate of offending. Particular emphasis is placed on the education of looked-after children, described as 'perhaps the most significant measure of the effectiveness of local authority parenting' (DoH, 1998d, p. 14). In pursuit of these objectives, local authorities must achieve 20 'key tasks' by March 2002.

All local authorities were required to submit Quality Protects Action Plans to the Department of Health (DoH) by January 1999 setting out how they proposed to address the key tasks. The government let it be known that it was prepared to punish councils who failed to realise their objectives in 1999 by withholding their allocations of the Children's Services Grant. At the time concern was expressed about this proposal which, in order to punish inefficient managers, would withhold resources from children relying on council services. In the event no local authority was sanctioned in this way.

Response to the Utting Report

On 5 November 1998 the government responded to the Utting Report. The Secretary of State for Health, Frank Dobson, commented that:

> Too many children taken into care to protect and help them have received neither protection nor help. Instead they have been abused and molested. Many more have been let down, ignored, shifted from place to place, school to school and often simply turned out to fend for themselves when they turned 16. The whole system has failed. If the whole system has failed these children, then the whole system has to be put right. (DoH, 1998e, p. 1)

As well as the changes introduced under Quality Protects, the government announced: the establishment of a new Criminal Records Agency to improve checks on people intending to work with children; a sum of £450,000 over three years in England to establish a group to provide a national voice for children in care and formerly in care; action to reduce placements; a more effective regulation of children's homes and residential schools; a Code of Practice and National Standards for Foster Care; initiatives to improve the school attendance and attainment of looked-after children; and additional resources to help the Prison Service to develop plans to hold all juveniles separately from adults (DoH, 1998a). Many of these initiatives have since borne fruit. In June 1999, for example, the government issued a draft circular on *The Education of Children Looked After by Local Authorities* (DfEE, 1999b), and in July 1999 the first UK *National Standards for Foster Care* and a national Code of Practice were launched (DoH, 1999b).

Some reservations have been expressed about the adequacy of these measures. While the government identifies 'listening to the views and wishes of children' (Templeton, 1998, p. 10), as one of its six priorities, some organizations have argued that additional changes are needed to ensure that their views are fully taken into account. For example, where children are dissatisfied with aspects of their care, they are more likely to challenge the local authority successfully if they have an independent advocate. However, looked-after children still do not have a *right* to an advocate nor does the local authority have a *duty* to provide one. Concern has also been expressed about targets for the objectives set out in Quality Protects. The target for reducing the numbers of placement changes, for example, is depressingly low: by 2001 local authorities are required to reduce the proportion of looked-after children who have three or more placements in one year to 16 per cent. Even if this is realized, much instability will remain. Similarly, the educational targets for looked-after children are hardly ambitious: 50 per cent of children leaving care should have at least one GCSE or GNVQ qualification by 2001, rising to 75 per cent by 2003.

The government has continued to develop policy in this area. At the time of writing, for example, a Care Standards Bill is before Parliament. This will establish an independent body to oversee the regulation of social care (as well as private and voluntary health services) in England. It will be known as the National Care Standards Commission (the Welsh National Assembly will be the regulatory body for these services in Wales). A Children's Rights Director will sit on the Commission and will be accessible to anyone who wishes to raise concerns about a children's home or other residential setting. However, the remit of the Children's Rights Director covers only children in residential settings. Critics argue that if the whole range of children's services is to be adequately overseen, there needs to be a statutory Children's Rights Commissioner.

Child protection

The issue of child protection is a central one for initiatives targeted at looked-after children. There is also concern about abuse within the family setting and a range of other childcare environments. The government has been active in addressing these issues on three principal fronts: an increased surveillance of known sex offenders; improving safeguards to ensure that unsuitable adults are prevented from working with children; and measures to make it easier for children to give evidence against abusers.

Under Part 1 of the Sex Offenders Act 1997, introduced by the Conservative government, offenders who have been convicted of sex offences against children are placed on the Sex Offenders Register. Known sex offenders must notify the police of any change of name and address if they are resident in an area for 14 days or more, failure to do so being a criminal offence. Offenders who have been sentenced to 30 months or more imprisonment are required to register for life. There has been some concern that children themselves have been placed on the Register and treated as sex offenders in circumstances in which this is wholly inappropriate. In 1999 an 11-year-old boy who pleaded guilty to indecent assault on a 2-year-old girl and a 10-year-old boy found guilty of indecently assaulting an 8-year-old girl were placed on the Register. It is doubtful that the legislation ever intended to brand children as sex offenders at such an age.

In July 1998 the government set up the Interdepartmental Working Group on Preventing Unsuitable People Working with Children and Abuse of Trust. Its first report appeared in January 1999 (Home Office, 1999). It recommended a single point of access in the form of a Criminal Records Bureau to enable organizations to check the records of people working with children. Other recommendations included introducing a new criminal offence to allow the prosecution of unsuitable individuals who apply for work with children. A second report, in July 1999, developed these proposals and addressed some of the problems arising from them (for example, how 'working with children' should be interpreted) (Home Office, 1999).

That same month the Protection of Children Act 1999 received Royal Assent, introducing a number of changes to the system for identifying and vetting unsuitable persons. In particular, following the recommendations of the Interdepartmental Group, it provides childcare organizations with a single point from which to check on those whom they are proposing to employ (whether on a paid or a voluntary basis). One limitation of this Act is that it covers only childcare services that are to some extent covered by statute. These include local authority social service functions relating to children (including schools), children's homes (including those which are privately or independently run), nursing and mental health service homes that accommodate children, registered child-minders and some NHS Trust services. However, voluntary groups and cadet forces, while able to use the new system to vet employees, will not be required to do so. The MP who introduced the Bill, Debra Shipley, could therefore do no more than express 'sincere hope' that organizations such as the Scouts would use the vetting mechanism.

If abusers are to be successfully prosecuted, children must be able to give evidence in court. The government has introduced important changes to ease the ordeal for children testifying in these (and other) cases. New arrangements for child witnesses were introduced under the Youth Justice and Criminal Evidence Act 1999. All child witnesses, not only those involved in abuse cases, now qualify for special protection up to the age of 17. Special measures available to them include screens so that they do not see the accused, clearing the press and public from the court, the judge not wearing a wig and gown, allowing child witnesses to be cross-examined prior to the trial and having the cross-examination submitted to the court on videotape, and permitting an approved intermediary to assist the witness in communicating with legal representatives and the court. There is a presumption in favour of permitting young witnesses to give their evidence via a live television link and to have their interviews video-recorded before the trial. Greater protection is, however, being given to children in sex abuse trials than in those dealing with other offences: for example, only in sex abuse cases is provision being made for videoed cross-examination and re-examination. It is unclear what justifies this restriction – violent offences can be just as traumatic for children as sexual ones.

Conclusion

The aim of this chapter has been to provide a general sense of the recent development of childcare policy in the UK. In conclusion, and as a basis for further discussion, it is worth highlighting four more general points about law and policy affecting children.

First, the various areas of childcare policy are 'joined up' in complex ways. The emphasis placed on this in the government's programme to tackle social exclusion was discussed in the relevant section. Other links are less obvious but equally important. There is, for example, an established relationship between poor parenting skills and social exclusion. As a recent report from the Mental Health Foundation, *Bright Futures*, observed 'poverty, unemployment and bad housing do not necessarily produce inadequate parents, but poverty makes good parenting more difficult' (Mental Health Foundation, 1999, p. 12). Another example is physical and sexual abuse within the home. There is an increasing awareness that attempting to explain this in terms of the 'wickedness' or pathology of individual abusers is often counter-productive. As the government acknowledges in the Second Report, such abuse is often triggered by pressure on families and 'real benefits could arise if there was a focus on the wider needs of children and families rather than a narrow concentration of the alleged incident of abuse' (p. 59). Even such an apparently 'private' issue as sexual abuse raises important issues for public policy.

Second, and related to this, the trajectory of childcare policy is partly determined by much wider cultural, economic, social and political developments. Those identified here include a shift in economic orthodoxies that has placed a much greater emphasis on the responsibility of individuals to help themselves – and on the role of education in equipping children and young people for economic independence in adult life – and the complex changes that have contributed to the erosion of the traditional family.

Third, the question of how responsibility for children's welfare and actions is divided between children, parents and governments remains deeply controversial. How is the responsibility for providing children with an adequate standard of living to be allocated between the government and the child's parents? What should governments do when parents fail to fulfil their obligations to children, and to what extent are parents responsible for their children's behaviour? A related area of controversy concerns the extent to which governments should intervene in family life as opposed to respecting the judgments of parents and carers on what is in the best interests of children. It is partly on the grounds that it would represent an undue intrusion into the 'private sphere' that the government has ruled out a ban on physical punishment. To take another example, despite the government's recognition that sex education is vital in tackling the problems of teenage pregnancy and the high incidence of sexually transmitted disease among young people, it has refused to reconsider the right of parents to withdraw their children from sex education classes (regardless, incidentally, of the wishes of children themselves).

Finally, the emphasis in childcare policy has up until recently been on the protection of children and the promotion of their welfare. However, as we have seen, children's rights organizations are increasingly concerned to promote policies that empower children. The government's campaign against poverty and social exclusion, as well as its programme to improve provision for looked-after children and protect them from abuse, welcome as they are, do not represent a departure from a more traditional view of children as recipients of adult help and benevolence. It will involve a more radical change in social attitudes and government policies to implement Article 12 of the Convention and recognize children not simply as recipients but as participants in the running of institutions and the making of the decisions that most closely affect them. The government and public authorities are taking some positive steps in this direction, but there is still some way to go.

7

Towards a 'Children's Policy' for the European Union?

Sandy Ruxton

Since the 1980s the theme of children's rights has emerged globally, reflecting growing concerns about the impact on children of dramatic economic and social change, and shifting perspectives on children and childhood (Qvortrup *et al.*, 1994). The adoption of the UNCRC in 1989 – now ratified by 171 states worldwide[1] – has crystallized this new awareness and interest, and has helped to stimulate the development of laws, policies and institutions to promote children's rights (International Save the Children Alliance, 1999).

Although haphazard, some progress has been made at national and local levels within the Member States of the European Union (EU; Ruxton, 1996). At EU level, however, the focus on children within Community policy-making has been largely non-existent since the establishment of the European Economic Community by the Treaty of Rome in 1957. Forty years on, the Treaty of Amsterdam (1997) is the first EU Treaty ever to refer specifically to 'children'.[2]

Against this background this chapter sets out the limited action that the EU has taken to benefit children and gives examples of the impact of existing law and policy on young children in the UK. It goes on to argue that children's lack of visibility within its legislation, policy and structures is mainly due to the low political priority accorded to them. Having identified the key aims and components of 'children's policy' and its relevance for the EU, the chapter then examines key issues in more depth as well as the potential for positive advances in law and policy. Finally, it sets out the benefits that would result from a coherent and comprehensive EU children's policy.[3]

The chapter is based on the report *A Children's Policy for 21st Century Europe*, which was published by Euronet (the European Children's

Network) in 1999 with financial support from the European Commission. The report sets out a children's agenda for the EU, based on information derived from a series of conferences and seminars across the EU and interviews with key decision-makers at EU and Member State level.[4]

EU action that has benefited children

In recent years the EU has undertaken some action that has had direct benefits for children. Most of this, however, has been targeted at the 15–25-year age range through education or youth employment programmes and initiatives to prepare young people – especially those from disadvantaged backgrounds – for participation in the labour market. A significant legislative initiative relating to this age group has been the 1994 Young Workers Directive, designed to promote the health and safety of young people in the workplace.[5]

In relation to younger children the most prominent theme at EU level has been tackling violence towards them, the profile of this issue rising dramatically across Europe as a result of public revulsion at the 'Dutroux' case in Belgium in 1996. While respecting the primary responsibility of the Member States in this area, it has been widely accepted that the EU can make a contribution, particularly by addressing child protection issues with a transnational dimension. In response various directorates of the European Commission have developed a range of funding programmes to tackle violence, child sex tourism, bullying in schools and the transmission of child pornography via the Internet. The most well-known of these are the Daphne and STOP Programmes run by the Secretariat General.[6]

Concerns over child safety have been the reason for a more long-standing involvement at EU level in consumer issues affecting children, which has been reinforced by the Single Market's emphasis on the free movement of goods and services. Some specific action has been taken by the European Commission since the late 1980s to target children as a vulnerable group (by, for example, directives on minimum safety requirements for toys and playground equipment, and on harmful television programmes). More recently increasing emphasis has been placed on developing practical strategies for educating children in school with regard to consumer issues.

Alongside the initiatives outlined above, which have focused on children and young people as a target group, the EU has also taken some action that has benefited children more indirectly. Within the field of family policy, there has been a very fragile and limited basis since 1989 for information and the exchange of good practice in relation to children,[7] but the action taken has centred on families rather than children. For example, only limited attention has as yet been paid to children as a separate category within households by Eurostat (the EU's statistical agency) and the Commission-funded European Observatory on National Family Policies. Similarly, the strong focus within the EU Treaties on removing barriers to participation in the labour force means that some action has been taken to help working parents (see below). The main thrust has, however, been on helping parents to reconcile work and family responsibilities rather than addressing children's interests directly.

The impact of EU policy on children in the UK

As yet the impact of EU policy on children in the UK has been very limited. This is partly because of the restricted 'competence' of the EU in relation to social policy, but also because of the long-standing scepticism, shared by politicians, media and the public in the UK, towards any significant EU intervention in this field domestically. This opposition appears to be particularly strong in relation to policy towards children and families, especially as a result of the endurance – and dominance during the 1980s and early 1990s – of the ideology of individualism and non-state intervention in the lives of families. This approach contrasts significantly with the corporatist or universalistic traditions towards child welfare within other EU states (Pringle, 1998a).

Yet the UK has during the past decade increasingly been influenced by the EU's social dimension. Although the UK originally opted out of the 1989 Charter of Fundamental Social Rights (the 'Social Charter'), UK employers and trade union organizations in particular have played a growing part in debates about the future development of social provision within the EU. And despite the hostility of the previous UK government, EU policy has clearly had a knock-on impact on social policy matters, with some indirect positive effects for children. The 1992 Pregnancy Leave Directive, for example, introduced as a health and safety measure and therefore not requiring unanimous support from all Member States, led to an improvement in maternity leave entitlement for women in Britain. Similarly, the 1993 Working Time Directive to protect workers from excessive working hours (also agreed under the umbrella of health and safety), has provided a stronger legal framework for workers in the UK since transposition into national law by the Working Time Regulations 1999. This latter provision is potentially particularly important for British fathers, who currently work on average 47 hours per week – the longest hours in the EU.

Although the current Labour government remains wary of the potential impact on UK public opinion of any significant increase in EU intervention in domestic social policy, it has opted in to the 1991 'Social Chapter' (which consolidated the provisions of the earlier Charter – see above). As

a result the 1999 Employment Relations Act has implemented the 1996
Parental Leave Directive so that parents with one year's continuous
employment will qualify for three months' leave to look after their
children.[8] Although this right is a significant step forward, it will not,
however, apply to parents who already have children under five years old.

It is not within the scope of this chapter to outline all the initiatives the
EU has taken that affect children in Britain. However, the above examples indicate that, backed by increasing pressure at national level, EU
action has had a small but significant impact on the lives of working
parents in the UK, and indirectly on their children. The remainder of this
chapter suggests that such initiatives could potentially be extended to
other areas where the EU has a degree of competence, including violence
to children, social exclusion and discrimination against children.

Weaknesses of the EU's current approach to children

Although EU initiatives have to some extent benefited children in the
fields set out above, children's interests remain in general invisible within
the policy-making process. For example the legal and political protection
of 'EU citizenship' is largely irrelevant to those outside the labour force,
especially children. Children have received little attention in negotiations
over the enlargement of the EU, and although the environmental threat to
children (by, for example, increasing traffic, inaccessible play space and
environmental degradation) is growing, EU legislation has not systematically addressed their needs. Moreover, while children can benefit from
some EU budget lines, overall they receive a negligible proportion of the
available resources, and what money there is is largely targeted at
children over the age of 15.

One consequence of this invisibility is that there is no focal point within
the EU structure for developing an overall policy direction and mainstreaming a children's perspective across all the policy areas. In the European Commission, there are at least 10 directorates,[9] and in the Parliament
at least seven Committees,[10] that have an interest, yet in neither case is
there a unit responsible for giving a policy lead.

Another effect is that children's rights are often overridden by more
powerful economic interests. The free movement provisions of the Single
Market, for example, take little account of the potentially damaging
consequences for children. Advertisers are exerting increasing commer-
cial pressure on children and employing new and more sophisticated
marketing practices to link children from a very young age to particular
products and services. Although there are some directives that have
sought to take children's specific interests into account, the 1984 directive
on misleading advertising fails to acknowledge the ways in which adver-

tisers are increasingly seeking to target children, and that children need special protection from this because of their vulnerability.

As a result of these weaknesses the EU has a very limited legal base for its action in relation to children. Although the 1997 Amsterdam Treaty inserts the first-ever reference to children into the EU Treaties, the focus of Article 29 on tackling offences against them remains very narrow. Other Articles – 137 on combating social exclusion and 13 on non-discrimination – are helpful too and should be used to benefit children. But the EU's overall 'competence' in relation to children's issues is restricted and lacks coherence.

Why is an EU children's policy needed?

'Children's policy' focuses on children as a specific group in society rather than the family, women, the labour market or the community/neighbourhood. It attempts to make children more 'visible' within policy-making and wider society and is usually based on UNCRC principles of protection, provision and participation. Building on an increasing awareness of children's specific interests, efforts to explore and define 'children's policy' have gradually emerged, the key components of a 'children's policy' (Euronet, 1999) being:

- the 'best interests' of the child as a guiding principle
- increasing investment in children and ensuring fair distribution of resources between social groups
- overall co-ordination of policy, based on cross-departmental working to agreed strategies
- policies addressing both the direct and indirect interests of children
- the systematic collection of information on children to identify their needs and policy priorities
- the establishment of independent bodies to monitor children's rights
- the participation of children in decision-making, both within the family and beyond

The need for a specific 'children's policy' at EU level is frequently misunderstood. It is sometimes argued that children's policy is purely a matter for the Member States; while this is true for the vast majority of policy areas, there are several in which the role of the EU in relation to transnational matters, developing joint action or exchanging information and ideas between Member States could be highly effective. Indeed, other social groups, such as women, have benefited significantly from such approaches despite having a limited legal base to draw upon.

Alternatively, it is claimed that the public would not support EU action in relation to children, although research suggests that the public will do so where it can see the need for it. According to one survey published last year, 84 per cent of Europeans believe EU intervention to combat child sex tourism to be desirable, 88 per cent believing it necessary (INRA (Europe), 1998).

It is sometimes suggested that as the family is the place where most children grow up, issues concerning children can be most effectively addressed under the umbrella of 'family policy', but 'family policy' attempts to span the needs of parents, elder people, other relations, step-families and lone parent families as well as those of children, and this broad focus can easily obscure the interests of the child.

Perceiving the best interests of the child as automatically the same as those of their parents is also unsatisfactory. There are instances in which what is best for the child may conflict with what is best for other family members. This can be particularly evident in cases involving adoption, separation and divorce, or child protection. An example within the EU context is the EU's emphasis on the childcare needs of parents (especially mothers) as workers. From this perspective children can tend to be seen as 'barriers to work', 'dependants', a 'cause' of family poverty – as burdens on families and society rather than as actual and potential contributors. Moreover, children's perspectives can easily get ignored.

It is also important to acknowledge that children have interests that go beyond what the family can do for them. This is evident in relation to their rights as consumers, citizens and recipients of services. For example, the fact that today's children spend more time in institutions such as day care centres, crèches, schools and youth clubs increases the importance of developing policy that addresses their particular needs as social actors.

Although there are obvious overlaps with 'family' or 'gender' policy, what is needed is an EU children's policy that, respecting the principle of subsidiarity, ensures the promotion of their rights. Such a policy should complement and build upon policies towards families and women.

Implementing children's rights at EU level using existing legal bases

The development of an EU 'children's policy' would be greatly assisted by the insertion of a clear reference to children within the EU Treaties. While this remains a long-term goal, however, there are other steps that could and should be taken as soon as possible which would improve the position of children and build the case for a comprehensive reference.[11] Most obviously, the relevant legal bases in the Amsterdam Treaty should be used to benefit children to the full (Euronet, 1997).

In relation to violence against children, Article 29 will encourage the development of police and judicial cooperation in tackling crimes against children that cross transnational borders. Although this Article provides a clearer statement of objectives, it is, however, part of the 'Third Pillar'[12] of the Treaty on European Union. This considerably weakens its impact as any action has to be agreed by the Member States on a case-by-case basis outside Community application of the Treaty.

The available evidence suggests that the trafficking of children into the EU is an increasingly serious problem. For example Albanian children are being brought into Greece and Italy illegally to be economically and/or sexually exploited and in France there are cases of children from China being forced to work in sweatshops and children from Sierra Leone being forced into prostitution. In addition, trafficking routes to the Netherlands appear particularly well established, children being brought from Eastern Europe, China and Nigeria by organized gangs to work in the sex trade (Ruxton, 2000).

While the European Commission has taken some limited action in relation to these issues,[13] the scale of the problem indicates that such action should be extended. Despite the practical restrictions on the application of Article 29 there is a considerable political will among the Member States to strengthen action in this area. For example, at a recent summit of the European Council (the heads of Member State governments) a new priority was given under the Finnish Presidency to fighting crimes against children.[14]

Another key area of potential EU activity is social exclusion. Children are particularly vulnerable to the effects of social exclusion as it can significantly damage their physical, mental and social development. Yet across the EU, one fifth of children already live in households with an income of below 50 per cent of the average in their country (Eurostat, 1993), and many live in families where no parent or carer is employed. Moreover, children in particular social groups (for example, ethnic minorities, homeless people, travellers, asylum seekers, refugees and those living in rural areas) often encounter particular difficulties with education, health, welfare and leisure services.

Although EU social policy initiatives have in the past often been blocked by Member States (especially the previous UK government and the German regional governments), Article 137 of the Amsterdam Treaty provides a new legal foundation from which to combat social exclusion. As this clause can be agreed by majority voting in the Council of Ministers, it provides an important basis for further EU action. The impact of this Article is already being felt. At a recent summit of Employment and Social Affairs Ministers in Lisbon under the Portuguese Presidency,[15] it was agreed that tackling social exclusion requires major coordination at European level in relation to two forms of action: the mainstreaming of social inclusion in education, training, employment and social protection policies; and the development of integrated, targeted programmes for groups experiencing major exclusion, the top priority being to eradicate child poverty by 2010. Following the summit the European Commission has also now pledged to examine the issue of child poverty in its forthcoming social inclusion programme.

The other area in which there is currently the most potential for EU action to benefit children is in relation to combating discrimination against them. Whereas discrimination against many social groups (for example, women, disabled people, ethnic minorities and elderly people) is usually acknowledged, there are common features with the experience of children. All these groups tend to receive different and unequal treatment compared with the 'majority' group against which they are defined. They often have judgments made about their needs and receive welfare based on what other people consider their needs to be, being denied the opportunity to participate in decisions that affect them. They are also seen frequently as being in need of protection rather than empowerment, and as 'dependants' who are 'unproductive'.

Article 13 of the Amsterdam Treaty gives the EU new powers to combat discrimination, and the European Commission has subsequently published a 'communication' to set the general framework, two draft directives (on discrimination and employment, and discrimination and race) and an Action Programme (2001–06). While these measures are welcome, the needs of children must be recognized under the broad umbrella of 'discrimination'.

Towards an EU 'children's policy'?

More than any other population group, it will be children who will experience the long-term consequences of the key issues facing the EU and its Member States, such as the euro, enlargement, welfare reform and demographic change. It is also children who – as workers and carers – will provide the mainstay of Europe's response to these dramatic economic, social and political challenges. There is therefore an urgent need for further EU action to prepare children for these challenges by developing a coherent EU children's policy, rooted in the principles of the CRC. Such a policy would:

● enable the impact of EU policy on children to be assessed systematically;
● ensure that a child perspective was included in the drawing up of EU policies;
● promote a greater exchange of good practice between the Member States;

- ensure that greater resources were invested in children;
- provide the basis for monitoring and evaluating the impact of social, economic and demographic change on children within the EU;
- strengthen the role of children's non-governmental organizations (NGOs) at EU level, and ensure that the voices of children are heard in EU policy-making;
- help EU institutions to recognize and respond to the particular vulnerability of children.

So what should be the key components of an EU children's policy? Most importantly, the EU Treaties should provide a clear legal basis to ensure that children's interests are fully respected within EU policy-making, taking into account the lead role of the Member States in this area. The Amsterdam Treaty represents a significant advance for children's rights, but what is really needed is a more comprehensive reference to children to be added to the Treaties.

At the end of 1999 the European Commission took a first hesitant step towards this goal by announcing in a debate on the 10th anniversary of the CRC[16] that it would consider publishing a 'Communication'[17] on children. Although there are indications that the Commission may back away from such a commitment, ideally a communication would be wide-ranging and would set out the context, key policy themes, and further measures to be promoted to EU and national level. Defining an appropriate policy framework could then in time be followed by the development of a well-resourced EU Action Programme for children.

To strengthen EU structures a Children's Unit should also be established, based centrally within the Commission. Its role would be to promote the development of an overall EU children's policy and to coordinate action across directorates. To develop a liaison between the EU institutions and children's NGOs, an NGO Advisory Committee should be established, as already exists in relation to other social groups.

It is also vital to improve the available information on children and to monitor their circumstances more effectively across all policy areas, especially the impact of macro-economic policy-making on children (Atkinson, 1998; Mickelwright and Stewart, 1998). To close gaps such as this, the mandate of Eurostat[18] should be extended to include a wider range of basic data on children. In addition, the reports of the European Observatory on National Family Policies should regularly be presented to the European Parliament and used as the basis for debates.

Finally, a policy on children's rights must be rooted in children's participation. The EU institutions should build on the rich and diverse range of pilot initiatives within the Member States and explore further ways in which they can take the interests of children – especially those below the age of 15 – more directly into account in decision-making.[19]

These recommendations form the basis of a vision for children's future in the EU. To translate this vision into practice will require the mobilization of considerable political will among the relevant actors: key decision-makers at EU and national level; civil society and, in particular, children's organizations; and – last but not least – children themselves. The twentieth century has shown what can be achieved with popular support: improvements in the living conditions of working people, progress towards equality between the sexes, an increasing awareness of the importance of environmental issues. At the beginning of the new millennium, it is time to put children on the European agenda too. Time for a children's policy for twenty-first century Europe.

Notes

1   Only Somalia and the USA have failed to do so.
2   The Treaty of Amsterdam was signed in 1997 and fully ratified by the EU Member States in 1999. It consolidates the 'Three Pillars' (the European Community; common foreign and security policy; and cooperation in the fields of justice and home affairs), which have been the foundation of the EU's work since the 1991 Maastricht Treaty. In practice the Amsterdam Treaty has resulted in limited but significant changes: new anti-discrimination and social exclusion provisions written into the Treaty; the addition of a chapter on employment to the Treaty; and further moves towards a common EU asylum policy.
3   For reasons of length the approach of the Council of Europe is not explored in any depth.
4   The full text of the report and further information is available on line via the Euronet website (http://europeanchildrensnetwork.gla.ac.uk)
5   Education programmes include SOCRATES (cooperation in education), LEONARDO (vocational training policy) and Youth for Europe III (cooperation in the youth field), all led by the Education, Training and Youth directorate. The employment needs of young people have been addressed through the Structural Funds (particularly the European Social Fund), led by the Employment, Industrial Relations and Social Affairs directorate. Some attention has been paid to activities to support younger children in school (e.g. a European network of schools, programmes for the training of teachers and 'Netd@ys' to explore the contribution of the Internet), but this action has been far more limited.
6   In addition to the Daphne and STOP funding programmes, specific projects have been initiated to combat child sex tourism (DGXXIII), to prevent and tackle violence in schools (DGXXII) and to protect children from harmful material transmitted via the Internet and other forms of new technology (DGX and DGXIII).
7   See the Council of Ministers 'Conclusions on family policy' of 29 September 1989 (together with an accompanying Commission 'Communication on family policies').
8   The 1999 Employment Relations Act also introduces new rights to time off to care for dependants and improves existing maternity provision.

9   Justice and Home Affairs; External Relations; Employment and Social Affairs; Development and Humanitarian Aid; Information Society; Education and Culture; Regional Policy; Health and Consumer Protection; Enlargement; and Environment.

10 Legal Affairs and Citizens' Rights; Employment and Social Affairs; Culture, Youth, Education and the Media; Development and Co-operation; Civil Liberties and Internal Affairs; Human Rights; and Women's Rights.

11 This section looks at violence against children, social exclusion and non-discrimination. Other areas of EU policy are, however, also relevant, including: citizenship and participation; the free movement of people; the media and Internet; consumer policy; education; health; the environment; employment; economic and monetary union; enlargement; and information on children. For a discussion of these areas, see Euronet (1999).

12 Under the 1991 Treaty on European Union (the 'Maastricht Treaty'), the 'European Community' became only the first of the 'Three Pillars' of the 'European Union', the second being foreign and security policy, and the third justice and home affairs. Activity under the Second and Third Pillars is conducted largely on an intergovernmental basis.

13 See note 6 above.

14 Council of Ministers of the European Union, Presidency Conclusions, Tampère European Council, 15–16 October 1999, SN 200/99.

15 Conclusions of Inter-ministerial summit of Employment and Social Affairs Ministers, Lisbon 23–24 March 2000, www.portugal.ue-2000.pt

16 Commissioner Vitorino, debate in the European Parliament, 15 November 1999.

17 A 'Communication' is an advisory statement produced by the European Commission that examines the context and content of particular policy issues and explores policy objectives. It is not binding on Member States.

18 Eurostat is an EU statistical service, based in Luxembourg, that covers – among other areas – issues such as agriculture, industry, trade, social trends, demography and the labour force.

19 See the 1998 Council of Ministers of Youth, Resolution on Youth Participation, Brussels, 26 November 1998.

Part II

Quality of Life for Children

8

Quality of Life for Children

Jeremy Roche

In this chapter I explore the meaning of the concept of quality of life (QoL) and how it might impact on work with children. Such an exploration is valuable because, in the childhood context, the concept of QoL provides an opportunity for a re-think of policy matters affecting children and a consideration of different ways of working with them. It also allows us to question whether a traditional concern with the welfare of children is a sufficient basis for work with children and families.

Thinking about the quality of children's lives can be disruptive to the extent that we accept the invitation to question the assumptions of the adult world. The argument of this chapter is that a QoL approach entails a shift in focus from the needs of particular children to a wider, more eclectic concern that addresses the social, cultural, economic and political aspects of our society, which determines the QoL of all children, including a concern with the emotional as well as psycho-social dimension of their lives. Thus such an approach emphasizes the opportunity that children have to realize their potential, in the broadest sense, and whether such opportunity is denied or restricted by poverty and oppressive ideas and practices.

The first section looks at the different uses of the concept and the practice issues it raises. Next the obstacles in the way of promoting children's QoL are examined before considering how QoL for children can be developed. I conclude by identifying the key principles that can inform work with children in order to contribute to their quality of life.

Quality of life – what does it mean?

There is a growing body of literature addressing the idea of QoL. The concept appears in many fields, including those of health, development economics and moral philosophy. Its definition is, however, not settled; there is no one agreed definition and it is a somewhat elastic concept. Very different kinds of issue are covered by the term, and the issues to which it gives rise are thus varied.

A supposedly objective measure of wealth and well-being such as a 'standard of living' index takes account of only material resources, whereas 'quality of life' includes social, psychological and political factors (see, for example, Jackson and Marks, 1998). In the field of health the concept has been associated with controversial debates: for example, an assessment of the subsequent quality of life of a severely disabled child becomes necessary when health care decisions are made. It has, however, also been used in relation to an individual's sense of well-being – and in this sense it is subjective and individualistic.

The Patient Generated Index (PGI) is a good example of this. The PGI is a 'patient-centred approach to measuring quality of life' (Garratt and Ruta, 1999, pp. 106–7) that seeks to give the concept more meaning by focusing on those aspects of life which sustain the individual. Thus Garratt and Ruta describe the PGI as an instrument that 'could be used to quantify the difference between individuals' hopes and expectations and reality in a way that has meaning and relevance in their daily lives' (1999, pp. 106–7). Certain aspects of QoL that are valued highly by one person might be of little importance to another. So in the field of health the discussion centring on the concept leads to a questioning of the 'doctor knows best' assumption and links with wider debates about people's health and well-being, the weight to be given to patients' view of their situation and the intersection between patients' subjectivity and medical science.

In the field of development economics Dasgupta and Weale (1992) point out that quality of life can be measured in two ways. The focus can be on either the 'constituents' of well-being, for example indices of health and welfare, or the 'determinants', for example access to food and clean water, and education provision. They argue that, at one level, it does not matter which route they take, but they go on to observe that some indices of well-being are restricted to the socio-economic sphere: 'the political and civil spheres are for the most part kept separate'. A fully rounded measure requires both aspects to be considered.

The World Health Organization (WHO) set up a working party to examine quality of life, which proposed the following definition:

> Quality of life is defined as an individual's perception of their position in life in the context of the culture and value systems in which they live and in relation to the goals, expectations, standards and concerns. It is a broad ranging concept affected in a complex way by the person's physical health, psychological state, level of independence, social relationships, and their relationships to salient features in their environment. (World Health Organization's Quality of Life Group, 1993, p. 30)

This definition emphasizes the subjective as well as the objective aspect of QoL (see Offner, 1996).

Within economics Sen (1993) has adopted a 'capabilities approach' to measuring QoL. Rather than examining the actual distribution of social goods (for example, health, education, housing and employment) in a society, the capabilities approach requires an examination of what people in a given country are actually able to do and to be. For Sen it is not enough to look at the subjective preferences of people because these preferences may be distorted by deprivation and oppression. As Glover points out (1995, p. 123), 'people's desires may be so shaped by their situation that their satisfaction is a poor guide to justice. Long established deprivation may lead to a "realistically" low level of desires.' What needs to be focused on is the differing needs of individuals for resources to realize their potential.

Sen further argues that freedom is an essential component of quality of life. He argues that assessments of simply material life indices cannot explain the choices that people make in life. This is because people value the freedom to make decisions and to participate in the processes that lead to the making of decisions and to changes in the choices that individuals make. This freedom, while important to the immediate life choices of individuals, is also important in another way. The exercise of freedom, with which comes a sense of responsibility, allows human capabilities to form, develop and be enhanced. For Sen it is these capabilities which make us human, but what are these 'capabilities'?

Nussbaum identifies a number of 'basic human functional capabilities' including being able to be adequately nourished and have adequate shelter, being able to avoid unnecessary and non-beneficial pain, being able to laugh and play, being able to have attachments to things and persons outside ourselves and being able to 'form a conception of the good' and to engage in critical reflection about one's own life (1995, pp. 83–5). Nussbaum advances a universal human rights position in relation to QoL. The concept 'human being' is a normative ethical concept. All human beings have these capabilities and the task of politics and social organization is to secure their realization.[1] The concept of QoL deployed in this chapter makes use of Sen's capabilities approach and focuses on children's lives and the claims they, and others acting on their behalf, make.

The position of children

While the literature reviewed above does not specifically look at children it raises issues that are of direct relevance to children and their environment. In the above accounts children appear but only as indices of health and well-being. For example, perinatal and infant mortality rates will often be taken as one key index of national quality of life. Children need to be brought into the social accounting process. In others words what is needed is both research and statistical information that is child-centred and recognizes that children are both 'receivers and doers' (Saporiti, 1994, p. 192). Yet beginning the process of compiling the contributions that children make and their socio-economic entitlements is only half the story. To have access to decent education and health services is a necessary condition for QoL – but it may not be sufficient. While it is obviously of fundamental importance to have access to such services, it does not address the issue of how those services are experienced and seen by all children. While the concept of QoL retains its concern with the welfare of persons, it at the same time stresses the perspective of children and seeks to understand the ways in which different children are affected by oppressive ideas and the uneven distribution of social resources; these disadvantaging circumstances bear down on children in different ways.[2]

It is not merely a question of the experts having their say or even of working in partnership with parents and others to safeguard and promote the welfare of children. A dominant assumption in our society is that children can be subsumed under the family. Yet some quality of life literature exploring gender inequality makes it clear that the unit of analysis can no longer be taken as the family (Nussbaum and Glover, 1995). The interests and behaviours of the 'head of household' are not necessarily coincidental with those of all its members (Blumberg *et al.*, 1995). In most instances family members, especially women, make very great sacrifices for the well-being of their children (Joseph Rowntree Foundation, 1999) and are determined fighters for their children's welfare rights. Nonetheless children are not visible in the QoL debates save as the dependants of other family members. So why might it be important to consider children separately as well as part of a family or kinship network?

Children themselves might have something particular to say about their own world and to contribute to decision-making in relation to this environment. Their view of their world and their QoL is essential if QoL is to mean something beyond the concerns of adults. Thus QoL for children has an objective material aspect to it, for example access to decent housing and education, as well as a subjective, or psycho-social, aspect. A child's parents might like the school their child goes to because it is well maintained, it does well in the league tables and the children seem to be well behaved. In contrast the child might not like the school because he routinely experiences unfairness and injustice in the classroom, the dining hall and the playground. In this sense listening to children and enhancing their participation is a 'good in itself'. Adults do not always know best.

What the model of QoL emphasizes is the importance of the development of human capabilities. These capabilities develop when the socio-economic context is supportive of individuals' needs, both material and psycho-social. The support that individuals need is both within the family and within society. In relation to the familial and the social contexts, what is at issue here is how children's capabilities to develop through participation in the processes that affect their lives can be best promoted at the same time as ensuring that the requisite material bases of these participative processes are in place. Children are social actors in their own environment with views on what they do and do not like. The traditional view is that the child, especially the younger child, is not able to participate in the world, that he or she is deeply dependent on adults, and properly so, and that although not the property of their parents, children are objects of concern. This positioning of the child is one of the obstacles to QoL for children.

Obstacles to QoL for children

There are two factors peculiar to children that serve to undermine their QoL. First, as noted above, children are subject to those socio-economic and environmental conditions which act upon and are influenced by their parents. For many children and families poverty is a dominant feature of their lives. Holman observes that 'lives are spoilt not just by the hardship of poverty but also by the impact of inequality' (1998, p. 61). Prejudice impacts on the lives of many children, and initiatives to improve the QoL of children will have to take on board not just the material conditions in which they are living, but also the psycho-social dimension. Lane captures the importance of this dimension in the context of her discussion of working in the Early Years sector in a way that effectively counteracts prejudice; she writes (1999, p. 4): 'To feel secure, confident, comfortable, content and able to pursue our ambitions as members of society, we need to be valued for ourselves, to be respected and treated with dignity and fairness'. She argues that it is important for adults to develop strategies to counteract prejudice as children 'have a right not to learn such negative attitudes' (p. 4). In this context, as in many others, the QoL question also raises issues about the ways in which adults see and discharge their responsibilities towards children.

Second are the attitudes and practices of adult society, which tend to see children as incompetent and irrational. It could be argued that, as long as adults care properly for children, how they perceive children is irrelevant. However, there are too many instances in the private as well as the public sphere in which children's trust in adults has been abused (see Parton, 1985; Reder *et al.*, 1993). As noted above this is more than a project to protect children better. The importance of thinking about children in the context of QoL is to disrupt accepted ways of seeing the issues associated with childhood. An acceptance of the idea of including children and treating them with respect in order to fashion a better world involves a reversal of many cherished practices. De Winter writes (1997, p. 163):

> What children can handle at a certain moment in their development is not a constant factor, but is partly the result of the space for learning and experiencing offered to them. By widening the field of development, for instance by involving children from a very early age in the organization of the world in which they live, their repertoire of behavioural capabilities grows.

He goes on to observe that if we take this view, children turn out to be capable of much more than adults think. Adults might need to be creative and think in terms of asking even very young children what they feel about a situation. Children as young as two years of age have been able to tell researchers from the Day Care Trust that the things they liked about their day care included good food, their friendships with other children and being able to make their own choices (see Moorhead, 1999).

Strategies for promoting children's QoL

Strategies to promote QoL for children operate at a number of levels: the national, the community and the individual. These are interconnected, initiatives at one level having an effect on the other two. For example, a community-based strategy to promote QoL for children might have a knock-on effect in the home, where there might not be the same emphasis on the child's participation or involvement in decision-making.

A community-based example provides a useful example of why QoL is important to all children. The Investing in Children initiative, established by Durham County Council in 1998 to improve the QoL of children living in County Durham, is premised on two linked ideas. First, those organizations concerned with the well-being of children should work in a coordinated way, and second, adults do not always know best. As a result the initiative adopted a 'statement of intent' identifying the aim of the initiative as being to 'work in partnership with children and young people to promote their best interests and enhance their quality of life' (Durham County Council, 1999). The statement describes how this aim will be achieved by consulting with children and their families, promoting partnerships, developing accessible children- and family-centred services and ensuring that 'child impact' statements are attached to Council decisions.

Child impact statements are statements that clearly indicate the impact of the proposed decision on the lives and well-being of children. Their existence can prompt decision-makers to see, perhaps for the first time, how what they are considering might impact on the lives of children. This can lead them to a greater commitment to consultation with, and the involvement of, children in decisions that concern them, for example on local transport policy. The introduction of child impact statements thus opens up new relations and public conversations between public authority, the organizations concerned with the well-being of children and the children themselves. The statement concludes by making explicit the link between QoL and children's rights:

> The values which underpin our work with children and young people are consistent with the United Nations Convention on the Rights of the Child.

This emphasis on children's rights is a necessary aspect of a commitment to QoL for children. The welfare rights contained in the UNCRC are directly concerned with both protecting children and enhancing their welfare. Article 4 of the UNCRC requires parties, with regard to the economic, social and cultural rights contained in the UNCRC, to undertake all 'appropriate legislative, administrative and other measures' to secure these rights, and states 'parties shall undertake such measures to the maximum extent of their available resources'. This carries within it a positive agenda for children. Furthermore the participation rights contained in the UNCRC link with the subjectivity that is integral to the QoL debate. Respect for the voice of the child is an essential part of any project that seeks to enhance the well-being of children; it is part of a strategy of inclusion that is one of the foundation stones of QoL.

In Durham the Investing in Children initiative has identified four pivotal aspects of community services that would make County Durham 'a good place to grow up': health, safety and protection, personal development and learning, and promoting independence to adulthood. Initiatives such as these acknowledge the impact and power of the problematizing discourses – visualizing certain children and families as being problems rather than having problems – that surround children today, and argue that Investing in Children must challenge these negative images of children and publicize their positive achievements.

At a national level initiatives such as Quality Protects and the Children's Commissioner for Wales can be seen as having been informed by events at the community level, for example concerns about the quality of public care, as well as debates at the international level surrounding children's rights. Taking children's rights seriously is part of a solution to the problems posed by the abuse of power by adults. On an individual basis, rights and the law can improve the lives of children. The Children (Scotland) Act 1995, for example, emphasizes the rights of the child within the family by imposing on parents a duty to consult with children on major decisions affecting their lives – this acknowledgement of the child's distinctive and potentially separate interests and perspective can be seen as part of the 'democratization' of family life (Beck, 1997) and as symbolically elevating the child as a citizen (De Winter, 1997; Roche, 1999); it might also operate to support QoL for children within the private sphere.

Conclusion

So what principles for practice can be derived from the above discussion of children's QoL. Given that children live under the same environmental conditions as adults, measures taken to support disadvantaged families will benefit children. Community-based action to provide positive and non-stigmatizing support to children and families has a key role to play here. Colton *et al.* (1997), in their research into child welfare services and stigma in three European countries, found that in the UK the cost of making use of the child welfare services can be to be labelled a scrounger or a malingerer. Those services which were best received by the families concerned were those assisting them 'to prevent problems from arising or becoming unmanageable' (Colton *et al*, 1997, p. 279). Further measures that assisted families to 'extend and improve their own coping mechanisms', were preferred to those which required a continued reliance on others. Stigmatizing service delivery is thus highly problematic.

So it is not just a question of the child's material well-being in terms of health, welfare and education, but also an issue of their self-esteem and respect, this of necessity including the child's family and community. Work that is concerned to promote the QoL of all children will have to have regard to this psycho-social agenda. This might entail proactive anti-racist work in day care settings and schools (see for example EYTARN, 1998) or developing inclusive ways of working with disabled children. Children's own resources, self-reliance and resilience might thus be enhanced.

Finally, the child's right to participate is central to any commitment to a broad notion of QoL for children. In this sense QoL for children raises more general issues about children's rights and the often-denied role they play in the lives of their families and communities.

Notes

1   Nussbaum (1995) notes that the term 'person' has in the past been withheld from certain groups of people, for example women. Historically, many 'others' – most obviously slaves – have been excluded from 'personhood'.

2   Sen (1995, pp. 259–79) comments on the research on the extent to which women occupy a disadvantaged position in traditional socio-economic arrangements through a comparison of the survival rates of women and men in the West and the Third World. He calculates that if the European and North American ratios are taken as the standard there are 100,000,000 women missing worldwide.

9

Children's Welfare and Children's Rights

Gerison Lansdown

Children, as minors in law, have neither autonomy nor the right to make choices or decisions on their own behalf. Instead, responsibility for such decisions and for the welfare of children has traditionally been vested with those adults who care for them. It has always been presumed not only that adults are better placed than children to exercise responsibility for decision-making, but also that in so doing they will act in children's best interests. In addition this presumption has been established as a legal obligation on the courts, which for many years have been required to give paramountcy to the welfare of the child in making decisions concerning their day-to-day lives (Children Act 1989). This model of adult–child relationships constructs children as the passive recipients of adult protection and good will, lacking the competence to exercise responsibility for their own lives.

In recent years we have begun to question the adequacy of this approach and to re-examine the assumptions on which it has been based: first, that adults can be relied on to act in children's best interests; second, that children lack the competence to act as agents in their own lives; and third, that adults have the monopoly of expertise in determining outcomes in children's lives. There have been a number of factors contributing to this process of change. Certainly, over the past 20 years, we have witnessed a growing body of evidence concerning children's lives that challenges any capacity for complacency about the extent to which children's welfare is being protected by adults.

The limitations of a welfare approach

Adults can abuse their power over children

Adults in positions of power over children can exploit and abuse that power, to the detriment of children's well-being. During the 1970s we first became aware of the extent to which children are vulnerable to physical abuse within their own families. The extent and scale of violence that parents were capable of perpetrating on their own children emerged through the work of Henry Kempe in the USA and was brought home forcefully in this country with the case of Maria Colwell, a young girl who was returned from care to live with her parents, who subsequently beat her to death (Howells, 1974). It was not, however, until the 1980s that the phenomenon of sexual abuse within families, as a day-to-day reality for many thousands of children, hit the public consciousness in this country with the Cleveland scandal into the sexual abuse of children (DHSS, 1988). There was, and probably still is, considerable resistance to the recognition that parents and other adult relatives could and do rape and assault their children. It challenges the very notion of family life that we wish to believe exists for all children – the view that children are safest within their families. It also challenges the legitimacy of the powerful cultural desire for protecting the privacy of family life because it undermines the comfortable assumption that parents can always be relied on to promote the welfare of their children.

It took until the 1990s to uncover the next scandal in the catalogue of failure on the part of responsible adults to protect and promote the welfare of children. In a series of public inquiries it became apparent not only that children in public care in a number of local authorities had been subjected to systematic physical and sexual abuse by staff in children's homes, but also that these practices had been surrounded by a culture of collusion, neglect, indifference and silence on the part of the officers and elected members within those authorities. It is now acknowledged that this experience of abuse was not simply the consequence of a few paedophiles entering the public care system (DoH/Welsh Office, 1997). Rather, it is an endemic problem, affecting children in authorities across the country and symptomatic of a fundamental failure to provide effective protective care towards vulnerable children.

One of the most forceful lessons to emerge from the series of public inquiries into the abuse of children in public care was the extent to which the children involved were denied any opportunity to challenge what was happening to them (DoH/Welsh Office, 2000; Kirkwood, 1993; Levy and Kahan, 1991). They were systematically disbelieved in favour of adult versions of events. They were denied access to any advocacy to help them articulate their concerns. Indeed, if and when they did complain, they risked further abuse. In other words the adults involved could, with impunity, behave in ways entirely contrary to the children's welfare.

We can, then, no longer disregard the fact that children can be and are both physically and sexually abused by the very adults who are responsible for their care, both within families and in state institutions. And in confronting that reality, it becomes necessary to move beyond the assumption that a simple reliance on adults to promote the well-being of children, because of their biological or professional relationship with the child, is an adequate approach to caring for children.

Adults do not always act in children's best interests

Actions detrimental to the well-being of children do not merely occur when adults deliberately abuse or neglect children. During the course of the twentieth century adults with responsibility for children across the professional spectrum have been responsible for decisions, policies and actions that have been inappropriate for, if not actively harmful to, children while claiming to be acting to promote their welfare. One does not have to look far for the evidence. We separated children from parents in the war evacuations. We excluded mothers from hospital when their children were sick, in pain and frightened. We failed to acknowledge that small babies experience pain and denied them analgesics. We undertook routine tonsillectomies that were unnecessary and often distressing to children. We promoted adoption for the babies of unmarried mothers with no possibility of future contact. We placed children in care and cut them off from their birth families. We looked after them in large, unloving institutions that stigmatized them and denied them opportunities for emotional and psychological well-being. We removed disabled children from their families and placed them in long-term institutional care. In all these examples, there is now public recognition that children were more harmed than helped by these practices.

In addition the existence of public policy that serves to act against the best interests of children is not simply a matter of history. We continue to place disabled children in special schools on grounds of the 'efficient use of resources' rather than the promotion of the child's best interests (Education Act 1996 s316). In this situation it is the law which condones practice that can operate against a child's best interests. However, in the field of public care, and despite the Children Act clearly requiring courts to give paramountcy to the best interests of children, there is growing evidence from organizations working with looked-after children that local authorities, when implementing care orders imposed by the courts, are making placements decisions based on cost rather than best interests (Children's Rights Office, 1998). Additionally, the curriculum being introduced by the government prescribing attainment targets for children at ever earlier ages has the potential of jeopardizing the right to play.

Parents' rights are protected over those of children

Public policy often supports the rights and interests of parents ahead of those of children, even when the consequences of so doing are detrimental to the welfare of children. There is, for example, a clear conflict of interest between children and parents in the field of assisted reproduction, in which both law and practice favour the interests of the parents. Our present legislation fails to protect the right of children born through assisted reproduction techniques to access to knowledge of their biological identity. The law actively prohibits children access to identifying information about their biological parents, and there is neither an obligation on the part of nor any encouragement from the relevant professionals for parents to be open with their children about the origins of their birth (Human Fertilization and Embryology Act 1990). The desire for a pretended normality, the fear of children not loving the non-biological parent, the fear of a reduced supply of donors if anonymity were not preserved and the difficulty in confronting children with the truth all play a part in perpetuating the current collusion against a commitment to respecting the fundamental right of the child to a knowledge of his or her identity (Blyth, 1990; Freeman, 1997).

It is evident that it is not children's welfare but rather the directly competing interests of parents to maintain secrecy and to have a child that is the overriding factor determining legislation and practice in this field. There is, for example, ample evidence from the experience of adoption on the importance of honesty and openness with children about their origin. All adoption agencies would endorse this approach as fundamental to good practice. Additionally, in the context of our enhanced understanding of genetics, there is a growing need for children to have accurate information about their biological make-up. Furthermore, there is a growing likelihood of individuals undergoing genetic testing at some stage in their lives, when the truth about their true parentage will emerge. How much more painful it would be to discover the reality in adulthood. If the welfare of children were the pre-eminent factor in decision-making, there is little doubt that the law would be amended in their favour.

In 2000 the government issued a consultation paper setting out proposals to change the law on the physical punishment of children in order to comply with the findings of the European Court of Human Rights that the law in this country failed to protect a child from inhuman and degrading treatment under Article 3 of the European Convention on Human Rights (ECHR, 1998). The consultation sets out three questions for consideration. Should the defence of 'reasonable chastisement' be removed from certain forms of physical punishment, such as hitting children around the head in ways that might cause brain injury or damage to the eyes and ears? Should the defence cease to be available against a charge of actual bodily harm and should the defence be restricted to those with parental responsibility? (DoH, 2000).

However, the consultation document fails to ask the central and most significant question – should parents be allowed to hit their children at all? The absence of this question is not accidental. There was considerable pressure on the government, from an alliance of some 250 organizations, to include in the consultation paper the option to change the law to remove the defence of 'reasonable chastisement' for parents and to give children the same protection from all forms of assault as adults. The government refused to do so. It is clearly recognized under international law that the continued practice of hitting children represents a breach of their human rights. The Committee on the Rights of the Child, the international body established to monitor government progress in implementing the UNCRC, has already criticized the UK government for its failure to introduce legislation to protect children from physical punishment by parents and recommended a review of the law to introduce appropriate protection (CRC, 1995). When the government appears before the Committee again in 2002, it will be censored if it has failed to act on this recommendation. The reality is that the government is not willing even to consult on a proposal to end all physical punishment of children because to do so would be seen to interfere with the rights of parents.

There is considerable evidence that the physical punishment of children is not an effective form of discipline, that it can and does cause harm, and that as a form of punishment it can and does escalate (Leach, 1999). In addition almost every professional body working with children is unanimous that we should change the law to protect children better and give parents a positive message that hitting children is both wrong and unnecessary (Barnardo's, 1998). It can also be seen from the experience of the eight countries that have banned it that it does not lead to a rise in prosecutions of parents, it does change parental behaviour in favour of more positive forms of discipline and it does not lead to worse-behaved or ill-disciplined children (Durrant, 1999). Again, then, it is not the welfare of children that informs the law and its proposed reform, but the need to assuage adult public opinion.

Children's interests are often disregarded in public policy

Children's interests are frequently disregarded in the public policy sphere in favour of those of more powerful interest groups. It is not necessarily the case that children's welfare is deliberately disregarded but that children, and the impact of public policy on their lives, are not visible in decision-making forums and, accordingly, never reach the top of the political agenda. Just consider, for example, the impact of public policy on children during the 1980s and 90s. In 1979 one in 10 children were living in poverty. By 1991 the proportion had increased to one in three (DoH, 1993b). That alone is a sufficient indictment of our neglect of children. Even more significantly, however, it is children who bore the disproportionate burden of the increase in poverty during that period: no other group in society experienced a growth in poverty on a comparable scale. The consequences of that poverty on children's life chances are profound, impacting on educational attainment, physical and mental health, emotional well-being and employment opportunities. At a collective level, then, our society failed to promote and protect the welfare of children over two decades.

There is little analysis of public expenditure to assess whether the proportion spent on children and their well-being reflects either their level of need or their representation within the community. What little we do know indicates that the lack of data is likely to cover very significant inadequacies in spending on children, indicating their weak position in the lobbies that influence public agendas and expenditure. We know, for example, that health authorities spend 5 per cent of their mental health budgets on children and adolescent mental health services, even though this age group represents 25 per cent of the population (Audit Commission, 1999). It is of course likely that services for older people will necessitate a disproportionate claim on these budgets, but no systematic assessment has been made of whether the current balance in any way reflects comparative levels of assessed needs. Also, as long as children lack powerful advocates in the field of health, such discrepancies will not be effectively challenged.

Similarly, in the field of housing, countless estates have been built in which the needs of children have been completely disregarded – no play spaces or facilities, dangerous balconies, and lifts with controls out of the reach of children (Freeman *et al.*, 1999). We have also grown increasingly intolerant of children in the public arena. Far from developing towns and cities that are designed with children in mind, that are child-friendly, as befits a society with the welfare of children at its heart, we now tend to view children as undesirable in streets and shops, particularly when they are in groups. The introduction of powers to impose child curfews, the refusal of many shops to allow children in and the decision by the Millennium Dome to refuse entry to the under 16s if they are not accompanied by an adult are all testimony to a perception of children as threatening, hostile and outside the legitimate bounds of society. Public spaces are seen to be 'owned' by adults, young people's presence in those spaces representing an unwanted intrusion. Yet these are the adults on whom children rely to promote their best interests. These are the adults who are responsible for protecting children's welfare.

Children's competence and contribution

The welfare model of childcare has perpetuated the view that children lack the capacity to contribute to their own well-being or do not have a valid and valuable contribution to make. Yet a failure to involve children in decisions that affect their own lives has been the cause of many of the mistakes and poor judgments exercised by adults when acting on children's behalf. There is now a growing body of evidence that children, both in respect of individual decisions that affect their lives and as a body in the broader public policy arena, have a considerable contribution to make to decision-making (Alderson, 1993; John, 1996; Marshall, 1997). Children, even when very young, can act, for example, as peer counsellors, mediators or mentors for other children. Local and health authorities have successfully involved children in the development of new hospitals, anti-poverty strategies and advice services. In other words far from being 'in waiting' until they acquire adult competencies, children can, when empowered to do so, act as a source of expertise, skill and information for adults and contribute towards meeting their own needs.

Moving beyond a welfare perspective

Once it is acknowledged not only that adults are capable of the abuse of children, but also that children's welfare can be undermined by conflicting interests, neglect, indifference and even hostility on the part of adults, it becomes clear that it is not sufficient to rely exclusively on adults to define children's needs and be responsible for meeting them. Indeed, the welfare model has failed children. The traditional perception of children as having needs – for love, care, protection – is now challenged by a recognition that children are subjects of rights, a concept that has gradually developed during the course of the twentieth century, culminating in the adoption by the UN General Assembly in 1990 of the UNCRC. The Convention now has almost universal acceptance, having been ratified by 191 countries throughout the world. Only the USA and Somalia have not yet made the commitment under international law to comply with the principles and standards it embodies. The Convention is a comprehensive human rights treaty encompassing social, economic and cultural as well as civil and political rights.

The recognition of children as the subjects of rights rather than merely the recipients of adult protective care introduces a new dimension to adult relationships with children. It does not negate the fact that children have needs but argues that children therefore have rights to have those needs met. The rights contained in the Convention fall into three broad categories, each of which impose different obligations on adults: freedoms to protection from the state, protection by the state to ensure respect for individual rights, and rights to the fulfilment of social and economic needs. The discourse in respect of human rights traditionally centred on the need for boundaries to the abusive exercise of power by the state to protect the civil and political rights and freedoms of individual citizens. While those protections remain important – there is still a need for powers to constrain the intrusion of the state into individual liberties – there has been a growing recognition that rights are not only abused by the state but also perpetrated by individuals against other members of a society. There is thus a need for the state to play an active role in protecting the rights of citizens from violations of their rights by others. This is particularly true of children. Because they lack autonomy, and their lives are substantially circumscribed by the adults who have responsibility for them, there is a clear onus on the state to intervene actively to protect those rights. In addition, children have socio-economic rights that impose obligations on the state to make available the necessary resources to ensure that children's well-being is promoted.

For example, if a child has a right to protection from discrimination, the government has the responsibility to introduce the necessary legislation, backed up by enforcement mechanisms, training and public education. If a child has a right to free full-time education, it is the responsibility of the state at a local and national level, as well as the child's parents, to ensure that education is made available and that the child is able to benefit from it.

Implications of respecting children's human rights

One of the underlying principles of the Convention is that the best interests of the child must be a primary consideration in all actions concerning the child (UNCRC, 1989, Article 3). This principle does not, however, merely take us back to a welfare approach: a commitment to respecting the human rights of children requires an acceptance that promoting children's welfare or best interests requires more than the good will or professional judgment of adults. The Convention injects two fundamental challenges to traditional practices in respect of children.

First, the means by which the best interests of children are assessed must be the extent to which all their human rights are respected in any particular policy, action or legislation. In other words the rights embodied in the Convention must provide a framework with which to analyse the extent to which proposals promote the best interests of children (Hodgkin and Newell, 1998). This approach also extends both to matters affecting the rights of an individual child and to children as a body. In providing child protection services, for example, do interventions that seek to protect the child from abuse also respect the child's right to privacy, to respect for the child's views and evolving capacities, to continuity in family life, to contact with the immediate and extended family? In a proposed local housing development, have the rights of children to adequate play facilities, safe road crossings and leisure services been properly considered? Similarly, one can apply a comparable analysis to decisions taken within families. Many parents currently drive their children to school and justify so doing in terms of the potential dangers of both traffic and abduction or assault to which the children might otherwise be exposed. A rights-based approach would necessitate a broader analysis of the rights of children. What impact does driving children to school have on their right to the best possible health, to freedom of association, to play, to a growing respect for their emerging competence?

In all these examples it can be argued that unless a comprehensive rights-based approach is taken, there is a risk that a decision or intervention is made that responds to one aspect of the child's life and in so doing fails to acknowledge other rights or needs. Indeed, it may inadvertently impact adversely on the child.

Second, if children are subjects of rights, they themselves must have the opportunity to exercise those rights and be afforded the means of seeking redress when their rights are violated. In other words they must have opportunities to be heard. Article 12 of the Convention embodies the principle that children have the right to express their views on matters of concern to them and to have those views taken seriously in accordance with their age and maturity. It is a procedural right that has increasingly been recognized as necessary if children are to move beyond their traditional status as recipients of adult care and protection and become social actors entitled to influence decisions that affect their lives (Lansdown, 1996; Willow, 1997). Children are entitled to be actively involved in those decisions which affect them as individuals – in the family, in schools, in public care, in the courts, and as a body in the development, delivery, monitoring and evaluation of public policy at both local and national levels.

Listening to children and taking them seriously is important because children have a body of experience and views that are relevant to the development of public policy, improving the quality of decision-making and rendering it more accountable. Beyond this, it is an essential element in their protection. Children who experience respect for their views and are encouraged to take responsibility for those decisions they are competent to make will acquire the confidence to challenge any abuse of their rights. The active participation of children must also be backed up by clear and accessible complaints and appeals procedures and the availability of independent advocacy if they are to be able to challenge failures to respect their rights.

It is in the field of education that the failure to recognize the importance of listening to children as an essential component of promoting their best interests is perhaps most evident. The current government has placed a considerable emphasis on education whose focus has been almost exclusively the issue of academic attainment. Certainly, the UNCRC includes the right of children to an education on the basis of equality of opportunity, and the determination of the current government to ensure that high aspirations and opportunities exist for all children is consistent with the fulfilment of that right.

However, unlike children in most other European countries, children in the UK are denied the right to express their views and have them taken seriously within the education system (Davies and Kirkpatrick, 2000). There is no right to establish a school council, and children are expressly excluded from sitting on governing bodies. Children are not consulted over the National Curriculum, teaching methods, school policies or proposed legislation. Children, as opposed to their parents, have no right of appeal against a permanent school exclusion. There are no complaints procedures that can be followed in the event of injustice, discrimination or abuse. There are no regional or national networks of school students to act on behalf of pupils. In other words the government agenda in respect of children perpetuates the view that education is something that adults do to or for children, the child being constructed as the recipient. It fails to recognize the obligation to respect children's human rights within the education system – the right to be listened to, to be respected, to learn through day-to-day experience about the meaning of democracy and human rights. Children's best interests can only be promoted if these rights, alongside the right of access to education, are realized.

Conclusion

There is a continuing resistance to the concept of rights in this country, particularly when applied to children. It is a resistance shared by many parents, politicians, policy-makers and the media. It derives, at least in part, from a fear that children represent a threat to stability and order if they are not kept under control. Furthermore, it reflects the strong cultural tradition that children are 'owned' by their parents and that the state should play as minimal a role as possible in their care. Attempts by the state to act to protect children are thus viewed with suspicion and hostility.

But promoting the rights of children is not about giving a licence to children to take complete control of their lives irrespective of their level of competence. It is not about allowing children to ride roughshod over the rights of others, any more than adult rights permit such abuses. It is, rather, about moving away from the discredited assumption that adults alone can determine what happens in children's lives without regard for children's own views, experiences and aspirations. It means accepting that children, even very small children, are entitled to be listened to and taken seriously. It means acknowledging that, as children grow older, they can take greater responsibility for exercising their own rights. It involves recognizing that the state has explicit obligations towards children, for which it should be held accountable. A commitment to respecting children's rights does not mean abandoning their welfare: it means promoting their welfare by an adherence to the human rights standards defined by international law.

10

'Our Bodies, Ourselves'?: Mothers, Children and Health Care at Home

Pam Foley

As the body of research and writing associated with the sociology of childhood grows, it combines an emphasis on children's agency with a focus on the nature of children's social environments. Children, as social actors in ongoing social life, engage with different sets of people in different social settings, acquiring a knowledge of the social world and adopting multiple responses and identities (Hutchby and Moran-Ellis, 1998). Such identities are both the cause and the effect of the environments within which they engage (James and Prout, 1996). The family remains one of the most important social and emotional environments of everyday life for children.

While the increasing use of the verb 'parenting' is useful since it recognizes the fact that care may be provided by a variety of adults or older children (Tatum and Tucker, 1998), its widespread use may obscure the gendered nature of parenting. It cannot be insignificant that most of what we understand as 'parenting' activities are carried out by women. The majority of children continue to live with and be primarily cared for by their mothers. Maintaining a child's health and healthy development is understood as a crucial component of parenting, or more accurately mothering, and is the central means of assessing maternal competence, both by mothers and by the wider world. Mothers attend to daily health maintenance, recognize the early stages of illnesses, carry out treatment and mediate with their children's health care services. And women bring to the health care dimension of mothering their own, gendered, experience and understanding of health and health care. Within the social space of the home, health and healthy development are among the ways in which the competence of children is explored, negotiated and defined. This chapter thus looks at mothers and children as co-constructors of knowledge and identity with regard to children's health and development and discusses how mothers' and children's perspectives and competence are made explicit and contested.

'Knowers' and knowledge: standpoint theory

While there is no reason to argue with the fact that children are, for a time, relatively dependent on adults, there are good reasons to resist the argument that dependency equals passivity (Alanen, 1994). Children, right from their earliest days, take part in the social world. Babies are born with not only extremely powerful abilities to learn, but also the ability to tap into adults similarly 'programmed' to teach them what they need to know. Interacting with other people is at the top of a baby's agenda. Adults and children across most cultures work together to adapt children's knowledge to new situations, to aid problem-solving and to regulate children's assumption of responsibility for managing this process (Rogoff, 1991).

An understanding of children's lives as engaged with the social world is central to the maternal perspective because the home is a place in which children are constantly learning and exhibiting an extensive range of social competencies. To mothers, health and healthy development are understood not only through observed bodily signs such as growth, eating and sleeping, but also in social terms – mainly the sociability of a child (Cunningham *et al.*, 1991; Lauritzen, 1997).

Christensen's (1998) work showed how children and adults use particular methods to establish the presence or absence of illness, including taking the child's temperature, noting whether the symptoms persist over a period of time, deciding whether to miss school and using therapies to mark the boundary between being well and ill and back again. Such procedures are not carried out by the adult in isolation but require at least the cooperation of the child. Usually more than cooperation is involved as signs and symptoms such as a raised temperature, aches and pains, coughs, hunger, nausea or rashes are detected, discussed and attributed by both mothers and children. Children become actively engaged in what is understood in their culture as health and illness. They become engaged in the co-construction of the social organization of illness. Mothers do not contribute to the objectification of the child or contribute to the idea of a child's passivity but interact with the child on the basis of he or she being an active participant in both learning and social life. Engagement with the social world, in this example working out what it means to be well or ill, leads to both mothers and children participating in the generation of knowledge about and an understanding of children's bodies.

A transition towards recognizing children as 'knowers' – able to generate knowledge as well as being the recipients of knowledge, or being the objects of knowledge – seems a highly significant one. 'Standpoint epistemology', a defining feature of thinking within women's activist groups and among feminist academics in the 1970s and 80s, mounted a strong challenge to medicine's claims to be providing an objective, universal, 'scientific' knowledge about women on which the female specialities of obstetrics and gynaecology were premised (Stanley and Wise, 1993). Defining all knowledge, including medical knowledge, as interpretative constituted a profoundly destabilizing move for existing systems of knowledge concerning the human body. Harding (1996) argued that what counted as 'knowledge' was what socially advantaged groups wanted to know and what it would benefit them to know. Feminist academics and researchers began to document women's experience and understanding of their bodies and their health care from a woman's 'standpoint'. This challenge to the principle of objectivity – an attempt to separate the 'knowers' from the things they claim to know about – and this dispute of the validity of claims to an impartial, universal under- standing of human experiences, was rooted in the belief that people act as both the *objects* and the *subjects* of knowledge (Alanen, 1994). Children are active in the determination and construction of their own lives and of the lives of others around them – including their mothers.

However, a perspective that sees children as subjects rather than objects is contested by two wider discourses and classifications within which children's lives are embedded. First, child development theories of the past have framed a vision of childhood as the time of a gradually increasing integration with society, as opposed to seeing children as already being active participants in social life. The idea that children are in the process of *becoming* has made them of particular interest to psycho- logical and educational theorists and to welfare and social policies. These draw upon traditional sociology and developmental psychology as a resource that then becomes recycled into 'common-sense' norms about what a normal child and normal mother are like (Burman, 1994). Children are essentially characterized as the subjects of developmental processes, dependent on mothers for their socialization. Maternal input is judged by the mother's ability to steer her child successfully through a series of developmental stages, and her ability to deliver an adequately developed and socialized child into the education system at around the age of five.

The concepts of a key role for mothers (and fathers) in the integration and socialization of children have led to a series of heated debates about women as mothers, social relations and social change. While lone mothers and teenage mothers may receive the greatest amount of social and polit- ical disapprobation, even mainstream mothers need to account for their mothering skills and outcomes (Smart, 1996). These debates and issues have, necessarily, influenced the maternal perspective: mothers are expected to draw upon wider societal and cultural understandings of what constitutes the healthy development of children, and these understandings deflect attention away from children's present and lived experience.

An awareness of wider cultural norms and goals must also be maintained, in parallel with a sense of continual and ultimate responsibility for the health of the child, already evident among mothers in the months before birth (Foley, 1998) and continuing throughout childhood (Blaxter and Paterson, 1982; Cunningham-Burley and MacLean, 1991; Lauretzin, 1997; Mayall and Foster, 1989). Women understand their roles as mothers as simultaneously being *responsible for* and *responsible to*; being *responsible* for the health and well-being of the child does not necessarily put the mother in the driving seat but instead forms a basis for dependency since she must be responsible to both the health and welfare agencies (Foley, 1998). Not all mothers will have the resources, personal or material, to meet their own or others' expectations. Other mothers will struggle to reconcile how they understand the child's point of view with their other role as a representative of the wider adult society, responsible for, perhaps, bringing the child into line (Ribbens, 1994). While the health and development of children are understood as political and societal issues, they are at one and the same time constructed as a familial, primarily maternal, responsibility and concern.

Second, in social settings other than the home, children are generally constituted as incompetent in speaking about their own bodies in terms of translating a bodily sensation into a disease state or condition. The persistence of ideas that deny children an active social presence in relation to health and illness has meant that relatively little research has been carried out concerning health, illness and development from a child's standpoint. Notable exceptions include the early and ground-breaking research by Bluebond-Langer (1978), whose work with dying children revealed children as not only knowledgeable about the progress of their own disease, but also actively managing adults' experiences and perceptions of the situation.

Alderson's (1993) research with children in hospital undergoing surgery looked at children's rights to integrity, finding both understanding and uncertainty shared between people of varying ages and experiences. Work around children's experiences of medical encounters revealed how they are effectively silenced and bypassed by both parental and medical staff clinical dialogue (Silverman, 1987; Strong, 1979). Mayall's (1996) study showed how children experience contrasting contexts, within which health issues are differently handled, the more responsive and flexible environment of home contrasting with the ambiguities of school life, where other agendas can take priority over children's health maintenance and where children's struggles to detect and self-assess illness fall upon very stony ground. Perspectives on children's health and development can, then, be understood as central to the discourses that shape what we understand as 'childhood' and 'a child'.

'Our bodies, ourselves'?

For children, as well as for men and women, an awareness and 'owner-ship' of the body is central to our sense of ourselves as distinct and separate persons. With our bodily selves we negotiate our own and each other's identity. First becoming aware of your own physical self is a profound experience, as anyone who has seen the expression on a baby's face as she gazes at herself in a mirror becomes aware. Our bodies are of central importance to the ways we interact with others and see ourselves – to the ways in which we are social beings. The fundamental nature of the body is not natural and universal but produced by social processes:

> We do not have bodies, rather we become embodied as particular types of people. Our embodiment is a historical creation. (Turner, 1995, p. 235)

Historically, philosophical conceptions of the body have centred on the male adult body as the norm, representing the female body as different, 'other' and essentially inferior (Lupton, 1994). Work on gender discourses has shown how systems of knowledge about the body differentially constitute particular kinds of body and empower them to do different things (Butler, 1993; Gatens, 1992; Grosz, 1994; Lupton, 1994). This analysis reveals the manner in which particular cultures and societies mark out particular bodies for specific categories:

> Gender itself may be understood... not as the effect of ideology or cultural values but as the way in which power takes hold of and constructs bodies in particular ways. Significantly, the sexed body can no longer be conceived as the unproblem-atic biological and factual base upon which gender is inscribed but must itself be recognized as constructed by discourses and practices that take the body both as their target and as their vehicle of expression. (Gatens, 1992, p. 132)

When feminists called for a social theory of the body they meant a theory which took gender *and power* into account (Davis, 1997). The ways in which the competing claims of biology and society/culture determine the lives of women in terms of perceived differences between their bodies and their minds, and those of men, remain an ongoing part of social and polit-ical life worldwide. Like women, children are also understood as essen-tially *different*, represented as 'other' (non-adults), and the classifications of the child's body available in our culture (incomplete, immature, vulnerable, etc.) can be understood as a result of the ways in which power is structured around their lives. Shifting the analysis down to this micro level of bodies could open up some interesting avenues of discussion for the sociology of children. If we were to work from the premise that biological disadvantage can be posited as such only in a cultural context, what might this mean for how we understand the body in childhood?

Any future development of the rights and roles of children must take into account the ways in which their bodies are constituted, particularly the languages and practices that are used within everyday life. The child's body, largely absent from many major sociological works about the body (Shilling, 1993; Turner, 1995), needs further analysis in terms of its historical and discursive associations. We can already glimpse how the body of a child has its meaning and capacities constructed, and some of the ways in which children act within contexts that constrain or enable competence (Hutchby and Moran-Ellis, 1998). It is in the variety of settings – school, family, day-care, health care – and the ways in which such settings reinforce each other, that difficulties for effective contestation will lie. Children's lives are enmeshed in professional and private discourses, which strengthen each other:

> Because [of] notions such as socialisation, – the institutional ways of thinking produce self conscious subjects (teachers, parents, care takers, children) who think and feel about themselves in terms of those ways of thinking. The 'truth'... about themselves, their activities, situation, and relations with others is self validating; and the more tightly the truth-producing discourses intersect and penetrate each other, the more difficult it is for alternative 'truths' about children and childhood to break into the contemporary institutional realities in which children live. (Alanen, 1994, pp. 40–1)

Conclusion

This chapter has briefly discussed two of the frameworks within which levels of competence and understanding among mothers and children are constructed and disputed in relation to children's health and development. Perspectives around who counts as a 'knower' and the lived and social experience of the body are, it is argued, crucial to the changing social identity of the child, as they were and are crucial to the changing social identity of women. A 'child-centred' approach to services has advanced children's services only to a limited extent because it draws upon adult assumptions of what children are and feeds into ideas of what children 'need'. It fails to counteract processes that position the child as object, children remaining the objects rather than the subjects of policies and practices. However, a 'child standpoint' approach to services would address the issue of the diversity of childhoods that affect social positioning, shaped by such other variables as gender, class and ethnicity, while projecting children as 'knowers' and focusing on the organization and detail of daily life. It is the day-to-day lives of children that implicitly determine what it means to be a child, taking us closer to more accurate conceptualizations of what children can be and do and what 'childhood' is.

11

Listening to Children

Nigel Thomas

Why listen to children?

In this chapter I want to look at what is involved in communicating with children and including them in decisions. This will mean thinking about how adults can communicate with children, and about some of the different ways in which children may be involved in decision-making. It will also mean thinking about some of the reasons why children are not always listened to, and about what can be done to improve things. We will look at some of the research that has been undertaken with children, and at some practical initiatives that aim to involve children more effectively. First of all, however, we need to ask some basic questions. Why is it important to listen to children? Is it:

- because they have a right to be heard?
- because it is good for them?
- because it leads to better decisions?

I want to suggest that all these reasons apply. Let us consider each one in turn.

Children's right to be heard

When we say that someone has a right to something, we are making a value statement. It is not something that we can prove in the way that we prove a factual statement. We can point to legal rights, founded on legal principles and embodied in actual laws, or to moral rights, based on ethical principles that command a more or less general agreement. In the case of children there is sometimes disagreement about what kind of rights they have.

Certain kinds of rights, such as the right to food and shelter, to health and education services, to protection from harm, can be seen as rights of the vulnerable or powerless, and it is rights of this kind that are often meant by 'children's rights'. Many charters of children's rights emphasize such rights to welfare and protection. Some people argue that rights to participate in society, to exercise free speech, to vote and to enter into contracts are dependent on having the capacity to make and carry out rational plans, and that these rights are therefore restricted to individuals with this capacity. The question of whether children have these kinds of right is therefore more controversial and may depend on what view we take of children's competence – something to which we will return later.

It is now, however, widely accepted that children do have a right to be heard and to have their views taken into account in decisions that affect them. This is expressed in Article 12 of the UNCRC, which was adopted by the United Nations in 1989 and ratified by the UK in 1991.

How listening to children can enhance their welfare

There is considerable evidence from psychological research that having a sense of control over our lives is associated with other measures of well-being, both for adults and for children as young as babies (see Maccoby, 1980). Many children grow up feeling that they have little control or that important decisions about their lives are being taken without really consulting them or even explaining to them what is happening. This applies to children at home and at school, and it often applies especially to children whose parents separate or who find themselves in public care. Taking the time to explain things properly to children, giving them a chance to express their own thoughts and feelings, and creating opportunities for them to influence what happens, can give them a feeling of being more in control and enable them to move on successfully in other areas of their lives. It can also be argued that everyone benefits when children are listened to and included in decisions. This should not, however, allow us to forget that there is sometimes a real conflict of interest between children and adults, and that children have a claim to be heard in these situations too.

How giving children a say can produce better decisions

Although the extent of research in this area has been limited, there is some evidence that allowing children to influence decisions that affect them improves the quality of those decisions. For example, Priscilla Alderson's study of children facing a major surgical procedure suggested that decision-making and success could be improved if children were given a real part in the discussions (Alderson, 1993). Projects that involve children in designing schools, play areas or other community facilities have produced good results in terms of the level of use or incidence of vandalism. It is a sound general principle that plans and decisions are better for being based on the knowledge and opinions of those directly involved, and this surely also applies where children are concerned. There may sometimes of course be conflict between a child's wishes and what adults think is best for her or him. This issue is discussed later in this chapter.

Ways of communicating with children

Communicating with children is too often seen as a specialized skill when it should be part of the basic repertoire of everyone who works with them. What is involved is in some ways no different from the skills involved in communicating with adults, but there is a difference in children and their situation, which has an effect on the communication process.

First, children's communicative skills and styles are often different from those of adults: less verbal, more demonstrative and less formal, for example. Second, children are relatively powerless, which can in some cases make them susceptible to saying what they think adults want to hear. Third, children have learned their own ways of managing adults, and these need to be understood. In particular, they are often suspicious of adults' questions and reluctant to answer openly. Finally, of course, children are all different. Of course a child of four is likely to communicate differently from a child of 10; in addition, individual children have their own strengths, their own styles, their own ideas of what is relevant. The key to successful communication lies in having a genuine interest in the child and what she or he is thinking, as well as the ability to communicate that genuineness to the child (see Crompton, 1980).

Brynna Kroll, discussing work with children in care, points out that it must start by acknowledging the power imbalance between adults and children (and also the difficulty of working directly with a child without alienating the parents). She suggests that the key issues are: how do we talk to younger people?; how do we clear our minds sufficiently to pay proper attention to the child?; how do we make real contact with a child, create a safe place and establish a good enough relationship?; what can be achieved in the few sessions that are often all we get?; how can a focus be maintained while at the same time leaving room for the child's own contribution?; how can 'leading the witness' be avoided?; how can the way in which the child makes the worker feel be used to assist the work?

Kroll argues that workers' needs include a child-centred philosophy, a range of helpful theories and useful techniques, in addition to training, supervision and support. The *philosophy* must accord value to the child's point of view as an individual and not just as a member of a family (although parallel or interpretative work with the parents is often extremely important). *Theories* need to encompass cognitive development and emotional processes including attachment and mourning. *Techniques* include play, drawing and other creative activities, but perhaps most important is what Kroll calls 'the art of "being" rather than "doing",' of simply spending time with a child and being receptive to what he or she may want to communicate (Kroll, 1995, p. 98).

Jan Thurgood, reviewing the contribution that social workers can make to listening to children who have been abused, argues for the importance of consistent relationships and of acknowledging children's individuality. She goes on to explore a number of ways in which workers can facilitate communication with children. Play can be used as a medium of communication as well as in therapeutic intervention: 'In play, children will open up areas of feeling they may not be able to put into words or would deny in conversation.' Painting and drawing 'may be an easier way of communicating than talking', as may writing for some children. Activity-based work 'offers a way for workers to build relationships with children and young people who would have no interest in a talking relationship'. The provision of primary care can be a sound basis for communication. Life story work can provide 'a focus for the child to achieve an understanding of their past and to work through feelings about it'. Group work can make it easier for some children to communicate more freely than in an individual setting. Finally, Thurgood emphasizes both styles of talking to children and the importance of looking for non-verbal communication (all quotes from Thurgood, 1990, pp. 59–64).

The skills and qualities needed when working with children are very similar whether one is a social worker, a teacher, a counsellor or a researcher, as the experiences of different professionals vividly demonstrate (see Milner and Carolin, 1999). Claire O'Kane and I (Thomas and O'Kane, 1998a) studied participation in decisions by children aged 8–12 years in local authority care. We talked with 47 children, both individually and in groups, as well as with adults involved in looking after them. One of the things they told us about was what makes for good communication between adults and children. The things that children found important were:

- *Time*: it is essential to have enough time to spend with a child: children do not necessarily want to talk by appointment. Time also means working at the child's pace, allowing him or her to stay in control.

- *Relationship, trust and honesty*: children communicate best with people with whom they have relationships of warmth and trust. It is important to be friendly and open, empathetic and above all 'straight' with children.

- *Active listening*: the skills of 'active listening' developed in counselling can be helpful in work with children. This means responding to cues, restating and drawing out the meaning of what the child is saying, combined with the expression of warmth, empathy and acceptance. It should also be remembered that body language – an adult's tone of voice, facial expression, and even style of dress – can affect how children communicate.

- *Choice, information and preparation*: children must have a choice about whether and how they participate in a decision-making process. They are more able to have their say if they have been prepared for the discussion and given time to think about things beforehand.

- *Support and encouragement*: children need support and active encouragement to speak up, especially when they have something difficult or negative to express. An adult may sometimes need to offer to express children's views for them. Children do not like it when they feel they are being judged or criticized, and they do not like to be 'put on the spot'.

- *Activities*: many children find it very boring to 'just sit and talk'. Games, writing, drawing and other activities can be used to make the process more interesting. 'Life story work' can be an excellent way to involve children in reflecting on their situation (see Ryan and Walker, 1993).

- *The child's agenda*: it is important to give children space to talk about issues that concern them rather than just respond to adults' questions.

- *Serious fun!*: the fact that serious matters are being discussed does not mean that everyone has to be po-faced. Some children find this threatening, and most find it alienating. If decision-making processes are made more enjoyable, children are more likely to get involved.

Finally, children's participation requires an element of *risk-taking*. Risk-taking allows children to learn from their mistakes, to take responsibility for their own actions, and to gain a growing sense of autonomy; adults need to learn to 'let go' sometimes. The implications of this are discussed further below.

Including children in decisions

The single most important element in listening to children and including them in decisions is probably *respect*. This takes several forms: first, a genuine interest in the child's views as we saw earlier; and second, respect for the child's preferred ways of communicating, which may be different from, but are not necessarily inferior to, those used by adults. Third, respect implies being open to the child's own 'agenda'. It is all too easy for adults to concentrate on getting the answers to the questions that concern them without considering that a child may have other issues to discuss that may be equally, if not more, important.

In recent years considerable advances have been made in including children in decisions about their personal lives. The impetus for this has been provided by the UNCRC and by laws such as the Children Act 1989, which applies to England and Wales, and the Children (Scotland) Act 1995. The greatest advances have probably been in decision-making in the care system, where it is now common for children as young as 8, 9 or 10 to be consulted and included in meetings (see Thomas and O'Kane, 1999). However, these discussions still usually take place in settings determined by adults, and children are not routinely given a chance to help to set the agenda or determine the form that these meetings take, so they may experience them as alien, tedious or intrusive.

Progress has also been made in consulting children about more public issues, whether it is the planning of child welfare services, the nature of their local environment or the way to deal with bullying in school. Development in this area is more patchy, but there are examples of good innovative practice from different parts of the UK and beyond.

The other way in which respect is an important issue has to do with how adults respond to children's wishes and feelings once they have been ascertained or expressed. Article 12 of the UNCRC claims for children 'the right to express those views freely in all matters affecting the child, the views of the child being given due weight in accordance with the age and maturity of the child.' Section 1 of the Children Act 1989 requires courts to have regard to 'the ascertainable wishes and feelings of the child concerned (considered in the light of his age and understanding)' and Section 22 makes a similar requirement of a local authority looking after, or proposing to look after, a child. What happens when the wishes of a child appear inconsistent with his or her 'best interests' – when a child wants something that adults believe would be harmful? Nothing in the law or the UNCRC requires us to do whatever a child wants, but we should listen carefully to what children tell us and make sure we understand the thinking behind it. Children are experts on their own lives and their own families, and we should not be too ready to dismiss what they say as the result of 'immaturity' (Thomas and O'Kane, 1998b).

Children's competence

At what age are children competent to make choices about their own lives? The short answer is that it depends on the decision and on the child.

Even small babies and toddlers can be given choices about food and drink, clothing, play activities and so on, and quite young children can contribute to more difficult decisions if they are consulted sensitively. Gerison Lansdown (1995) suggests that decision-making involving children needs to be linked to an assessment of the competence of the child in relation to a particular decision. If a child lacks the competence to understand the implications of a decision, the adult should still only over-ride the child if to do so is necessary to protect the child or to promote his or her best interests. If the child is competent, the parent should only over-ride the child if failure to do so would result in serious harm.

Psychological research and practice with children can help us to under-stand how children's competence can vary and how it can best be elicited (Garbarino *et al.*, 1992). Sociologists such as Pia Christensen (1998) and Nick Lee (1999) have shown how judgments about children's compe-tence miss the point if they are too static – that a child's competence is not only variable, but is determined in processes of social interaction and negotiation. If communication is done well, if situations make sense to children and if there is a presumption of *competence* rather than incompe-tence, children often turn out to be more capable and sophisticated than they are given credit for. This applies to all children, including those with learning disabilities.

The advantages of working with a presumption of competence, and with respect for children and what they may wish to communicate, are apparent in both childcare work and social research. Both researchers and practitioners have found that giving children control over the pace and context of a discussion produces good-quality results. It is interesting that much of this work has been done with children on the margins – children in care, in trouble, going through family separation – who might easily be thought to be less capable of expressing coherent views because of their difficulties or distress. If children like these can be listened to and given choices about their lives, the same should be possible for all children: in their families, in their schools, even in public life.

Points for practice

When we talk to children in the care system about decision-making and communication with adults, they are often very clear that what they want is dialogue rather than simply to get their own way. Given the opportunity to rank different aspects of participation in order of importance, they consistently put 'to have my say' and 'to be listened to' above 'to get what I want' (Thomas and O'Kane, 1998a).

We have seen that there are some important things that adults can do to enable children to be involved in this kind of dialogue:

- The first is to accept that all children have the *right* to be included in this way.
- The second is to look actively for children's *competence*, not to assume their incompetence.
- The third is to use *methods of communication* that children find helpful or enjoyable.
- The fourth is to give children *time* to express their views in their own way.
- The last is to treat children, and their views, with *respect*.

Effective dialogue between adults and children is not always easy to achieve. When it happens, it is usually of mutual benefit: rights for children do not have to be at the expense of rights for adults (see Roche, 1999; Thomas, 2000). When children have an effective voice, services can be delivered more effectively, and the foundations are being laid for a better, more democratic society in the future.

Let us finish with some of children's own words on the subject. The following quotes are taken from the audiotape *Voices with Volume* (Thomas *et al.*, 1998):

I don't think you should be any age to be listened to. I don't care what age it is, because if *you* are getting problems people should listen to *you*. Say if you're eight years old, it still matters doesn't it?

It's your life, you've got to learn from your mistakes. And if you don't make any mistakes, you're a lucky person!

Basically the review meeting was about them – it was about what they thought was best for me. I could say what's best for me as well, like you could say what's best for you. I don't need – well, I do need sometimes, but most of the time I don't need people to say what's best for me.

Do you think you should help to decide where you live and things like that, or do you think grownups should decide for you?
No, because if they decide for me they might decide to put me somewhere I don't like, and what's the point in me going somewhere I don't like? I'm just going to misbehave then, aren't I, to get out of there?

Whatever age you are, you should be able to have a say in what you should be able to do, because it's as much your right as anyone else's.

12

Community Development: a Strategy for Empowerment

Stanley Tucker

In this chapter some of the ideas that have influenced community development work as a strategy for empowering children and families are explored. Emphasis is placed on the need to understand both the nature of community development activity and how it can serve to alter patterns of decision-making and service delivery within community contexts. It is not being argued that community development should be seen as a panacea for all social ills. Structural inequalities such as poverty, poor housing and inadequate health services, or the experience of racism and discrimination, will not be swept away merely by raising the level of local participation. Indeed, it is important to be mindful of the fact that the impact of these kinds of inequality, for children in particular, can produce a widening of the 'health gap' and later 'difficulties' in education and employment (Smith, 1999, p. 269). Yet it is hoped to demonstrate that some level of social change can be achieved through the implementation of community development approaches that attempt positively to engage families in the wider issues that face the communities in which they live.

What, then, are the advantages to be gained from promoting community development work as a platform for empowering children and families? To answer this question it is important briefly to review some of the key ideas that influenced the introduction of community development programmes. Community development work in the UK became increasingly influential during the 1960s. Born out of parallel experiences in the USA, the primary intention was to make 'the state work better' by focusing attention on an 'inflexible bureaucracy' that had produced community-fracturing high-rise developments in urban areas (Taylor, 1995, p. 100). The 'birth' of community work as a form of 'social work intervention' also has its roots in the same period. Official recognition of the strategy was offered through the Seebohm Report (DHSS, 1968).

During this time, in what Popple (1995, p. 15) describes as the 'golden age' of 'British community work', government interest in community development as a strategy for working in 'deprived' urban communities was to grow rapidly. By 1969 the government of the period had created 12 national Community Development Projects (CDPs). The main purpose of the CDPs was to stimulate self-help, re-create community identities and thereby generate local social and economic resources. However, this proved to be a difficult task, not least of all when those employed on the CDPs began to make controversial and potentially embarrassing links between local inequalities and wider structural, social and economic deficiencies (Derricourt, 1983).

Community development as a strategy for empowering local communities has at its heart a range of issues and concerns. One central concern is that of facilitating an increased level of democratic involvement. In essence it is argued that people living in communities can be collectively encouraged both to express and to respond to local needs and issues. As Twelvetrees (1982) points out there is a clear 'political dimension' attached to such work, insofar as it encourages individuals and groups to act together to advocate and advance the case for locally driven social change. The approach is, in reality, heavily influenced by notions of 'self-help' and the requirement for an increased level of partnership in decision-making between local communities and the statutory and voluntary sectors. There are, it is argued, clear advantages to be gained from the introduction of such a strategy. These include:

> Enabling community members to participate in aspects of community development and community life that concern them by setting priorities, developing programmes, and participating in them. (Gittell and Vidal, 1998, p. 49)

In addition, particular groups have used community development work as an awareness-raising platform. For example, community development has been influential in promoting anti-racist practice by enabling 'autonomous black community-based groups' to campaign about 'contentious issues, such as police relations with the black community and the education of black children' (Popple, 1995, p. 70).

Profiling community development work with children and families

It is possible to categorize a range of approaches that have been adopted in community development work with children and their families. At different points in time the analysis of local need, and the development of various forms of community-based action or intervention, has been stimulated by parents, carers and children, local community activists, community work personnel, service managers and local and national politicians. It is also important to acknowledge the fact that community development work is frequently driven by a variety of motives, intentions and priorities. Here I offer a brief overview of some of the different approaches that have been pursued. These approaches can be broadly divided into three categories:

• local resource development and community regeneration;
• needs assessment and consultation;
• an increased level of voluntary sector activity.

Local resource development and community regeneration

A range of strategies to encourage local resource development and community regeneration has been introduced throughout the UK. Crucially, as Henderson (1997, pp. 34–5) points out, attempts have been made to link the social and economic aspects of community life. Such work is concerned with giving children and families a greater say in how their communities should be developed and managed. In particular it is argued that many parents and children feel 'socially excluded' from everyday community life and the 'distribution of material, cultural and social resources' (Craig, cited in Henderson, 1994, p. 53). The approach to such forms of development work often involves the active linking of locally assessed needs (undertaken in partnership with children and families) and resource allocation.

In some areas the main concern has centred on the need to regenerate social activity and community participation through education and leisure programmes. A variety of community-based groups, often led by parents and residents on urban housing estates, have, for example, lobbied for the development of play facilities – playgroups, playgrounds, play buses, summer play schemes and so on. Others have advocated the importance of developing educational programmes to increase parenting skills, the knowledge and understanding of child development and coping with the stresses of family life. Elsewhere emphasis has been placed on introducing locally managed economic and social initiatives. These have included the development of local food purchasing cooperatives for families on limited incomes, the introduction of credit unions and community banks to provide low-interest loans and, in rural communities in particular, the tackling of environmental issues to improve the quality of family life (Durrant, 1997).

The impetus for the development of such initiatives varies considerably. The level of disgruntlement and anger felt by an individual or group about a lack of community facilities can stimulate community development activity. At other times a particular problem or issue, such as children having nowhere to play, will act as the catalyst for intervention. Or the actions and activities of a community development worker may serve to raise local interest, expectations and willingness to become involved in community life. The main focus of this kind of work is, however, frequently directed towards improving life in a tangible way. Crucially, local community members are often involved in both the creation and the delivery of services as members of management or project steering groups, volunteers or workers.

Needs assessment and consultation

Urban policy initiatives such as City Challenge and the SRB [the Single Regeneration Budget] require consultation with communities and their participation in partnerships. The setting up of user panels and neighbourhood forums as part of decentralization strategies have also necessitated active participation by members of the community. (Percy-Smith, 1996, p. 85)

Born out of central government concerns to raise the focus of public consultation activity and a requirement to foster partnerships with local community organizations and groups, community development strategies have been utilized to respond to recent public policy initiatives. During the 1980s and 90s the functions of local government changed radically. Acting sometimes in the role of service purchaser or inspector, and sometimes in the role of provider, policy-makers and managers are, in many instances, required actively to canvass the views of actual and potential service users. Moreover, public authorities have also been required to take on strategic planning functions in the development of new social and economic programmes. Emphasis has in particular been placed on introducing and developing policy-making activities, as Percy-Smith notes above, which are directly influenced by public involvement in compiling 'evidence' of community need. In addition, processes of decentralization (moving resources, decision-making powers and personnel into local communities) have involved the introduction of various neighbourhood area committees and councils.

The impact of such consultation strategies has been significant in terms of directly involving children and their families in decision-making processes and policy formulation. The drawing up of local Children's Services Plans, for example, has required social service departments to canvass the views and opinions of children and young people (DoH/DfEE, 1996, p. 3). The introduction of the Single Regeneration Budget programme involved local government in direct discussions with community organizations about their requirements for pre-school education, family support, leisure facilities, economic regeneration activities and so on. In the case of the development of local childcare partnerships (for which local authorities have a coordinating responsibility) specific mention is given in planning guidance to ensuring that steps are taken to:

> obtain the views of children and young people about their preferences for childcare and other parent/child support services... Particular attention should be given to canvassing the views of older children, children with disabilities and children of ethnic minority origin. (DoH/DfEE, 1996, p. 75)

At a less formal level, consultation exercises with children and families have taken a variety of different forms. Local authorities, for example, community work personnel and community organizations themselves have used a variety of opinion-surveying tools to canvass views about quality of life issues such as play, environmental pollution and attitudes to crime. Schools, as part of their National Curriculum activities, have developed project-based work aimed at involving children in auditing local community resources and commenting on how they meet their needs and aspirations (National Curriculum Council, 1990), whereas voluntary organizations, such as the Children's Society, have set up targeted projects aimed at specific groups of children, such as 'young carers', to explore their views as to how caring impacts on their day-to-day lives (Frank, 1995).

Increased levels of voluntary sector activity

The role of the voluntary sector in promoting community development work with children and families has increased markedly in recent years. Many of the larger national charities, such as NCH Action for Children, have, under the banner of what might be usefully described as family support services, developed a range of locally based initiatives to actively promote the social care and welfare of children and their families. The growth of family centre work has been particularly significant in this respect. As Cannan and Warren (1997, p. 9) comment, the work of such centres in many instances takes on a 'holistic approach'. The development of individual parents and their children is placed within a wider community context. Family poverty, for example, is viewed as a 'multi-dimensional' issue that might require:

> counselling, credit unions, health advice, training and adult education, leisure activities and environmental improvements.

At a local level various voluntary groups representing the interests of black families, children with disabilities and lone parents have attempted to develop work aimed specifically at challenging and countering oppression, discrimination and social exclusion. Examples of the promotion of this kind of activity can be seen within many black communities. In some areas the development of cultural identity work through language teaching has figured significantly, while efforts have also been made to counteract the educational disadvantaging of black children via the provision of 'Saturday school' initiatives (Gore, 1997).

An issue-based agenda, then, often drives much of the community development work of the voluntary sector. Development programmes and initiatives are frequently underpinned by concerns to counteract family poverty, ill-health, the poor educational performance of specific groups of children or the lack of affordable, good-quality childcare for working parents. From the perspective of the larger voluntary sector charities, work carried out in local communities can also be used to provide evidence to support specific national campaigning activities around, for example, the need to promote child protection, the impact of domestic violence or the experience of homelessness.

Not all plain sailing

Perhaps one of the greatest challenges that faces the sponsors of community development work is the potential that it can have to falsely raise the local level of community expectation. Put at its simplest, if children and their parents make an investment in any consultation process, or programme of community activity, it is not unreasonable for them to expect that they will be listened to and that their views will, whenever possible, be acted on. The dynamics of decision-making, however, are both complex and complicated. Different forms of competing interest will sometimes come into play in decision-making processes. Messages from academic research or 'expert' opinion, for example, may differ from community perceptions of need. Those involved in managing community consultation activities are frequently required to weigh and balance a range of differing views and opinions. This can be a difficult task, particularly when alternative perspectives are being offered on how services should be developed, extended or maintained.

The issue of the relinquishment of power is also an important one to consider. Community development work directly involves, in many instances, the devolution of power – to make decisions, allocate resources and set priorities – down to the level of the local community. Such devolution of power will, of necessity, mean that it has to be either 'voluntarily' or 'forcibly' relinquished elsewhere in the decision-making structure. Politicians, administrators, service managers and practitioners may lose power. There is also the danger that if community activities do not go according to plan, attempts may be made to reassert the authority of centralized bodies and institutions.

There is also the difficult issue to consider of how newly acquired power may be used at the level of the community. How representative are the views of those who claim to speak on the behalf of particular communities? In an 'adultist' world are parents more likely to assert that they 'know better' than their children when it comes to voicing community needs? Is sufficient time always given to exploring the views of those children and parents who find it difficult to express their views? These are important questions that require some degree of resolution if effective forms of community development work are to be promoted.

Some concluding thoughts

Community development as a strategy for empowerment has the potential to improve the life of many children and families living in local communities. Empowerment can take many different forms – active involvement in consultation activities, decision-making, service delivery and so on. It may mean that people generally feel better about the communities where they live and that they will want to improve the quality of life for both themselves and others residing there. It may also mean that children and their parents gain new skills, knowledge and outlooks that will assist in the development of self-esteem, confidence and awareness.

The greatest advantage of pursuing a community development strategy, however, may well lie with the fact that individuals begin to see what it is possible to achieve by working together in partnership. Such partnerships can take many different forms. They can involve local authorities, voluntary organizations, community organizations, schools, play activity groups, family centre users and so on coming together for a particular purpose. Or children working with each other to express their thoughts and feelings about the place in which they live. Or parents joining forces to lobby for the development of particular facilities or resources. Community development involves learning by experience, listening, respecting the views of others and treating people with dignity and respect.

Part III

Conceptual and Practice Frameworks

Part III

Conceptual and Practice Frameworks

13

Working Towards Consensus: Children's Hearings in Scotland

Anne Griffiths and Randy Frances Kandel

Recent years have seen an increasing discussion about the way in which the legal system deals with children and the issue of children's rights. What is valuable about the children's hearing system in Scotland is that it represents an attempt to engage vulnerable children and their families in decision-making processes that concern a child's future in a non-judgmental, informal and supportive environment. This is one that aims at reaching a decision based on consensus rather than through coercion of the kind that results from the imposition of a court order. Children involved in the process include those who are offenders as well as those who have been subject to neglect and/or abuse. By bringing families together with support services offered through social workers and others, to discuss what is in the 'best interests of the child', it is hoped that more constructive solutions involving the child and family can be found for dealing with these children's welfare and the problems that they face.

Working towards participation and consensus, however, raises questions about 'the child's voice in legal proceedings', including the ways in which such a voice is constructed, either directly or indirectly, and the extent to which it is empowered or constrained by the forum in which it operates. These questions form part of an ongoing, comparative research project involving Glasgow's children's hearings and the more formal setting of a family law court in a New York state county. It is data from the former that provide the basis for the discussion of children's hearings in this chapter.[1]

What is special about the children's hearing system in Scotland, implemented in 1971 under the Social Work (Scotland) Act 1968, is its focus on children as vulnerable beings in need of assistance.[2] This perspective derives from the philosophy underlying the recommendations made by the Kilbrandon Committee (Kilbrandon, 1964), which led to the creation of the hearings system, that where children have difficulties their best interests are served by working with them and their families to alter their situation so that state intervention is rendered unnecessary. In pursing this aim the Kilbrandon Committee refused to distinguish between children as offenders and children who have been offended against, on the grounds that both sets of children required care and protection because their 'normal up-bringing process' had 'fallen short' (para. 15).

The Committee considered that in both cases special measures of education and training were required to overcome the child's problems, and that this could best be achieved through a non-punitive model of treatment that took account of the whole circumstances of the child's life and where welfare would be the paramount concern in making a decision about the child. For this reason the Committee concluded that both types of child should be dealt with in the same forum.

How the system works

These considerations continue to underpin children's hearings in Scotland, now regulated under the Children (Scotland) Act 1995. Under this Act (to which all references apply except where otherwise specified), hearings comprising children's panels exist to deal with children under 16 who are in need of compulsory measures of supervision. State intervention in this context covers a wide range of circumstances including the neglect and abuse of children, and the commission of offences by children, as well as dealing with children who are 'beyond the control of a relevant person' or who fail 'to attend school regularly without reasonable excuse'. Panel members are public volunteers working on a part-time, unpaid basis who make decisions about whether or not children are in need of compulsory measures of supervision.

Local authorities play an important part in the hearings system in terms of administration and support, and in the implementation of the hearings' decisions. Cases are, however, referred to a children's hearing by a reporter who draws up the grounds for referral and who is employed by the Scottish Children's Reporter Administration, a national body charged with the management and deployment of reporters throughout Scotland. Reporters (who act independently from local authorities) act as gate-keepers to the system investigating cases brought to their attention by agencies such as social work departments, schools and the police. After reviewing the situation the reporter decides whether to drop the matter, whether to encourage a child and family to work with social services on a voluntary basis or whether to proceed to a hearing. When a hearing is held it is the panel members who must decide whether or not to discharge the referral, whether a child is in need of compulsory measures of supervision and, if so, what conditions if any should be imposed.[3] While panel members make decisions about whether or not a child is in need of compulsory supervision, reporters play a central role in the operation of the hearing system for it is they who make the initial decision about whether or not a child should go before a hearing, who organizes the timetable and necessary documentation for the hearings, and who has responsibility for ensuring that the administrative and legal requirements of the process are met.[4]

Key features of the system

Although a legal forum, every effort is made to encourage children and families to participate in proceedings by dispensing with the kinds of legal formality associated with courts. Thus, in keeping with Kilbrandon's recommendations, a determination of the facts is separated out from a disposal of the case by the requirement that no hearing can proceed unless the child and family accept the grounds for referral.[5] In this way the demands of formal legality – requiring a determination of the facts with regard to due process – are kept distinct from a disposal of the case. The latter, which is concerned with the welfare and development of the child, is more appropriately placed within the jurisdiction of the hearing system. In cases of dispute a hearing can either discharge the referral or refer the matter to the sheriff court for a finding on whether the disputed grounds are established.

This approach, premised on consensus as the starting point for discussion, seeks to avoid the adversarial nature of legal proceedings. It is one that minimizes the role of lawyers so that children and families are not subject to confrontation with and intimidation by the kind of legal process that operates in ordinary law courts. Rules of evidence and procedure are much less stringent, and while lawyers may be present at a hearing they do not act as advocates speaking on behalf of their clients.

Throughout the hearing the dialogue is one that is managed by panel members, who engage children, families and any other professionals present, such as key social workers, in the decision-making process concerning what is in the best interests of the child. In keeping with the open nature of proceedings panel members relay their decision and the reasons for it directly to the child and family at the end of the hearing. They do not retire to discuss the matter with one another prior to reaching their decision, which is based on the views expressed by the majority. It is then made clear to the child and family that, if they are dissatisfied with the decision, they have three weeks to lodge an appeal with the sheriff. After the hearing, the reporter forwards written confirmation of the decision, the reasons for it, and notice of the right to appeal to the child and any relevant person.

In this process three overriding principles apply. These are that:

1 the welfare of the child throughout his childhood shall be its paramount consideration (s16(1));

2 children must be given the opportunity to express their views and have them taken into account when they are sufficiently mature (s16(2)), with a presumption in favour of children aged 12 or over having such maturity (s11(10));

3 there should be minimum intervention, that is, that a hearing should only make an order if it is better for the child to make such an order than to make no order at all (s16(3)).

Making express provision for a child to express a view when he or she is sufficiently mature is in keeping with the terms of Article 12 of the UNCRC.

There is no doubt that, whether dealing with welfare and/or rights, children's hearings are 'child-centred', but to what extent do children really have a 'voice' in these proceedings, or rather, what factors facilitate or constrain their participation in the decision-making processes that affect their future?

Observations on the process

Children's panel members' views

A lack of legal formality may create a less intimidating atmosphere for discussion, but children still find their participation constrained by the framework with which they are faced. Brought before three adult strangers they are encouraged to express often quite intimate details about their lives within a limited time period, normally around 50–60 minutes. The following observations are based on the views expressed by the majority of the 40 Glasgow panel members interviewed as part of the study. From the panel members' perspective the narratives in the hearing are neither about the grounds of referral nor of an evidentiary nature (as, if contested, the matter is taken to the sheriff for proof). Nor are they about according recognition to a child's perception of his or her own circumstances. The hearings are, for the panel, a means of forming an independent assessment about the disposal of the case, measured against recommendations made by various professionals in reports circulated to the panel and family members or other relevant persons prior to the hearing.

Most panel members agree that they form a preliminary view of a child and his or her family from the reports and gain from these a sense of how they will handle a specific proceeding. All, however, are of the view that this may alter radically during the hearing when they are able to observe first hand the kinds of interaction that take place between family members and professionals. They stress the importance of body language and non-verbal communication in providing valuable information about family relationships (for example, how a child acts with his or her mother) as well as the family's attitude towards the various professionals who are involved (for example, the degree of rapport with the social worker).

In this process panel members agree that it is essential to hear a child's story about the circumstances giving rise to a referral directly from the child, but most admit that this is an uphill struggle. There are a number of reasons for this. Many panel members observed that, while some young children were happy to talk, adolescents were much more reluctant to participate. This was often put down to a child's stage in the life cycle. Adolescents' relationships with adults are generally viewed as being more problematic, and panel members are thus not surprised when they are non-communicative. Some adolescents, however, respond to panel members' attempts to engage them in dialogue.

Children's and young persons' views of the process

The children's and young persons' experience of panels varied. Those who had positive experiences commented:

- it's not too bad

- the people [panel members] they were all talking nice and that to you. Well, I thought they would be shouting an' that

- you think everyone will shout at you but they don't. They act normal

- they wiz listening like [you could tell they were listening] because of the way they were answering back.

Those who had more negative experiences commented that panel members were not really listening to them because:

- they shuffled papers and like while I was speaking

- they didn't look at you

- they were too busy writing on paper in front of them

- adults don't listen to young people

One 10-year-old boy from a residential school commented that panel members did not listen to him because 'they already had their minds made up'. When asked why he thought this was the case he explained, 'they didn't even leave the room... they just came straight out with the decision in front of you'. Ironically, while this boy considered that failure to adjourn indicated a failure to take his views seriously, panel members consider that their on-the-spot decision-making demonstrates transparency, openness and an independent opinion of what is genuinely in a child's best interests precisely because there is no conferring with colleagues prior to giving a decision.

When asked to give advice to other young people who might come before a panel for the first time, there were a variety of responses. These included advice such as:

- I'd tell them there was nothing to be nervous about. It's just people asking you about yourself

- Act normal and be yourself

- Speak up

- I'd tell them it will be OK.

Overall, children's and young persons' views of the panel were as follows:

- It was OK

- I was glad it was over

- [The decision was fine] because if they hadn't acted faster I would just get out of control

- When I came out I said to my Auntie, I'm lucky [when asked why that was so replied] I don't know [I thought that] they would put me away or something because I wasn't coming to school

- I wanted to live with my Auntie, they ended up giving my Auntie custody of me so that was alright. At least that's what I wanted.

What is clear, however, is that children's participation is constrained by the following factors.

Conflicting loyalties

Whatever the difficulties in his or her family, a child may be reluctant to lay these open to strangers for discussion, especially when either or both parents may be presented in a negative light (for example, because of failing to ensure the child's attendance at school, neglect or drug addiction). In the face of outside intervention children will often keep quiet about the difficulties they face, as in the case of a boy who was reluctant to admit that he was truanting because his disabled mother wanted to keep him at home to provide her with emotional as well as physical support. Preliminary research suggests that many of the children who come before a panel are from economically and socially deprived families with a high unemployment rate and/or alcohol or drug addiction; this is certainly the overwhelming perception of panel members and social workers who were interviewed.

Fear

Children, especially those who come before the panel for the first time, may be reluctant to talk because they are unfamiliar with the panel system and fear what the panel might do. There is a common misconception that panels exist to take children into care by removing them from their homes. In addition the presence of family members may inhibit children from speaking freely because of the repercussions that this might have for family relationships after the hearing: in most cases where children are placed under supervision this is carried out in the family home.

Under s46(1) of the 1995 Act the panel now has power to clear the hearing at any time in order to speak to a child alone. The substance of what is discussed in private must, however, be revealed to those who have left the room. The reason for this is to maintain an open process so that nothing is 'hidden' from the participants, but many panel members feel that an element of discretion rather than mandatory disclosure would encourage children to speak more openly in this situation.

In some cases children do take advantage of the opportunity to write to the panel with their views before the hearing. This is not often done as literary skills may be an issue for some children who have been in and out of the school system for years. The children most likely to write in to the panel are those living in a residential home or secure unit who are encouraged to express their views and get assistance in doing so from staff members. When children do write in they tend to use the letter as a means for giving their views regarding contact or residence with a particular parent, views that they might find difficult to express verbally in that parent's presence.

Disaffection

Proceedings may be less formal than those in court, but they still adhere to certain formalities, such as reading out the grounds for referral, which must be accepted by a child and family before the hearing can take place. These grounds are often quite technical; while the panel chair often attempts to put them in 'user-friendly' language, this does set a certain tone at the start of proceedings that is hard to displace. At this stage children may be asked to give their version of circumstances leading up to the grounds for referral, but even when they are willing to talk they find it hard to overcome the accounts that have preceded them in reports in which they are characterized as truants or trouble-makers. In a setting in which the ethos is one geared towards cooperation it is easier for children to go along with experts' descriptions of themselves than to dispute what is said about them as persons, as any dispute may make them appear to be confrontational. Children before a panel are there because they or their parents have failed to comply with social/legal norms relating to appropriate behaviour regarding attendance at school, drug use and so forth. These norms trump other considerations, for example a child's non-attendance at school being the result of bullying or having to pass though another gang's territory.

Communication for children is a problem especially when they are asked to speak after all the experts have had their say. Over half the panel members (who also sit as chairs) noted that it was their practice to turn to the social worker after the grounds of referral were established to initiate discussion. There are a number of reasons for this – to bring the reports up to date and to give a child/family time to get their bearings and relax, for example. However, by the time the child gets to speak he or she may be intimidated by the various presentations of 'self' that others such as social workers, and even parents, have constructed.

While it is generally stressed throughout the hearing that it exists for the benefit of the child, children do not necessarily perceive this. A number of children have suggested that it would be helpful to have an adult (who is not a social worker) speak on their behalf. The current system allows for this in that it permits a child to be accompanied by a person to assist him or her at the hearing, but it is not a provision utilized by many children observed at hearings or interviewed. While provisions exist for the appointment of 'a person to safeguard the interests of the child', such an individual, known as a safeguarder, has a duty not only to assist a child in expressing his or her views, but also to provide the hearing with an independent assessment of what is in the best interests of that child. Thus the advocacy role is always tempered by welfare considerations.

Children's strategies for dealing with the panel

Faced with a panel children adopt a number of strategies. They may:

- *Carry on as normal:*
  This is most likely to be the case when dealing with younger children aged 5 or under who have little understanding of what a panel is about and who play around or sit under the table during the hearing.

- *Pretend to be elsewhere and say nothing or keep their comments to a minimum:*
  In many cases children and young people feel embarrassed to be in the company of adults at a hearing and just long to 'get it over with'. Their body language and demeanour signal their desire to be anywhere but at the hearing.

  Take the case of Tom, aged 14. He came before the panel because he had not been to school for months and had serious health problems (which the reporter put down to anorexia). His mother had a drug problem and had difficulty in caring for him. He failed to attend one hearing because he was afraid that he would be taken into care. When he did come to a hearing he sat with his head bowed and when questioned gave monosyllabic answers.

- *Leave it to another adult to speak for them:*
  In Tom's case he left it to his social worker to speak on his behalf. Where a young person has a good rapport with and trusts the social worker or another adult to express his or her point of view, the young person's position will not be prejudiced by a relative silence. When this is not the case, however, the young person's lack of participation may be problematic.

- *Go along with the panel – play the game:*
  In this case, rather than distance themselves from the panel, children or young people adopt what they perceive to be the panel members' solution to their predicament so that they can get the meeting over as quickly as possible. As one 15-year-old from a residential school explained, 'It's like telling them what they want to hear.'

  Mary Jane, aged 15, and Sarah, aged 12, came before a panel for serious non-attendance at school. Their mother stated that this was because they did not have any clothes or shoes. While the panel was discontinued for lack of information about the family's position, both Mary Jane and Sarah agreed with panel members that they ought to be going to school and said that they would go in future. Their agreement seemed to be more about complying with the panel's wishes than reflecting a genuine change in attitude towards attending school.

- *Retain autonomy through defiance in language and behaviour:*
  In some cases young people attempt to retain control over their situation in a panel through defiance, refusing to acknowledge panel members' authority over them. An example is provided by Sue, aged 13, who came before a panel because she was beyond parental control. She was staying out all night at weekends without letting her parents (who were separated) know where she was. She refused to cooperate

with the panel, expressing the view, 'I hate people telling me what to do.' Discussion got so heated that she stormed out of the hearing shouting 'F— off the lot of yous'.

- *Participate as best they can:*
  Some children, once they have got over their nervousness, respond to panel members' attempts to engage them in discussions about their future and participate as best they can. Sam, aged 12, initially came before a panel as a victim of sexual abuse by his father. He was also truanting from school. He was placed on supervision and went to live with his uncle and aunt. He appeared to have settled into his new home and to be going to school regularly. He came back to the panel for a decision on whether his supervision order should be continued. Sam was quite open with the panel members and plainly stated that he did not want the order to be continued or 'to come back here'. As he was about to start secondary school the panel decided that supervision should be continued while he was adjusting to this change in his life, and he agreed to this when informed that a review could be called for in three months' time.

Conclusion

It is clear that working towards a consensus is an onerous task for children's hearings given the difficulties that arise in communicating with and in gaining the participation of children who appear before them. These difficulties to some extent reflect an uneasy fit between meeting the requirements of the legal process and creating a space in which children and families feel free to speak. The technical legal language, most apparent when dealing with grounds of referral at the beginning of a hearing and rights of appeal at the end, erects a barrier that must be overcome if there is to be proper participation based on a full understanding of what is taking place. In many cases chairpersons endeavour to translate the grounds of referral into a language that lay people can understand, but they are not always successful in their attempts. Despite their exhortations that parties should question anything that is unclear, some children and families accept grounds of referral that they do not really comprehend because they feel awkward asking for clarification or because they want to get the hearing over with as quickly as possible. Rather than relying on individuals' skills in making grounds comprehensible, it might be more effective to draft a comprehensive lay person's guide to the grounds, in age-appropriate language, to which panel members could refer for guidance.

A lack of understanding, which underlies some of the fear and disaffection that children experience, could be addressed by making sure that they are better informed about the role, powers and purpose of hearings. While many social workers consider that they have responsibility for making sure that children and families understand what grounds of referral involve and what a children's panel is about, their ability to convey this information varies enormously. Much depends on first, the type of relationship that exists between the social worker, the child and the family, and second, the amount of time that the social worker has at his or her disposal to provide this information. There is no doubt that children and families who have good, long-standing relationships with their social workers are better prepared to face a panel than those who do not. Cutbacks in the resources available to social workers mean that they have to prioritize their workload, with the result that less time is generally allocated to children and families in this situation given the other pressing needs that social workers currently face in Glasgow.

One way of overcoming this difficulty is to provide leaflets setting out basic information on the nature, powers and function of hearings, the appointment of panel members, their role and the various stages that form part of a hearing. Some leaflets already exist, but they are aimed more at meeting adults' needs and are not available in user-friendly language for children.

Another possibility would be to make this material available in schools and leave it to teachers to make it accessible to children as required. While panel members from some area teams in Glasgow go into schools to publicize the work they do, this tends to be on an ad hoc basis. A more sustained approach, creating a framework for promoting this information in schools across Scotland, would equip children with a better understanding of how hearings operate and their role in the process.

Participation involves not only an understanding of process but the ability to communicate and make one's voice heard. This chapter has outlined the difficulties that children face when dealing with children's hearings. Given the power imbalance that exists in a forum, where a young person faces three adult panel members and other adult professionals, some children's rights groups, such as Who Cares?, propose introducing child advocates. These adults would assist children to present their point of view and speak on their behalf when necessary.

While social workers and safeguarders claim to fulfil this role, it is one that is always tempered by their need to take account of what is in a child's best interests. From a young person's perspective this may defeat the purpose of advocacy. A number of children expressed the view that, given the choice, they would not opt for an advocate because, 'I think children should be able to speak for themselves' or because, 'they [i.e. adults] don't talk like you'. Some were afraid that adults would alter the meaning of what they said. Others, however, supported the idea of having an advocate. As noted above, current rules allow for someone to accompany a child to assist him or her at a hearing, but many children do not register this fact even though they are informed of this right in the letter that they receive from the reporter about their hearing. Making sure that children are aware of this right is important because it may provide them with a resource that they wish to use. Increasing awareness could be achieved by making sure that social workers inform children of this option and by highlighting this right in leaflets and videos.

Despite the problems children face at hearings the question must be asked of whether they would fare any better under the formal legal system with legal representation. Do children have more power to make their voices heard and have them acted upon in a more formal legal setting? Some surveys conducted among lawyers in the UK who work with children reveal that they operate on the basis of a welfare and rights perspective, so that in practice the child's views continue to be accommodated within a best interests framework (Gallagher, R., 1998, p. 69; Masson and Oakley, 1999, pp. 97–117). Such an approach gives rise to heated debates about the extent to which adults should speak for children or rather on their behalf, and what role, if any, lawyers should play in this process (Gallagher, R., 1998; Hallett *et al.*, 1998). Whatever the difficulties children's hearings in Scotland continue to command a high degree of support (Hallett *et al.*, 1998; Lockyer and Stone, 1998; Sutherland, 1999) as representing an enlightened and humane approach to dealing with state intervention in the lives of vulnerable children.

Notes

1   This research project, funded by the Annenberg foundation in the US examines children's participation in children's hearings and the more formal setting of a family law court in a New York state county.

2   For detailed information on children's hearings see Edwards and Griffiths, 1997; Lockyer and Stone, 1998; Norrie, 1997; and Sutherland, 1999.

3   Under s70 the hearing has a wide range of powers including the power to make a residential supervision requirement placing the child in a foster or local authority home, or even in secure accommodation.

4   Reporters may be, but need not be, legally qualified. Some come from a background in social work or education.

5   Under s65(9), where a child is too young to understand the grounds for referral, or has not in fact understood them after an explanation has been given, the hearing can either discharge the referral or direct the reporter to apply to the sheriff for a finding on whether the grounds of referral are established.

14

Parental Responsibility

Lesley-Anne Cull

Historically, the concepts of 'parental rights' and 'parental duties' have formed the basis of family law in England and Wales, Scotland and Northern Ireland. As recently as 1986 the Law Reform (Parent and Child) (Scotland) Act was based on the concept of the rights of parents in relation to their children. The parental rights were adult-centred and focused on the rights of the parent vis-à-vis the child. In the mid to late 1980s, however, the concept of parental rights and duties in the old legislation and case law came under scrutiny as the legislation relating to children began to be reviewed. In this chapter we will explore the way in which 'parental responsibility' became an important new concept in the legislation relating to England and Wales, Scotland and Northern Ireland from the late 1980s onwards. We then go on to look at who has parental responsibility and the ways in which it can be acquired by different individuals, and consider the significance of this for children and families in particular, but also for any individual who has care of a child. Finally, we will look at why it is important for those working with children and families to have an understanding of the meaning and importance of parental responsibility.

The arrival of the Children Act 1989 in England and Wales, followed later by the Children (Scotland) Act 1995 and the Children (Northern Ireland) Order 1995, marked a profound change of approach to questions concerning the parent–child relationship. There was a move from a proprietal frame of reference 'to one which implies that parental use of authority is valid only if employed for the benefit of the child' (O'Halloran, 1999, p. 81). This reasoning was illustrated in the House of Lords judgment in the Gillick case in the late 1980s. The fundamental issue in this case concerned the extent to which a parent has the right to the final say in any decision regarding children and young people under the age of 18:

> Parental rights to control a child do not exist for the benefit of the parent. They exist for the benefit of the child and are justified only in so far as they enable the parent to perform his duties towards the child. (*Gillick* v. *West Norfolk and Wisbech Area Health Authority* [1986] AC 112 Lord Fraser at 170D)

There was a move from the language of 'parental rights' to that of 'parental responsibilities', and at the same time an acknowledgement that 'parental rights yield to the child's right to make his own decisions when he reaches a sufficient understanding and intelligence to be capable of making up his own mind'.[1] Nonetheless, the effect of having parental responsibility is to empower a person to take most decisions in the child's life (DoH, 1989).

What is parental responsibility?

What does the term 'parental responsibility' mean? The law in England and Wales and in Northern Ireland describes the concept loosely and refers to 'all the rights, duties, powers, responsibility and authority which by law a parent of a child has in relation to the child and his property' (s3 Children Act 1989; Article 6 (1) Children (NI) Order 1995). In Scotland the legislation provides more guidance on what is meant by the term. The responsibilities of a parent to a child under 16 are set out in s1 of the Children (Scotland) Act 1995. They are to safeguard and promote the health, development and welfare of the child; to provide appropriate direction to the child according to her age; where parents are separated to maintain regular contact and personal relations with the child, and to act as the child's legal representative (for example in relation to entering contracts and managing money). A further provision, not included in the legislation in the other two jurisdictions, is the requirement to 'have regard to' what the child's views and wishes are.

Although the courts have not been definitive in their interpretation of the term 'parental responsibility', certain key elements have been identified. In *Re H (Illegitimate Children: Father: Parental Responsibility)* (No 2) [1991] 1 FLR 214, the Court of Appeal stated that the crucial ones are, 'First, the care and control of the child or children. Secondly, the protection and discipline of them. Thirdly, the maintenance of them. Fourthly, the education and religious upbringing of them.' The nature of the responsibilities will clearly depend on the age of the child and the particular circumstances to be considered.

Who has parental responsibility?

In each of the three jurisdictions a mother has automatic parental responsibility for her child and this cannot be surrendered or transferred to anyone else unless by way of adoption or parental order. Where the father of the child is married to the mother (either at the time the child is conceived or at a time after the birth) he will also have automatic parental responsibility and this will not be lost if the couple separate or divorce. If

the father is not married to the mother, however, he does not have automatic parental responsibility in relation to the child. The reasoning behind
this can be seen in part in the Law Commission's consultation paper
which stated:

> the Act did not automatically confer parental responsibility on unmarried fathers
> because of a perceived need to protect vulnerable mothers, especially those whose
> children had been born as a result of violent or coercive relationships. (Lord
> Chencellor's Department Consultation Paper, 1998, p. 2)

Unmarried fathers can acquire parental responsibility either by written
agreement with the mother (which must comply with certain procedural
rules) or, in the absence of any such agreement, by an order of the court.
The reality is that the number of written agreements each year represents
only a very small fraction of the total number of births outside marriage.
Statistics show that in 1996 there were 649,485 births, 232,663 (35.8%) of
which were registered outside marriage. Of those 181,647 (78%) included
the father's details on the birth register. In the same year, however, only
3,000 parental responsibility agreements were registered – 1.2% of all
births outside marriage. The figures suggest that 'fathers (and probably
also mothers) have no idea what parental responsibility means and that
[unmarried fathers] do not have it' (Ashley, 1999, p. 175).

There have been strong arguments in support of unmarried fathers
having automatic parental responsibility. It has been argued that the
genetic link between parent and child should normally carry a social and
legal relationship (Fortin, 1998). This is implicit in the words of J. Ward,
who said that the effect of a parental responsibility order is to confer
'upon a committed father the status of parenthood for which nature has
already ordained he must bear responsibility'.[2] The conferring of automatic parental responsibility would reflect the reality of the statistics in
that the majority of unmarried fathers are living with the child's mother.

Following consultation in early 1998 the government decided that an
unmarried father whose name appears on his child's birth certificate
should have parental responsibility under the Children Act 1989. This
raises a number of serious issues, not least in relation to the 'vulnerable
mother' who may be coerced by the father into allowing him to put his
name on the birth register. A mother's consent in adoption proceedings is
ineffective if given within 6 weeks of the birth. It could be argued that the
same considerations should apply to the issue of the mother's agreement
to the father's name being included on the birth register (which must at
present be completed within 6 weeks of the birth). There may also be
cases where the couple agree that the father should be included but where
he may not be able, for whatever good reason, to attend the registering of

the birth; it is not known whether the register will be capable of amend-
ment at a later date (Ashley, 1999).

It should be noted that the government's decision was presented as a
measure designed to encourage the commitment of unmarried fathers by
giving them status as legal parents rather than as one taken in the context
of human rights:

> The Government's view is that the current law, which does not give parental
> responsibility automatically to unmarried fathers on the birth of the child, complies
> with Articles 8 and 14 of the Convention. The wide range of types of relationship
> outside marriage means that the interests of the child and mother have to be
> protected. The law gives this protection while still permitting the unmarried father
> to acquire parental responsibility by agreement or court order. (LCD Consultation
> Paper, 1998, p. 17)

However, the implementation of the European Convention on Human
Rights in domestic law under the Human Rights Act 1998 makes it more
likely that the position of unmarried fathers will be debated in terms of
their human rights. In 1994 the European Court held that Irish law *had*
infringed an unmarried father's rights by denying him the right to challenge his child's adoption (*Keegan* v. *Ireland* [1994] 18 EHHR 342). It
should therefore be possible, following the incorporation of the Convention into UK law, for unmarried fathers without parental responsibility to
claim that their rights have been violated[3] and ask the court to make a
declaration that domestic law is incompatible with Convention law. The
defence that the interests of the child and mother are being protected by
the law as it currently stands will presumably be relied upon (Branchflower, 1999). It will be interesting, however, to see whether an illegitimate child will have more success by claiming that *her* rights have been
violated where her father does not have automatic parental responsibility.

It has been argued that where couples separate and it is feared that a
father could use parental responsibility to attempt to interfere inappropriately in a child's life, certain orders, for example a prohibited steps order
(under s8 of the Children Act 1989), could be used to prevent this
happening. In a Court of Appeal decision, however, it was held that irresponsibility in a father's behaviour, or his abuse or probable abuse of
parental responsibility, could disqualify him from obtaining a parental
responsibility order. The Court took the view that it was not sufficient to
argue that the father could be prevented from interfering inappropriately in
his child's life by making an s8 order; where it was feared a father would
behave in this way, he should not be granted parental responsibility at all.[4]

The case against automatic parental responsibility for an unmarried
father is based on a number of grounds. A father with parental responsibility has, for example, a right to be a party in proceedings involving the

child and would have to be traced in order to ensure that he was given an opportunity to participate in those proceedings, thereby causing a possible delay to the resolution of the case. In addition there are some fathers who, for whatever reason, will never play a role in their child's life. 'It remains questionable whether a reform which attaches so much significance to the blood tie between parent and child will benefit those children whose fathers are not cohabiting with their mothers, particularly where the parental relationship is an extremely stressful one' (Fortin, 1998, p. 323). Deech argues that 'to a child too young to understand the background [to the biological claim] it is meaningless unless accompanied by physical and social intimacy' (Deech, 1992, p. 3). Deech also argues that none of the international instruments, including the European Convention on the Status of Children Born out of Wedlock, require states to grant unmarried fathers automatic legal status.

Acquiring parental responsibility

In 1998 the Court of Appeal reviewed the principles followed in previous decisions on whether to grant parental responsibility.[5] It had been held that the court was required to consider the degree of commitment that the father had shown to the child, the degree of attachment between the father and child, and the father's reasons for applying for the order. It was made clear, however, that these requirements, albeit a starting point, were not intended to be exhaustive. The court has a duty in each case to take into account all the relevant circumstances and to decide whether the order proposed is in the best interests of the child, bearing in mind that the welfare of the child is paramount. Parental responsibility orders are made even where a father has no immediate hope of having direct contact with his child. In *Re C and V (Contact and Parental Responsibility)* [1998] 1 FLR 392, for example, the Court of Appeal agreed with the judge at first instance that there should be no contact between a father and his son but held that the parental responsibility application was an entirely separate matter, which had to be considered from a different perspective.

Acquiring parental responsibility can have implications for unmarried fathers beyond the declaration of the status of the applicant as the father of that child. For example, where a residence order is in force, no one can cause the child to be known by a new surname or to be removed from the UK for more than one month without the written consent of every person who has parental responsibility for the child. In addition, where a child might be the subject of an adoption application or a Hague Convention application (relating to abduction), a father with parental responsibility would in both cases have the right to be heard on the application *(Re H (Parental Responsibility)* [1998] 1 FLR 855 at 858H). With regard to the day-to-day arrangements for the child, however, the Children Act enables each person with parental responsibility to act independently of the other(s) in meeting that responsibility. It would be impractical to make joint decision-making in all aspects of the child's life mandatory. This does not mean that the parents (or anyone else with parental responsibility) may act unilaterally if to do so would be incompatible with any order made in respect to the child under the Children Act. Where a person other than the father of the child has acquired parental responsibility for that child, he or she does not have the right to consent, or refuse consent, to the making of an application for an adoption order, to the freeing order or to the order for adoption. Neither can they appoint a guardian for the child.

Sharing parental responsibility

More than one person may have parental responsibility in respect of the same child at the same time. For example, when a residence order is made to a person, that person has parental responsibility for as long as the order lasts. If a court grants a residence order to an unmarried father without parental responsibility, however, the court must also make a parental responsibility order. This does *not* come to an end even if the residence order is discharged (although any person who has parental responsibility for the child or, with the leave of the court, the child herself can apply for a parental responsibility order/agreement with the father to end).

In Scotland the legislation provides for any person who 'claims an interest' to be able to apply to the court to make an order dealing with parental responsibilities and rights. This can include an order depriving someone, including the mother, of some or all rights or responsibilities.[6] It could be argued that this is a more reasoned approach than that adopted by the legislation in the other two jurisdictions. In England and Wales and Northern Ireland, an unmarried father found to be 'unsuitable' to have parental responsibility for his child may have it removed from him by the court, but a mother found 'unsuitable' in the same way will not lose parental responsibility.

Local authorities in England and Wales and the Trust in Northern Ireland acquire parental responsibility (and share this with the parent(s)) in respect of a child while an emergency protection order or care order is in force. There is a significant difference, however, when compared with parental responsibility that is shared following an order in private family proceedings. When a local authority or the Trust has a care order it can determine the extent to which the parent(s) can exercise parental responsibility. In Scotland the local authority, on application to the sheriff, can be granted a 'parental responsibilities order',[7] the effect of which is to transfer all parental responsibilities and rights to the local authority (i.e.

not just from one parent). Not all rights are transferred, however, as the parent(s) will retain the right to consent or refuse consent to a freeing order or to an adoption order.

Where a child has been freed for adoption or an order made for adoption, the parent(s) loses parental responsibility. If the child has been freed all the parental responsibilities are vested by the order in the adoption agency until the adoption order is made whereby they are transferred to the adoptive parents. The effect is to extinguish parental responsibility in the birth parents. Although they retain parental status on the birth register as the child's parents, they are classed as 'former parents' (even at the freeing stage). Freeing a child for adoption has been criticized as consigning a child to 'legal limbo' (Adoption Law Review, 1990).

Parental responsibility and the day-to-day care of children

It has been argued that the definition of parental responsibility is not particularly helpful and that lawyers struggle to give parents a clear explanation of what it actually means (Ashley, 1999). What, then, are the implications of parental responsibility regarding the day-to-day decision-making and care of a child? Where more than one person has parental responsibility for a child, each of them may act alone and without the other(s) in meeting that responsibility. It should, however, be noted that parental responsibility does not carry with it the general right to be consulted about a child's upbringing, and it is usually the parent with whom the child lives who carries the main responsibility for day-to-day decisions. This clearly carries with it a potential for conflict where the relationship between the parents has broken down and may be a situation in which those working with children may find themselves involved, either directly or indirectly.

Earlier, we referred to the significance for unmarried fathers in certain situations (such as cases relating to adoption and abduction) of having or not having parental responsibility. For many parents, parental responsibility, or the lack of it, does not become an issue until a relationship breaks down or the mother becomes unable to exercise her parental responsibility (because of accident or illness, for example). It may then become clear, perhaps after taking legal advice, that the father does not have parental responsibility. This may of course be acquired in the ways outlined above, but does it mean that the father without parental responsibility has no powers or duties in relation to his child? In fact, although there may be no agreement or order, an unmarried father still has a duty to maintain his child. If the child is living with him he can exercise any powers that a carer has, including powers in relation to education and discipline.

For those working with children and families, it may be important to know who has parental responsibility, especially in those cases in which disputes arise between those with parental responsibility in relation to decisions being made about a child, as in certain circumstances the consent of everyone with parental responsibility is required. Where there is a residence order in force, for example, a child's surname cannot be changed without the consent of everyone with parental responsibility, and neither can the child be removed from the country for more than a limited period (unless by leave of the court). It would therefore be inappropriate for teachers to allow a child to be registered with a new surname or for the doctor's surgery to amend a child's surname on her records without such consent. Where a child is living with his or her father and the mother opposes this, she can remove the child from the father at any time if he does not have parental responsibility.

In England and Wales, however, s3(5) of the Children Act 1989 states that a person caring for a child who lacks parental responsibility 'may do what is reasonable in all the circumstances of the case for the purpose of safeguarding or promoting the child's welfare' (see Article 6(5) of the Children (Northern Ireland) Order 1995). It has been suggested that, on this basis, a father could object to the removal of the child by arguing that he reasonably believes that the child would be at risk if released into the mother's care (Allen, 1998). The Children (Scotland) Act 1995 has similar wording, although it goes further and specifies that the person may, subject to certain conditions 'give consent to any surgical, medical or dental treatment or procedure'. Teachers, childminders and other providers of childcare are therefore authorized under the legislation in each of the three jurisdictions to make decisions about a child, even though they do not have parental responsibility.

Conclusion

In this chapter I have looked briefly at the way in which the concept of parental responsibility replaced the old notions of 'parental rights and duties', and outlined the ways in which parental responsibility is acquired by parents and others. In one view it would be more accurate to refer to children's rights, especially following the decision in the Gillick case, the adoption in the UK of the UNCRC in 1989 and the implementation of the Human Rights Act 1998.

The competing rights of parents and children, and the courts' approach to decision-making in disputed cases, is the subject of much academic debate (see, for example, Barton and Douglas, 1995; Fortin, 1998); this is, however, beyond the scope of this chapter. What I have tried to show is that the significance of the concept of 'parental responsibility' lies partly in the fact that it provides a model of parenthood that is based on the welfare needs of the child and is consistent in both private and public family law. The inconsistencies in relation to the way in which mothers and fathers acquire parental responsibility and the issues surrounding automatic parental responsibility for fathers have also been considered. I have referred to planned changes in the legislation. It remains to be seen what the impact of these changes will be in terms of litigation, delay and costs, in particular to local authorities involved in care or adoption proceedings. It is probable, however, that the legislation will reflect the fact that many children are born to unmarried parents who are in stable relationships and that it is discriminatory to assume that unmarried fathers are irresponsible or uninterested in their children.

Notes

1   Lord Scarman *Gillick v. West Norfolk and Wisbech Area Health Authority* [1986] AC 112 at 186D.
2   *Re S (Parental Responsibility)* [1995] 2 Family Law Reports 648.
3   Article 8 of the Convention provides that everyone shall have a right to respect for their private and family life, and Article 14 guarantees this right free from any discrimination.
4   *Re P (Parental Responsibility)* [1998] 2 Family Law Reports 96.
5   *Re H (Parental Responsibility)* [1998] 1 Family Law Reports 855.
6   Section 11(2)(a), Children (Scotland) Act 1995.
7   Section 86, Children (Scotland) Act 1995.

15

The Impact of Domestic Violence on Children

Cathy Humphreys

> State Parties shall take all appropriate legislative, administrative, social and educational measures to protect the child from all forms of physical or mental violence, injury or abuse, neglect or negligent treatment, maltreatment or exploitation, including sexual abuse, while in the care of parent(s), legal guardians or any other person who has the care of the child. (UNCRC, 1989, Article 19, Para 1)

The right of all children to grow up in an environment protected from abuse is recognized within the UNCRC. While this may represent an ideal rather than a current reality, it nevertheless places freedom from abuse within the framework of children's basic human rights. A dimension of abuse now gaining recognition is that experienced by children living with domestic violence. Although this form of abuse is not new, the separation of the discourses on child abuse and violence against women have often led to children's experience of domestic violence being marginalized. This chapter will explore a number of areas relevant to children's experiences of domestic violence. This will initially involve a discussion of the issues of the definition and incidence of domestic violence. This will be followed by a discussion of the ways in which children may experience abuse, the factors that may create resilience for children faced with domestic violence, and a brief discussion of areas of intervention.

Definition and incidence of domestic violence

The term 'domestic violence' is a contested one with the potential to include as much within the terminology as it excludes (see Mullender and Morley, 1994). For the purposes of this chapter I will adopt the following definition:

> Domestic violence typically involves a pattern of physical, sexual and emotional abuse and intimidation which escalates in frequency and severity over time. It can be understood as the misuse of power and the exercise of control (Pense and Paymar, 1988, 1990) by one partner over the other in an intimate relationship, usually by a man over a woman, occasionally by a woman over a man (though without the same pattern of societal collusion), and also occurring amongst same-sex couples. (Mullender and Humphreys, 1998, p. 6)

This chapter will argue that the abuse of the child's parent (usually mother) cannot be separated from the lives of children and that in myriad ways they may either directly or indirectly be affected by the violence. The language in the chapter will often be gendered to reflect the dominant pattern of violence, namely violence against women by men known to them.

Estimates of the extent of the problem of domestic violence vary from 25% to 50% of male–female relationships (Kelly, 1996; Stanko *et al.*, 1998). Mooney's random sample survey of 100 men and women from North London reported that 30% of women had been at some time subjected to physical violence 'more severe' than being grabbed, pushed or shaken from a current or former boyfriend or male partner. Twenty-seven per cent had been injured, 27% threatened with violence and 23% raped, and 37% had suffered mental cruelty (Mooney, 1994). A study by the Exeter Family Study (Cockett and Tripp, 1994) found that, in divorcing or separated couples, one in four women separated because of domestic violence.

The picture of the gendered nature of the violence varies between studies often as a result of how the violence is measured or reported. Homicide figures show that, consistently over the past 10 years, on average almost two women a week die at the hands of their male partners and ex-partners. This accounts for half the women killed in the UK. In contrast, homicide by ex-partners accounts for only 9% of men who are killed (Mirrlees-Black *et al.*, 1996). Studies such as that undertaken by the Home Office (Mirrlees-Black, 1999), which on a self-completion questionnaire showed a relatively similar level of recent domestic assault over the previous year towards both men and women, makes the point that this did not mean that men were equally victimized:

> Men were less upset by their experience, considerably less frightened, less often injured, and less likely to seek medical help. (Mirrlees-Black, 1999, p. 61)

Domestic violence occurs across different social classes and ethnic groups. The cultural, religious and social context may increase the impact and range of abusive strategies that can be directed at women, and particularly affect their ability to seek help (Mama, 1996). Nor are women with disabilities immune. The disabled women's Network of Canada (Riddington, 1989) surveyed 245 women with a disability and found that 40% had experienced abuse and 12% had been raped. The perpetrators were primarily (although not always) spouses and ex-spouses (37%).

Children's experiences of domestic violence

No one thinks enough of the kids – thinks what effect it has on them. It doesn't just affect the mother – it's the kids… Because they're the ones that have got to see it, and hear it. (17-year-old girl)

I've seen him kick and punch, and pull her hair. Once he threw petrol over. I remember him cutting my mum's lip. (13-year-old girl)

Children are not immune from the violence between adults. There were 54,500 admissions to Women's Aid refuges in England in 1997/98, of whom 32,017 were children and 22,492 women (Women's Aid, 1998).

Research exploring the perspectives of children living with domestic violence is now being documented in the UK, bringing to light the details and diversity of children's experiences (McGee, 2001; Mullender *et al.*, 2000). This work complements a range of research, much based in North America, which compares the experiences of children living with domestic violence with those of other children, in order to identify the different ways in which they may be affected.

Child deaths

At the most extreme end of the continuum children are killed in situations of domestic violence. A study of 30 child death inquires acknowledges the association between domestic violence and child abuse (James, 1994). The most-cited UK child death inquiries (Maria Colwell, Toni Dales, Sukina Hammond and Kimberley Carlile) all involved violence by the child's father or stepfather towards the child's mother. As O'Hara (1994) points out, however, the seriousness of this link between domestic violence and child abuse tended to be overlooked until the 1990s in spite of the evidence emerging so clearly in the child death inquiries of the 1980s.

Physical abuse of children

Children may be injured or abused by men who are also violent to their mothers; they may be accidentally injured because they become caught in the violence directed usually at their mothers; they may be injured and disabled before they are born because of attacks on their mothers; or they may suffer a greater level of physical abuse by their over-stressed mothers.

The estimates of overlap between domestic violence and the physical abuse of children range widely from 27%, in a study by NCH Action for Children of 108 women who used their family centres (Abrahams, 1994), to 70% in a North American study by Bowker *et al.* (1988). In one study of 184 children in 120 families who had been living with their mother at a shelter for battered women, 35% of the sample had been physically abused in the previous year (O'Keefe, 1995). Research shows that an increasing level of male violence towards women was indicative of an increased level of physical violence towards children (Ross, 1996).

A growing concern is the reports of assaults on women during pregnancy. Mezey and Bewley (1997) have undertaken an overview of the research in the area. Findings include the following: domestic violence may commence or escalate during pregnancy (Bohn, 1990); pregnant women were more likely to have multiple sites of injury, including being struck on the abdomen, and the postpartum period was the time of greatest risk for moderate to severe violence (Gielen *et al.*, 1994). Physical injuries to fetuses, including bruising, broken bones and stab wounds, as well as death, have all been described in a range of studies (Pearlman *et al.*, 1990). Such issues point to child abuse occurring before the birth of the child. It also points to the complexity of separating child abuse from the abuse of women. Kelly (1996) talks about 'the double level of intentionality', a reference to the way in which offenders may abuse children in ways that will have a directly abusive impact on another, or vice versa.

Sexual abuse of children

The increased risk of child sexual abuse for children living with domestic violence has also been documented, although research in this area is less well developed. Farmer and Pollock (1998), in a study of substitute care for sexually abused and abusing children, found that, in a case file study of 250 children, 39% came from families in which there was domestic violence (primarily male violence towards the child's mother). A more detailed follow-up of 40 children revealed that 55% had lived with domestic violence. Other studies, such as that by Hester and Pearson (1998), showed that over half the children who had been sexually abused and were attending the NSPCC centre had also been living with domestic violence.

Emotional abuse

Increased attention has now been given to the emotionally abusive effects on children of witnessing domestic violence. A study by Dobash and Dobash (1984), who interviewed 109 mothers from refuges, reported that in 58% of cases the children were present when the mothers were being abused. The majority of children living in situations of domestic violence thus witness events that would terrify most adults.

Children suffer the effects of domestic violence in a number of different ways. These include the impact on their behaviour and emotional well-being, and the effects on their cognitive abilities and attitudes. Some of these effects may be the direct result of witnessing violence, sometimes as extreme as murder. At other times the indirect effects caused by their mother's impairment may deprive children of emotional and physical care. There are also the 'flow-on' effects of domestic violence, which involve children in relocation, losing their homes, moving schools and losing contact with friends, relatives and their communities.

Children witnessing domestic violence generally have significantly more behavioural and emotional problems than children who are not in these abusive environments. Children are reported to be more aggressive and antisocial – 'externalized behaviours' (Maker *et al.*, 1998; O'Keefe, 1995) – as well as having high rates of depression, anxiety and trauma symptoms (McCloskey *et al.*, 1995). Hughes (1988) showed that the combination of witnessing and also being abused was more detrimental to children. However, children who witnessed abuse, as well as those who both witnessed abuse and were themselves abused, were significantly more behaviourally disturbed than a control group in which domestic violence was not an issue.

Age difference is generally seen to be more important than gender difference in determining children's reactions and vulnerabilities. Children need to make sense of their experiences, and developmental abilities are crucial in determining how this may occur. Babies under the age of one who witness domestic violence have been characterized with poor health, poor sleeping habits and excessive screaming (Jaffe *et al.*, 1990). They are particularly vulnerable to any impairment in their mother that may affect her ability to look after them emotionally and physically after violence on the part of her partner or ex-partner. This is a particularly worrying finding when taken in conjunction with research showing that women are most vulnerable to moderate to severe violence in the postpartum period. Children of pre-school age tend to interpret most events in relation to themselves. They are therefore vulnerable to blaming themselves for adult anger (Jaffe *et al.*, 1990). This age group registers the highest levels of behavioural disturbance of any age (Hughes, 1988). School-age children continue to show a high rate of behavioural disturbance. As children move into adolescence other behaviours become more evident, such as running away and the use of drugs and alcohol (Mullender, 1996).

The extent to which 'race' and the experience of racism impact upon the experience of children has tended in many studies to be overlooked. In the USA O'Keefe (1994) found few differences between white, Latino, and African-American families other than that the last group of mothers rated their children to be more socially competent than the other groups. In the UK a study is being undertaken by Mullender *et al.* (2000) to explore the impact of ethnicity and racism on children in situations of domestic violence. There may be a number of compounding factors, such as the difficulty in seeking help (Mama, 1996), threats of abduction, language and interpreting problems, and the loss of a community that may protect children from racism, which may increase the difficulties for black children in the UK (Iman, 1994).

Children's resilience

Care needs to be taken not to assume how children will react to living with domestic violence. While there is an increased likelihood of problems for children living with domestic violence, not all children are negatively affected. Jaffe *et al.* (1990) have been careful to point out that there are children in their studies who show few negative symptoms and a higher level of competence than those in comparative groups. A study by Hughes and Luke (1998) of 58 women and their eldest children living at a women's refuge found that 60% of children were found to be not distressed or only very mildly distressed. Each situation therefore needs to be assessed individually to explore safety strategies that are in place for both women and children, the effects in all areas of a child's life, and the networks that may support children, including those at school and in the extended family.

Moore and Pepler (1998), in a study of 113 children of mothers in a women's refuge and a control group of 100 children in two-parent, non-violent families, found that the mother's behaviour and mental health played a key role in their children's adjustment. Children whose mothers were able to maintain positive parenting strategies (even in the face of sometimes horrific violence) showed the most positive adjustment among the group of children who had lived with domestic violence.

Violence-free lives

An optimistic finding from several studies is that many children have the ability to recover once they are living in environments free from violence

(Church, 1984). Church's study of 51 mothers and their children who had been in a women's shelter concluded that the children who recovered most rapidly (as shown in their behavioural adjustment) from living in situations of domestic violence were those who had no contact with their previously violent father or, in a small number of cases, where non-violent access arrangements had been successfully negotiated. The children who showed the least improvement were children who, although frightened of their father, were forced to visit him regularly, regardless of their fears.

These studies have implications for child contact arrangements following the separation of the child's parents. Consistent and serious problems arise in negotiating contact arrangements that are safe and free from violence, abuse and conflict (Hester and Radford, 1996; Humphreys, 1999a). Hester and Radford found, in their study of 53 post-separation families, that the men continued to be violent to their ex-partners in 46 out of 53 cases. The possibility of further violence to children remained, as did the problems associated with children continuing to witness and become involved in the violence towards their mothers.

Family law has generally established precedents in which the child's best interests are invariably seen to be met by maintaining contact with both parents. The right of the child to live free from violence and abuse has tended to be subsumed by the assumption that children need contact with both parents. However, the emerging evidence that children may recover from the worst effects of living with domestic violence if they are permitted to live in a violence-free context may require more careful consideration in the future negotiation of child contact arrangements.

The way forward

A wide range of interventions are now developing to tackle the serious problems associated with domestic violence. A number of principles can be used to guide the work in this area to ensure that work moves beyond good intentions to effective intervention.

First, the UN Convention can again be cited:

> protective measures should, as appropriate, include effective procedures for the establishment of social programmes to provide necessary support for the child and for those who have the care of the child, as well as for other forms of prevention and for identification, reporting, referral investigation, treatment and follow-up. (UNCRC, Article 19, para 2)

Prevention measures in the form of social programmes are acknowledged as a primary strategy for intervention in child abuse. This is a priority reflected in the rhetoric from the DoH to re-balance the focus of child welfare in order to emphasize family support and prevention as much as incident-focused child protection intervention (DoH, 1995).

Given the endemic nature of domestic violence, a focus on individual incidents of abuse will do little to tackle the wider issues of the attitudes of men, women and young people to abuse and violence in relationships (see Henderson, 1997). Zero Tolerance Campaigns and school-based prevention programmes are now available (Islington's STOP pack; North-ampton's Relationships Without Fear; and Hackney's RESPECT educa-tion pack), and the challenge for the future is to ensure that a more widespread dissemination of this work within schools occurs to support the community prevention of domestic violence.

Second, intervention needs to recognize that effective child protection also (usually) requires protection and support for the child's mother and strategies that challenge and appropriately confront offending behaviour. These principles require a shift in orientation from much of the current focus of work with children. At this stage child welfare intervention has little focus on engaging men, who are more frequently the domestic violence offenders. The needs of the children's carers (usually mothers) are similarly marginalized except in relation to women's mothering role. In this process effective intervention in relation to domestic violence may be lost (Humphreys, 1999b).

These principles do not imply that children's needs should be conflated with those of their mothers. Children have their own issues in relation to safety planning and recovery from the effects of living with domestic violence, which need to be recognized in their own right. Recognizing the adults involved in this process, and supporting women rather than admon-ishing them for their 'failure to protect', however, is an important under-lying principle that requires resources and training in the skills of safety planning, recovery work and a knowledge of the network of help which may be needed.

Third, integrated multi-agency responses are now developing in many areas throughout the UK. These responses recognize that domestic violence intervention requires prevention, protection and provision provided through a broad range of organizations cooperating together. While organizations such as Women's Aid have been providing safe houses and outreach services for more than 25 years, other statutory and voluntary agencies are now recognizing that only a broad-based, multi-agency response will be effective in creating safety and an appropriate response to violence. Research leading to the development of a frame-work of good practice indicators has now been undertaken to inform the development of services in this area (Humphreys *et al.*, 2000). These indi-cators include attention to services that are sensitive to the particular needs and problems of access for black and ethnic minority children and their mothers as well as other groups of children or their mothers who have specific requirements, for example in relation to disability.

In conclusion it needs to be reiterated that children's responses to domestic violence are not predictable. Although patterns emerge which repeatedly show that children are negatively affected emotionally, behaviourally and cognitively by living with domestic violence, each child's reaction is different. Assessments, safety planning and intervention need to recognize the child's unique response and the strengths he or she brings to the situation. Ideally, we are working towards a society in which children's rights to live free from violence and abuse are both recognized and respected.

16

Primary Education
in Scotland

Donald Christie

Context

Scotland prides itself on what it sees as its own distinctive institutions. Scottish culture has historically accorded particular prominence to education, which has enjoyed romantic associations with the ideals of egalitarianism and the 'democratic intellect'. In recent years some of the gloss may have rubbed off the traditional perception of the excellence of Scottish education in the face of accumulating evidence of mediocre attainment in international comparisons. However, it remains the case that public satisfaction with the education system in general, and with primary education in particular, remains high in Scotland. While there are frequent calls for more resources for schools, there has been neither the public outcry over falling standards nor the denigration of the teaching profession that seem to have characterized the education debate in England. In this chapter we shall examine the state of primary education in Scotland during the last decade of the twentieth century, the challenges it faced and whether the public confidence it enjoyed was well justified.

Distinctive features

It is perhaps important to clarify at the outset some of the distinctive structural features of primary education in Scotland. First, children attend primary schools for seven years between the ages of five and 12. All children are first admitted to primary school in a single cohort at the beginning of the school year in August. Since 1997 all children have been guaranteed at least one year of pre-school education, and this will soon be extended to all children aged 3–5. Second, apart from a very small private sector, virtually all primary schools are under the control of the 32 Scottish local authorities. Thus there is not the diversity of forms of school governance to be found elsewhere in the UK. Third, primary teaching has been an all-graduate profession in Scotland since 1984, and primary teachers enjoy a salary scale in common with their colleagues in the secondary schools. The professional qualification for primary teachers conferred by teacher education courses in Scotland is to teach children aged between 2 years 6 months and 12 years. This is achieved through either a 4-year BEd degree or a one-year PGCE course.

The challenges faced by primary education in recent years

During the 1990s the primary education system in Scotland has had to face a number of challenges which derive from two main sources. First, there have been challenges of curriculum reconstruction associated with the arrival of the 5–14 National Guidelines for curriculum and assessment. Second, primary education has been caught up in political restructuring at both the local level, with the reorganization of local government in 1995–96, and the national level, with the change of government educational priorities following the election in 1997 and the inauguration of the Scottish Parliament in 1999. Associated with these political events have been the challenge to primary schools from new forms of accountability, the advent of managerial styles of policy-making and an increasingly pervasive culture of performativity. Before examining the impact of curricular change on the work of primary schools in Scotland, let us consider some illustrative examples of political influence.

Political influences

During its period of government from 1979 the Conservative Party enjoyed little political support in Scotland, its decline culminating in not one Conservative member being returned to Parliament in the 1997 election. This did not deter successive Scottish Office ministers of education from attempting to introduce educational policies to mirror those being implemented elsewhere in the UK. Strenuous efforts were, for example, made to promote a self-governing status for schools in Scotland. These efforts were met with failure: only one primary school in the whole country 'opted out' of local authority control. Here we see but one example of the strong tendency to resist what might in Scotland be seen as the imposition of ideas from England. However, as will become apparent when we examine Scottish primary education in more detail, there are often what Stronach (1999) has described as 'ghostly equivalents' of key features of policy and practice in England and Wales to be found in Scotland. Since the New Labour government came to power in 1997, the political context has been transformed by the creation of a Scottish Parliament in Edinburgh with education and social inclusion as its principal concerns. The new designation of a Minister for Children and Education establishes a frame of reference that clearly aims to put the needs of children first and attempts to challenge conventional institutional priorities and professional roles.

A major influence, although it did not directly apply to Scotland, was the legislation contained in the 1988 Education Reform Act. From north of the border, the creation of the National Curriculum for England and Wales, the associated proposals for national testing and the prospect of the publication of league tables of schools' results were generally perceived as being inimical to the egalitarian and inclusive traditions of the Scottish educational system.

Nevertheless, Michael Forsyth, the then Scottish Office minister with responsibility for education, succeeded in initiating and driving through the most substantial review of curriculum and assessment for primary and early secondary education ever undertaken in Scotland. This began with a discussion paper (SED, 1987) and culminated in the publication between 1991 and 1993 of a comprehensive set of National Guidelines covering all areas of curriculum and assessment for children aged 5–14, the years covering primary schooling (5 to 12) and the first two years of secondary school (SOED, 1991a, b, c; 1992a, b, c; 1993a, b, c, d). The 5–14 Guidelines are different in several important respects but may nevertheless be considered to be the Scottish ghostly equivalent of the National Curriculum in England and Wales.

Background to curricular changes

In order to be able to judge the impact of the 5–14 Development Programme, it is important to establish the context from which it developed. As Darling (1994, 1999) has argued Scottish primary education has, since the 1960s, had a strong and enduring commitment to a child-centred philosophy. The landmark document epitomizing the progressive approach was published by the Scottish Education Department (SED) under the title *Primary Education in Scotland*, usually referred to as the 'Primary Memorandum' (SED, 1965). The advice it contained was to consider the needs of children first and to allow children to construct their own understanding and appreciation of the world around them through meaningful educational experiences that build on their interests and natural curiosity. Practical activity and discovery methods were encouraged. The traditional reliance on rote memorization and didactic teaching methods was eschewed. The curriculum itself was radically reconstructed.

Gone were the arbitrary subject boundaries, to be replaced by new integrated areas such as environmental studies, which not only included geography, history and science, but also incorporated mathematics, which was to be seen as simply another tool to enable children to understand the world around them. Above all, the personal development of the whole child was to be the central concern of primary schools.

Despite the fact that public satisfaction with primary schooling remained relatively high, official inspections by Her Majesty's Inspectorate (HMI) during the 1970s and early 1980s revealed a number of weaknesses in the implementation of the primary curriculum in Scotland. Drawing together the evidence from two years of HMI inspections, the SED published a harshly critical survey of the quality of learning and teaching in Scottish primary schools (HMI, 1980). The principal criticism was not falling standards: indeed, the document went out of its way to reassure the public on this score. Rather, it was over the lack of breadth and balance that primary schools were taken to task.

The curriculum as experienced by children was reported as being too narrowly focused on the basic skills of English language and arithmetic. This narrow focus produced a 'skills and frills' curriculum, the important work in language and mathematics (the skills) taking the lion's share of the available time, most often occupying the whole of the morning session within the school day, while everything else (the frills) was done on the discretion of the teacher in the more relaxed afternoon. The lack of breadth and balance in the primary curriculum was later put forward as one of the main justifications for the 5–14 Development Programme, along with a populist appeal to the need for greater accountability and consistency in terms of standards of attainment.

The 5–14 Development Programme

To facilitate its comprehensive review the curriculum was divided into five main areas: English language, mathematics, environmental studies, expressive arts, and religious and moral education. The process was implemented by a Review and Development Group for each of these areas. The generic areas of assessment, testing and reporting were also placed under review. A set of common principles governing the 5–14 curriculum were set out in terms of breadth, balance, coherence, continuity and progression. A shared language of levels, outcomes, strands and attainment targets was adopted to ensure consistency across the different curriculum areas. A 'draft' version of each set of guidelines was issued in a series of Working Papers for national consultation. The revised advice, which finally appeared in the form of the 5–14 National Guidelines, has been described by Clark (1997) and Darling (1999) as being not radically out of step with the principles laid down 30 years previously in the Primary Memorandum. However, in terms of the sheer volume of the documentation and the quantity of detail on offer, the 5–14 Guidelines were historically unparalleled in Scotland.

The structure and balance of the 5–14 curriculum is summarized by the Scottish Office Education Department (SOED, 1993d) in terms of the share of time available in primary classrooms for the different areas, as follows:

English language	15%
Mathematics	15%
Environmental studies (science, social subjects, technology, health education and information technology)	25%
Expressive arts (art and design, drama, music and physical education)	15%
Religious and moral education	10%
Flexibility	20%

Implementation of the 5–14 Guidelines: the challenge of curriculum overload

Research and evaluation commissioned by the Scottish Office during the 1990s has tracked the implementation of the 5–14 Guidelines. The early evidence indicated that progress was slow, and while primary heads welcomed the prospect of sharing good practice and having a clearer structure, classroom teachers were more sceptical (Malcolm and Byrne, 1995). Later evaluations have tended towards 'cautious optimism' about progress towards implementation (Malcolm and Simpson, 1997). In particular the guidelines for language and mathematics have largely been adopted.

However, the full implementation of the rest of the 5–14 Guidelines has yet to be achieved, and several challenges to key aspects of the framework have emerged. For example, local authority education departments have encouraged primary schools to depart from the suggested time allocations in the 5–14 Guidelines in response to calls from teachers for more time to be spent on literacy and numeracy in the first three years of primary school. In response to such moves the new Scottish Executive Education Department (SEED) has called upon the Scottish Consultative Council on the Curriculum to initiate a review of the Guidance on Structure and Balance of the Curriculum 5–14, and a task group has been set up to review the Guidelines for Environmental Studies, which have proved to be particularly problematic in terms of their implementation.

During the 1990s the Scottish Office has continued its practice of collating the information gathered by HMI from its school inspections to produce a periodic review of standards and quality in Scottish schools. The most recent of these, based on 10,000 class visits in primary schools and 13,000 in secondary schools between 1995 and 1998, paints a generally positive picture of primary education in Scotland (HMI, 1999), commending the breadth of the curriculum on offer and the standards of attainment in some areas but pointing out weaknesses in other areas and identifying concerns about assessment and pupil progression, particularly in the first two years of secondary school. From this kind of evidence, it would appear that the 5–14 Guidelines have had some impact on the weakness of lack of breadth identified in earlier surveys (for example HMI, 1980).

Balance and breadth have arguably been promoted within areas of the curriculum as well as across the curriculum as a whole. On the other hand concerns have been expressed over the erosion of some of the more intangible, but nevertheless essential, qualities of primary education that has accompanied the 5–14 Development Programme. In relation to expressive arts 5–14, Robertson (1999) highlights the twin dilemma confronting teachers, namely 'spontaneity versus linear progression' and 'enjoyment versus accountability' (Robertson, 1999, p. 372).

The challenge of accountability

While the 5–14 Guidelines were not a legally binding prescription, primary schools were nevertheless under pressure in other ways to comply. Since all parties, including teachers and the representatives of the local authorities, had been involved in the creation of the Guidelines, it could be argued that teachers were under a moral obligation to adopt the new curriculum framework through a sense of collective responsibility. However, even more powerful forces for compliance were exerted through the medium of HMI school inspections, which, as soon as the 5–14 Guidelines appeared, started to be carried out against their framework of outcomes and targets. The curricular strengths and weaknesses of schools were reported using the terminology of the Guidelines. Where weaknesses were identified, local authorities were expected to ensure that steps were taken to help schools make improvements, which were themselves defined in relation to 5–14 targets and levels.

While the importance of external inspection should not be underestimated, the Scottish Office has developed a twin-track approach to school evaluation involving what has become another distinguishing feature of Scottish education throughout the 1990s, namely the policy and practice of school self-evaluation. In the late 1980s the Scottish Office commissioned research into what makes a good school by systematically gathering the views of all parties, including parents, children and staff

(SED, 1989). From this work comprehensive resources were prepared to support the process of primary school self-evaluation (SOED, 1992d; SOEID, 1996). All schools are expected to carry out an internal audit using recommended approaches and to establish their development priorities each year in a School Development Plan. This would typically include the development of at least one written policy in a selected area of the curriculum and perhaps the drafting of a policy related to some aspect of school ethos, such as an anti-bullying policy. To this has been added target setting procedures in relation to National Test results.

The challenge of testing, targets and league tables

The original proposals for National Testing for all pupils in the middle and at the end of primary schooling, which would have enabled the construction of league tables, were substantially modified. Instead, the national tests were to be used as a means of confirming class teachers' own assessments. Testing was recommended for pupils when they were deemed by their teachers to be ready to progress from one level of the 5–14 programme to the next. Although the spectre of primary school league tables was erased, at least for the time being, the net result of this revised policy was in fact more testing in primary schools than had originally been proposed. Moreover, as Scottish primary teachers approached the end of the decade with 5–14 testing well established, they faced the new and significant challenge of target-setting as part of the New Labour government's avowed commitment to improving school attainment.

Target-setting is one of the means by which the Audit Unit of the SEED attempts to raise school standards. For primary schools this means being set targets in respect of the number of children achieving at the expected 5–14 level in National Tests in language and mathematics. These targets are set from year to year and are designed to maintain a momentum for improvement even in schools where the attainment level is already high. This has in turn led to concerns being expressed about the validity of classroom assessment procedures and to moves by local authorities to reintroduce traditional standardized tests in areas such as reading.

The challenge of children's rights

Since its ratification by the UK in 1991, the rights of children in Scotland have been protected by the UNCRC. It was not, however, until 1995 that specific childcare law analogous to the 1989 Children Act in England and Wales was enacted for Scotland in the form of the Children (Scotland) Act 1995. The UN Convention promotes three strands of rights: the right to provision, the right to protection and the right to participation. All three of these strands represent challenges for primary schooling in Scotland.

First, the right to education without discrimination challenges policy and practice regarding Scottish children with special educational needs, many of whom still attend special schools outside the mainstream despite policies promoting integration and, more recently, inclusion.

Second, primary schools are challenged on a daily basis by children's right to protection from all forms of abuse, including bullying. In the early 1990s the Scottish Office made a significant commitment to tackling bullying in schools by designating a national anti-bullying development officer and sponsoring the development of resources by the Scottish Council for Research in Education (Johnstone *et al.*, 1991; SCRE, 1993). However, the problem of bullying remains relatively intractable, and, after nearly 10 years of effort, imaginative solutions are still being sought.

Third, primary schools have to respond to the rights of children to participate in decision-making and to express their views on all matters affecting them. Pupil councils have been established in many primary schools as one channel through which participation can be achieved. Evaluation studies have been encouraging where it is clear that these councils have been allowed to make a difference to children's lives in school, even if only in what might be seen by adults as relatively minor ways, such as improving the school toilets. The evidence, however, also points to potential pitfalls where pupil councils have been seen by children as tokenistic (Dobie and MacBeath, 1998).

The challenge of social inequality and social inclusion

The pervasive challenge of social inequality in Scotland has been met by a number of significant educational initiatives instigated by the new local authorities. Responding to surveys that had revealed a significant inequality in measured attainment between relatively advantaged and disadvantaged areas, several local authorities have adopted Early Intervention strategies in literacy and numeracy. The Scottish Office, and subsequently the Scottish Executive, has lent its support to these initiatives by providing additional resources and sponsoring research and evaluation (Fraser, 1998).

An important ingredient in these initiatives was the introduction of additional peripatetic specialist teachers and auxiliary classroom assistance for teachers in the early years of primary school. In several schemes this assistance was provided by trained nursery nurses who assisted in Primary 1 (reception) classes. Additional learning resources and staff development opportunities were provided. The new Scottish Executive, in its 1999 Improvement in Scottish Education Bill, has indicated that £377 million will be made available over a three-year period to continue to raise achievement and promote social inclusion. It has already provided the resources to enable local authorities to reduce class size and to recruit hundreds of new classroom assistants, at least one assistant being provided for each primary school in Glasgow, for example, and more for schools with larger roles. A flagship policy centres on the concept of the New Community Schools, which are designed to foster multi-disciplinary working between teachers and other key professionals and agencies in order to meet the wider needs of children and families and to overcome existing barriers to learning. In 1999 pilot projects were already underway in 30 local authorities involving over 150 schools.

The benefits of the new Scottish politics have yet to be felt by children and families in many communities that have been consistently deprived of resources over recent decades through the operation of an 'inverse care law', by which those with the greatest need have paradoxically received the least in the way of services. This is evident in the resourcing of schools where core funding has increasingly failed to provide schools with basic necessities like books and equipment such as computers. Schools have had to rely more and more on their own fund-raising efforts to secure the essentials. Even more alarming is evidence that the social divide is manifest in unequal access to school psychological services, people using rank and influence to subvert systems in order to obtain scarce professional help for children in socially advantaged groups (Mackay, 1998). In the context of rapid expansion of the World Wide Web and the Internet, there are also concerns over the emergence of an 'information underclass' – those whose social conditions preclude access. The gap has grown, apparently inexorably and in many different ways, between the fortunate and the less fortunate in society. While current initiatives of the Scottish Executive have been designed to close this gap, only time will tell whether these will be effective.

17

Children, Sexual Abuse and the Child Protection System

Lorraine Green

This chapter aims to address and inform those studying or working with younger children and families in a variety of fields and to problematize the common misconception that child sexual abuse (CSA) is a minority problem and the result of family dysfunction, evil or extreme psychiatric pathology. It also treats CSA in a sequential manner, analysing not only the act(s) of abuse and how the child subsequently responds to and understands these, but also whether Western society deals with these in a way that children find fair and helpful. The key theme running throughout the chapter is the premise not only that the act of CSA is a common manifestation of adult and gendered power, but also that subsequent, typical responses to its disclosure or detection compound the initial abuse and disempower and invalidate children even further.

This chapter will synthesize and analyse relevant, contemporary research on CSA. It will additionally draw on two recent, empirical research projects, one analysing sexuality and sexual abuse in children's homes (Green, 1998, 1999a), and the other a cross-comparative research project, involving England, Belgium and the Netherlands, which analysed the balance between legal intervention and therapeutic support services in relation to sexually abused children (Green, 1999b). The methodology utilized in the former study was individual and group interviews, participant observation and documentary analysis, and that in the latter focus group techniques. The two research projects referred to above differ from much of the current research and theorizing on CSA in that, in both of them, the views of children were accessed and were seen as being of central and focal importance. Although most of the children involved in these two research projects were teenagers, many of them spoke about the abuse occurring pre-adolescence and of their feelings and others' responses at the time.

Introduction

The number of cases of CSA that come to the attention of the statutory services in England seem to represent the tip of an iceberg, reflecting the socio-economically disadvantaged profile of most welfare clients (Parton and Wattam, 1999). The number of children seen to be subjected to CSA will inevitably depend on how wide or narrow one's definition is and the research methodology utilized. According to one of the broadest definitions, one UK study found that 50 per cent of females and 25 per cent of males reported CSA before the age of 18 (Kelly *et al.*, 1991). Other research studies have also reported an endemic CSA level (see, for example, Baker and Duncan, 1985; Finkelhor, 1986). CSA is also often linked to physical and emotional abuse (Bifulco and Moran, 1998), although it could be argued that CSA in itself incorporates these aspects.

CSA, however, differs somewhat from other forms of child abuse because it is often conducted in an all-pervasive atmosphere of secrecy and lies (Green, 1999b; Hetherington and Cooper, 1999). It also more commonly commences in pre-pubescent children (Wattam and Woodward, 1996), those between 5 and 9 years of age being at greatest risk (Home Office, 1988), and the perpetrators tend overwhelmingly to be male (MacLeod and Saraga, 1988; Pringle, 1998a). It is also important to note that a high proportion of CSA (some estimates reporting over 25 per cent) is perpetrated by other children (National Children's Homes, 1992), although this particular dimension of abuse will not be included within the remit of this chapter.

In surveys the characteristics of adult, male sex offenders, such as their ethnicity, age, education, social class and mental health, are proportionally similar to those found in the general population (Fisher, 1994; Pringle, 1998a). These surveys thus seem to contradict not only the pathologization and psychiatrization of perpetrators, but also the contemporary demonization and marginalization of serial paedophiles and their emergence as folk devils (Cohen, 1973; Erooga and Masson, 1999). It could be argued that this furore surrounding serial paedophiles also masks the fact that most CSA is perpetrated within families or by those known to them (MacLeod, 1999). Additionally, it is not always possible to separate out intra-familial or extra-familial abuse as many abusers abuse both within and outside their families (MacLeod, 1999), often targeting settings and institutions where children reside, such as children's homes, schools and youth and social clubs (Gallagher, B., 1998).

Liddle (1993) argues that one reason why so many 'normal' males abuse children sexually is because they are, in gender terms, socialized to eroticize that which is small, dependent, passive, innocent and acquiescent – that is, the idealistic media presentation of women – so it is not such a large step to juxtapose that eroticization onto children. However, internal inhibitions, such as guilt and responsibility, and external barriers, such as the presence of others and possible resistance from the child, need to be eliminated before abuse can occur (Finkelhor, 1984; Wolf, 1984).

Contemporary research has shown the societal response to detected CSA in the UK to be at best inadequate and at worst extremely damaging to the children, sometimes mimicking the original abuse dynamics (Browne, 1995; MacLeod, 1999). Responses to CSA in the UK are overwhelmingly adversarial, evidentially based and legalistic (Hetherington *et al.*, 1997), and both therapeutic and legalistic responses are framed in adult-centred conceptions, which disadvantage, bewilder and disempower children (Green, 1999b). It is also generally agreed that, although therapeutic support for children, non-abusing parents and also involved professionals, is of vital importance, there are rarely adequate resources to provide it (Colclough *et al.*, 1999; Green, 1999b).

The following sections will explore the experience of CSA and professional and familial responses to it, mostly through the eyes of teenagers, the majority of whom had been abused pre-adolescence. It will also highlight what these children wanted in terms of help for them and their families and how they thought perpetrators should be treated. Some examples will be taken from focus group interviews with Dutch and Belgian children, but only where their responses paralleled those of English children (Green, 1999b). The main substantive difference in the three countries was that Belgium and the Netherlands were more inquisitorial and less legally adversarial than in England, resulting in disclosures not necessarily being immediately investigated by police. The adult-centred nature of the different child protection systems was similar, as were the inadequacy of therapeutic resources, the feelings expressed by the children and their experiences when the legal system was invoked.

An abuse shrouded by secrecy, ignorance and intimidation

The European study mirrored other studies, showing that children rarely voluntarily reveal abuse because they do not understand what is occurring, are terrorized, feel responsible or fear not being believed:

> I was only little [and was told] policemen will come and take you to prison and then you'll get hung and shot... and I used to be locked in a really dark, cold bedroom and he said over and over again your mum wouldn't believe you if you told, no one would. (female, 14)

> I was told this is normal and if your parents don't do this to you it's because they don't like it. (female, 18)

The main reasons why children were not understood when they disclosed were either a lack of adult understanding or disbelief:

> I tried to tell them this is why I did this and this is why I wanted out. I said 'My uncle comes over and he likes to play with me', and they said that's nice. I said 'He takes me a lot for walks down the cemetery and buys me ice creams', and they never picked up on any of it and I'm really mad they didn't. I just didn't have the vocabulary to say this man is abusing me. (ex-resident of a children's home)

When children disclosed, they did so overwhelmingly to peers, closely followed by disclosure to a mother or other close adult female. Many children also commented that they felt parents should be more vigilant and that the onus should not only be on the child to disclose:

> Adults are supposed to be the ones looking after you and they always say if anything's happening they'll know and look after you and that no one can hurt you... and there's someone hurting you at the time they're saying it. (female, 14)

Issues of confidentiality were also very important to children, and many denied or recanted when faced with the realization that an investigation would follow, as well as feeling that breaking confidentiality was a further betrayal of their trust.

Children's accounts of CSA and its effects

Although it is important not to be too positivistic when talking about the perceptions and effects of CSA, all 32 of the children interviewed in the European project (Green, 1999b) reported it to be a horrendous experience that had left them damaged, so that they felt tortured, manipulated and used. Many reported a subsequent lack of trust in others, depression, guilt and shame, being fearful of men and of being re-abused by the abuser, and a negative and destructive attitude towards their own lives, in which crime and drugs were sometimes implicated:

> You build up stuff inside you and you can't do anything with it until you explode and then no one understands why you've exploded. (14-year-old girl)

When looking at the earlier research on children's homes (Green, 1998), a slightly different picture emerged. A small number of children who talked of sexual abuse mentioned that, in some way, they had at the time viewed it positively. This appeared to be only the case if the abuse was accompanied by affection and there was no affection forthcoming from other sources. Some of them also linked this to the fact that many of them were very promiscuous as teenagers, and they tended to blur the boundaries between affection and sexuality (Green, 1999a).

Adult-centred conceptions were also evident in both studies in the type of help that children were commonly offered, as well as in the way in which they perceived themselves as being seen as stigmatized (Goffman, 1963) and 'damaged goods':

> I got counselling... they expect you to go into a room with someone you hardly know and pour your heart out and tell them all the details and I can't do that. (male, 16)

> Other people give you the name of an 'abused child'... they feel sorry for you and you don't want them to. (female, 14)

Many children in all three countries mentioned that help for non-abusing parents was important, and they felt that they themselves would benefit from group therapy with other abused children, both of which rarely occur in England. They also unanimously stressed the need for very early education on sexuality and sexual abuse as they felt that they would have been more able to understand, name and disclose the abuse:

> Start telling kids [about abuse] as soon as they can understand and let them grow up with it – so they know it's wrong, they can't get done for it or killed, and that they should tell someone. (female, 14)

Although children's conception of mental health is a poorly researched area, a recent research project on young people's conceptions of mental ill-health (Armstrong *et al.*, 1999) closely accorded with how sexually abused children see themselves, as well as finding that children were more likely than adults to internalize their worries. Positive child mental health was also strongly linked to relationships with family and friends, and thus abuse by the family is likely to destabilize the children even further, representing a grave betrayal of trust and responsibility. CSA can also be linked with some adult psychosocial problems, which tend to be dealt with in a medical model, psychiatric vein (often involving involuntary hospital admission). These responses frequently replicate the oppression and powerlessness of the original abuse (Warwick, 1999).

Children's views of the perpetrators and their treatment

In some accounts in the sexual abuse literature, the unsubstantiated claim is that children want the abuse to stop but that they rarely want to break links with the perpetrator if he is a close family member (Cooper *et al.*, 1997; Hetherington and Cooper, 1999). Although such a claim cannot be entirely repudiated, as some children may indeed want this, it is too deterministic and may reflect the authors' own value judgments rather than the children's wishes. In the European research, the antipathy of the children towards their abusers, irrelevant of family connections, was over-whelming. Many of the abusers of the 32 children were family members, although one was previously unknown and a small number of others were familiar to the children but not intra-familial. Not a single child in all three countries who had been abused by a family member corroborated the view that they wanted the abuser to remain within the family. All the children wanted justice for the abuse they had endured and advocated extreme punishment for the abusers, ranging from long-term imprison-ment to death:

> What do you think should happen to the people that abused you, if you had the choice? (facilitator 1)

> Shot. (female, 14)

> No, a more painful death, I think, with a bullet they don't know it. Stab straight up the body, like they've done to us. Why should they get off easier? (male, 16)

> *(the three other children nod heads in agreement)*

> At the end of the day what sort of punishment would you have found suitable for the perpetrator? (facilitator 2)

> The death sentence. Sexual abuse is the worst thing you can do to a child because you keep it with you and there are consequences for the rest of your life. (female, 15)

> But the death sentence is just an injection and he's gone and he didn't feel it. I want him to suffer like we've suffered. (male, 13)

> What's necessary is a prison sentence and strict control and then perhaps send them away, not the death penalty... put them on an island and leave them there. That's exile but not quite a prison. (male, 15)

Although it is possible that these childrens' views on punishment may be moderated in the future, what they do very strongly highlight is the fact that the children did not feel safe and protected by child protection systems and that they had little faith in the ability of society either to reha-bilitate the perpetrators or to ensure that they were adequately punished.

Legislation and the power of the law

In England if CSA is suspected or detected, health and welfare profes-sionals are obliged to report this to social services and/or the police, and a child protection investigation is instigated. CSA therefore falls under the forensic 'gaze' (Parton, 1991) and has been criminalized. Children are seen as potential witnesses, and the emphasis on finding and prosecuting the alleged perpetrator is the prime focus, superseding the needs or wishes of the child:

> The police interview was nothing about me, it was all about nailing him [the perpetrator] and they just fired questions at me... and when I was in court they just kept on trying to trip me up and get me to confess I was lying. And at one point his solicitor was standing in front of me and shouting at me. (male, 16)

In some cases the evidential needs of the legal system physically as well as emotionally damaged the child:

> She was two years old and was bleeding. I took her to the doctor who referred her to the hospital. Then it happened again and we found out it was her grandfather. They did an investigation and gave her another internal examination and since she's been through all of that being examined, she is still fearful of anyone coming anywhere near her. (mother)

The legal system is adult-centred which meant not only that children had to accede to its pace, but that they were often placed in situations they did not understand and found intimidatory, being obliged to think in adult concepts and language. Children's testimony was therefore judged as unreliable or incoherent if they were unable to conform to adult-centred conceptions of truth and fiction and comprehend the legal process:

> the police kept on saying big words... and I was only little... they'd say sexual abuse and I didn't understand what that meant then. (female, 14)

> At the police station there were too many adults and policemen and they were making me nervous... I thought they were going to trick me into saying stuff that he did and then lock me up or something. (male, 16)

In addition, the patriarchal nature of the legal system often also invalidated the claims of females if they were seen to be sexually active or to have been provocative, mothers sometimes being asked, in a way that they perceived as blaming, about their sex lives with the abuser:

> My 8-year-old daughter was raped and they said she had provoked it because she was wearing a mini skirt. (mother)

Children in all three countries in the European research, as well as in the research in children's homes, talked time and time again about being inadequately involved in and informed about police investigations and the court process, as well as about it taking an inordinate amount of time and rarely resulting in a conviction, or at least in one they thought was commensurate with their abuse.

Similarly, English health and welfare professionals talked frequently about being held hostage to the law in terms of what resources were at their disposal and how they spent their time. The law, conversely, showing no accountability for how it operated. The police talked about having to interview a child within 12 hours of a disclosure but the legal process then often taking over 12 months, and cases repeatedly being dropped and rarely resulting in convictions. Social workers similarly talked about all their time being taken up with investigations and this draining their resources, leaving little possibility of doing preventative or therapeutic work with families:

> We seem to be forced straight into a legal framework and if we don't work in that way, well, we'd be seen as incompetent and be sacked probably. (child protection social worker)

> We were called to court, and there was four of us sat there for three days, how much did that cost? (senior nurse, child protection)

Theoretical and practical implications

The findings of this research have very clear implications in terms of the vital necessity of early and ongoing sex education for children, the need to re-evaluate adult assumptions about how children think and feel, and the negativity of adult systems and organizations in terms of child participation, justice for children and their mental health. The lack of accountability of the law, its unequivocal control over other professions and its patriarchal, adult-centred, evidential and adversarial approach also need serious consideration, as does the manner in which health, education and welfare professionals approach the issue of CSA and respond to children.

These professionals should therefore be aware of and attempt to develop child-centred service perspectives. This may entail adapting and reformulating existing organizational structures and work practices so that they are able to effectively respond to children's needs, rather than expecting children to conform to adult conceptions and parameters, and dismissing or negating them if they can not. Understanding the widespread, manipulative and secretive nature of CSA, and the inherent adult/child and gendered power issues, should also help professionals understand the necessity of early and ongoing sex education for children and the need to communicate to children that they will be understood, believed, protected and non-stigmatized if they disclose. Support and education for non-abusing family members is also vital as this affects not only how well they respond to their child's needs, but also whether the child feels able to approach the family for support or, alternatively, that they need to shield the family from the abuse and its effects.

In terms of theoretical analysis and development these findings corroborate the notion of the inaccurate, social construction of childhood innocence and asexuality, and the gargantuan attempts that adults make to police the boundaries between sexuality and childhood and shield children from sexual knowledge (Evans, 1994; Meyer, 1996). Such a response leads to two versions of the sexual harm argument, one justifying such behaviour on the grounds of children's immaturity and ignorance, and the other linked to guarding them from the 'perversity of sexual indoctrination' (Evans, 1994, p. 17). Not only are children therefore wrongly posited as passive and innocent, but also their innocence becomes a fetishized and easily manipulated sexual commodity, and they often are seen as 'damaged goods' through abuse (Kitzinger, 1997).

The preceding sections of this chapter have therefore tried to show how children are initially disarmed in terms of understanding and disclosing abuse by an adult-fashioned culture of innocence and ignorance, imposed through sexual secrecy and sanction. Abusers subsequently use this to their advantage to manipulate, sexually abuse and silence children, who are thus often uninformed in any accurate way about sexuality or sexual abuse. Following this, if sexual abuse occurs and is disclosed or detected, the responses of the law and health and welfare professionals frequently further disempower the children. They do not feel that professional responses understand their perspective, are fair in terms of justice or enable them to feel protected from future harm or to recover from past abuse. Rather, there exists a continuum of abusive adult–child behaviour through which children are initially made more vulnerable to abuse, degraded and betrayed if abuse occurs and, later, often further violated and disempowered by the very systems that claim to protect them.

18

Foster Families

David Berridge

This chapter deals with children living in a variety of circumstances and family arrangements, which have over time become increasingly diverse. Foster care is one of the most complex forms of family life, requiring adjustments on the part of the foster children, foster carers (or foster 'parents') and members of their respective families. Although, as we see below, it takes many forms, foster care refers to a situation in which children live in other people's families. Fostering is usually distinguished from adoption in that the latter is intended to be a permanent arrangement, while the former is more temporary and most children eventually return to their birth family. Fostering can be 'private', in which parents arrange for children to live in another family, sometimes overseas. If this lasts beyond 28 days, the local authority is supposed to be informed as it then has certain responsibilities for the child's welfare; in practice, however, most people are unaware of these requirements. Private fostering is omitted from this chapter because of its specialist nature, although a number of the points discussed will still apply to it.

Most children separated from their families who are looked after by local authorities (formerly 'in care') live in foster homes – over 20,000 under 11s in England at the time of writing. This is, however, not a static group, and about 10,000 children return home from foster care each year. Indeed, many foster placements are of short duration: a quarter last less than a week and half under a month (House of Commons, 1998). Thus a lot of moving in and out occurs, which, irrespective of longer-term benefits, can be stressful for children, carers, carers' families and social workers alike.

Types of foster care

Foster care is often divided between, on the one hand, that which is intended to be temporary and, on the other, arrangements planned to be more long-term or permanent. The former can include planned short breaks as a form of family support for parents, and perhaps children, under pressure (this sometimes being known also as 'respite' or 'relief' care). Thus children might go to stay with a foster family (preferably the same one) on a regular basis, for example for a weekend a month, or when the pressure builds up. Each year over 6,000 children and young people of all ages experience planned short breaks with foster families. Short breaks have mostly been used as an option for families with disabled children, and there is scope for them to be used more frequently to deal with other problems. Although in some circumstances they might help to avoid family breakdown for parents who are particularly hard pressed, short breaks have been criticized because of the discontinuity affecting children. It is also pertinent to ask why, for example, if a family is under stress, a disabled child rather than another family member should be removed.

Emergency fostering fulfils an important role, especially as many children's homes have closed. Emergency foster carers accept children at very short or no notice, at any time of the day or night – a highly demanding task. Children may have been removed from their parents by the police because of physical or sexual abuse, or because they are seriously neglected and living in dilapidated housing. They may be recovering from injury or have recently been interviewed by social workers or the police and are likely to be confused and distressed. Foster carers will try to provide comfort, warmth and reassurance and help to manage the uncertainty that the children face. It may not be intended that the children stay in the emergency home very long, but delays can occur in trying to ascertain the next step. Carers will therefore face a delicate balancing act in trying to form relationships with children yet not make them too dependent as they will soon leave and might perceive this as, perhaps another, rejection.

In contrast, long-term or permanent fostering is, as the name implies, intended to last years rather than weeks or months. This type of foster care has become unpopular in recent years as it has been felt to provide inadequate long-term security for children compared with adoption or a return home. It may, however, be an appropriate option for some who maintain regular contact with their parents but cannot be reunited and do not wish to be adopted. The critics of long-term fostering highlight also the difficulty in recruiting permanent carers and the tendency for a significant minority of placements to break down or 'disrupt'.

Most of the above discussion implies that foster families are previously unknown to children, yet there is growing interest in children being fostered with relatives, usually grandparents or aunts and uncles, especially as the research evidence provides a positive endorsement of this. About one in seven of all under 11s fostered are living with a relative.

However, the use of relative foster carers varies considerably between local authorities, and not all have developed a policy concerning its use. There are, for example, different approaches to approval, payment, training and support. Anomalies can also arise if relatives are paid a significant sum to look after a child, one that was unavailable to the birth parent. Nonetheless, relative care has grown in importance in the US ('kinship care') and is likely to do the same in the UK.

The contribution of foster carers

Although, as shown above, there are several types, foster carers are involved in a range of common tasks. These have been summarized in Triseliotis *et al.*, *Foster Care: Theory and Practice* (1995), one of the best general introductions to the subject and to which interested readers might want to turn next. Foster carers, for example, seek to provide physical nurturing and care through a positive experience of family life, dependable relationships and adult role models. They respond to children's experience of separation, together with possible feelings of rejection and guilt. Furthermore, carers need to be alert to the temporary nature of fostering as a form of substitute parenting while, in association with the social worker, facilitating a return home or more permanent fostering/adoption arrangements.

In undertaking this, foster carers will usually need to liaise with birth families, encouraging contact and visits as appropriate in line with the care plan. This is often not straightforward as parents may have significant problems and needs of their own, and contact, albeit usually beneficial in the longer term, can be distressing as it evokes memories and powerful emotions. Consequently, foster carers will need to deal with a range of emotional and behavioural problems posed by the child, which might include low self-esteem, sullen withdrawal, poor social skills and possibly violent or other forms of challenging behaviour. In all this, carers will need to liaise closely with the social worker to implement the care plan.

Although this list covers the main contributions sought from foster carers, a couple of others can be added. We will return to the issue later, but reinforcing a child's ethnic identity i s important. It is usual nowadays to attempt to place children from minority ethnic groups with families from the same background, although one is often not spoilt for choice, especially when emergencies arise. Ethnic background and culture are key components of individual identity, and these should be maintained, especially when children's lives are disrupted by such profound change. A particularly vulnerable group is refugee children who, having fled a hostile country and sought sanctuary, can feel socially and psychologically bereft. Seeking continuities, therefore, can provide reassurance.

In addition it is worth adding that foster carers should promote children's educational experiences. As a group, children looked after by local authorities up to the age of 16 years do not do well at school, and few go on to achieve any success at GCSE. The reasons for this are complex, ranging from children's origins – family experiences of poverty, and lack of parental encouragement – an inadequate emphasis on education within social services, low expectations and a movement between foster placements. Educational success is one of the main routes to social mobility in the UK, and children looked after should not be denied this opportunity (for a detailed discussion of this topic, see Borland *et al.*, 1998).

Foster care standards

It should be apparent from the above discussion that foster families provide a difficult service. It is therefore disconcerting that, until recently, fostering received little professional attention. Government did not inspect fostering services in England for a decade, and researchers similarly gave it a wide berth (see below). There are probably several reasons for this, including the (misguided) perception that foster care has traditionally catered for mostly younger, unproblematic children. The average age of children now living in foster homes at any one time is about 11 years and, as the number of children's homes has diminished, behavioural problems are more common. Indeed, it has been observed that children who 20 years ago were living in children's homes would now be in foster care, and those in foster care currently remain at home. Encouragingly, this disregard has now been rectified. For example, a Parliamentary Select Committee of MPs discussed foster care at length, their conclusions beginning with the following statement:

> Foster carers are still an essential and under-valued part of the care system for looked after children. Their dedication and commitment should be saluted. (House of Commons Health Committee, 1998, p. xxxiv)

The following year a set of *UK National Standards for Foster Care* (UK Joint Working Party on Foster Care, 1999) was produced, with government endorsement. We live in an era of government bureaucratic regulation involving audit, 'best value', targets, standards, objectives/sub-objectives and the like, and social work is not exempt from this. While demonstrating strong political leadership, it risks undermining professional skills and judgment. If children's experiences improve as a result, however, it is presumably justified. The foster care standards begin by outlining some key principles. First, children should be entitled to high-quality care in a family setting. Children's needs should determine each foster placement and be individually met. It is important to recognize ethnic origin, cultural background, religion and language. In addition continuity in children's lives should be promoted. Partnership is important between carers, children, parents and agency. Furthermore, respect should be shown for foster carers as an essential part of the team.

Detailed sections follow that spell out the implications of these value positions for foster care. Hence children and their families should be provided with services that value diversity and promote equality. Placements should be based on an assessment of children's needs, which leads to a careful matching of children and carers. A key standard is that children in foster care are protected from all forms of abuse, neglect, exploitation and deprivation. Furthermore, information on placements should be carefully recorded and made available to children as appropriate. Adequate health care is necessary to promote physical, emotional and social growth. Children and young people need to be prepared adequately for adult life.

Other sections of the standards cover foster carers themselves: assessment and approval, supervision and support, training, carers' annual reviews and the payment of allowances and expenses (see below). In addition, a section is concerned with agencies' responsibilities. This covers the need for effective policies and management structures; appropriate training for social workers; the placement of children with other, including independent, agencies; and complaints procedures. Each of these areas is fleshed out in more detail. For example, in the first area, Equal Opportunities and Valuing Diversity, statements include:

> Each child has her or his identity and self-esteem valued and promoted; foster carers and social workers work cooperatively to enhance the child's confidence and feeling of self-worth (1.2).

> Each child is supported and encouraged to develop skills to help her or him deal with all forms of discrimination; black and minority ethnic children, and children of mixed parentage, are supported and encouraged to develop specific skills to help them deal with racism (1.4).

At the time of writing these standards are relatively new and we are unaware of their impact.

Research into foster care

There is now a stronger research base in child welfare, so what does this tell us? Unfortunately, compared with say residential care, researchers have paid relatively little attention to foster care. A recent research review showed that, over the past 20 years, barely 13 research studies in the UK had foster care as their main focus (Berridge, 1997). The position is now changing, and major studies are underway at the universities of Bristol, East Anglia and York. Some of what follows may therefore be modified when their findings are published (for a more detailed discussion of research findings, see Berridge, 1997, 1999; Sellick and Thoburn, 1996).

Researchers have commented on the current nature and scale of foster care. Although there are often appeals to expand fostering, the number of carers has remained remarkably static – some 25,000 in total in the UK. There are, however, recent signs of some increase in this number, and government initiatives such as Quality Protects (DoH, 1998b) seem to be having some effect. The recruitment of foster carers would be expected to be influenced by demographic and economic changes affecting women, such as a growth in co-habitation, divorce and step-parenthood; a trend towards smaller families and delaying the arrival of first children; more women working outside the home; and caring responsibilities towards elderly relatives. Yet the retention rate is higher than might have been expected and most carers show commitment over several years.

Research shows that placements are more difficult to maintain for the older child. Similarly, those with behavioural difficulties are, as one would expect, more challenging to foster than others. Nonetheless, outcomes are generally positive, and most children benefit from their time in foster care. A notable achievement has been the successful fostering (and adoption) of severely disabled children, many of whom would previously not have had the opportunity of family life.

A particularly controversial area has been foster care for children from minority ethnic groups, especially the merits of 'same race' or ethnic matching in placements. Issues become even more complex for those of mixed parentage, for example one black and one white parent. Evidence shows that white carers can successfully foster children from minority groups, although if agencies recruit effectively across all sections of the community, this should be needed less. In selecting placements colour should not override considerations of ethnicity, culture, religion and language. Most researchers would conclude that strict rules about placing children should be avoided and instead a careful assessment should always be made of individual circumstances. However, other things being equal and in line with Children Act 1989 guidance, a general conclusion is that 'children should be placed with families with as similar an ethnic, religious and linguistic background as possible' (Smith and Berridge, 1993, p. 33).

Researchers have often investigated children's links with their birth families. Interestingly, as stated earlier, fostering with relatives has generally been more successful than that with unrelated carers. Findings to date are not definitive but many researchers have pointed to the benefits for most children of continued, structured contact with their birth parents and other family members. Earlier research demonstrated the considerable barriers that parents often face in trying to maintain contact, including travel distance, carers' attitudes and anxieties relating to how to behave (Millham *et al.*, 1986). Children are more likely to return home where positive links are maintained. Similarly, good practice would include attempts to place brothers and sisters together or at least maintain contact if they are separated.

The qualities of successful foster carers have been found to include the following: enjoying being with children; being family-centred; flexibility but firmness, while tolerating difference and accepting the child; emotional resilience; open communication; and seeking and receiving support from outside the family. For their part, foster carers want social workers to be 'well informed, accessible, reliable and develop a relationship of trust with carers. Workers need to liaise effectively on their behalf' (Berridge, 1999, pp. 249–50).

Support to carers and relevant training play an important part. Furthermore, researchers have argued that carers need to feel that they are involved in or at least consulted about planning, as they probably know the child as well as anyone and will in any case have to implement decisions. We also know that fostering can have a profound effect on carers' own families, including their children, so appropriate support and compensations should be offered. No clear evidence has emerged yet of the benefits of particular types of organization of fostering services.

The future of foster care

We conclude this brief overview of foster care with a glance to the future. Fostering is at something of a crossroads at present, the National Foster Care Association (NFCA) has even referred to it as being 'in crisis'. Much of the debate centres around whether fostering should in future become more 'professionalized' and its status therefore raised. This hinges partly on payment. Although reimbursement varies, most local authorities currently pay below the NFCA recommended rate and do not even meet what are considered to be the essential living costs of children, let alone any element of financial reward. Foster carers, therefore, are subsidising the state to the tune of about £30 a week for each child (Oldfield, 1997). The same study concluded that the UK comes tenth out of 15 EU and three other countries in the level of generosity of fostering allowances, below countries such as Portugal and Greece.

The NFCA report (1997) recommended paying carers an average of £168 a week – £1 an hour. This would entail an extra commitment of

£236 million a year. Although this is a significant sum – a tenth of the total children and family services budget – it is interesting to observe that we spend twice as much annually on residential care compared with fostering, despite catering for a third the number of children.

Enhanced payments would make foster carers more accountable for their contribution: at present most are effectively volunteers. It would also then be possible to insist on attendance for training, which cannot at present necessarily be reinforced. There might be opportunities for carers to absorb some fieldwork responsibilities, such as report-writing, attending meetings and court, liaison with school and more direct involvement with parents. None of this is to denigrate the considerable contribution already made by foster carers as a group, but there is much scope for further development.

19

External Influences on Workplace Competence: Improving Services to Children and Families

Ronny Flynn

The focus on improving worker and workplace competence accelerated in the UK during the 1980s, driven by concerns that public services, notably education, health and social services, were under-performing and lacked clear goals and direction. Were children coming out of the education system well qualified, literate, numerate and skilled for employment? Was the National Health Service meeting the health needs of the population, and could it provide better value for money? Should social work focus more on prevention or intervention? Concerns highlighted by the public or media led to a series of public inquiries and reports (DoH/Welsh Office, 1997; Warner, 1992), and public services came in for a great deal of criticism. They were extremely costly and appeared not to assist economic growth or provide social stability (Ackroyd, 1995).

Part of the answer appeared to lie in an improvement to workplaces. Workplaces needed to be better managed, and workers needed to be clearer about their roles, their responsibilities and the skills they needed to do their jobs. This focused an increasing expectation on people to work to clearer standards, to become more accountable and to be better trained and more highly skilled in their work for children and families. The government of the day looked to the private and business sectors, with their emphasis on efficiency, effectiveness and economy, for different models of working and as a way of introducing radical change to the public sector. Added to this was the need for a better-qualified workforce to compete with those of other Western European countries. Considerable change took place in the settings where health and social care services were organized and delivered, the situation still continuing to change (Jones and Tucker, 2000). Challenges to how services are organized and delivered continue to come from both central government and service users, and legislation to improve and regulate children's services continues to proliferate.

Fundamental to the workplace is the quality of people who are working within it. People cannot, however, work competently as individuals without the support of a competent workplace (Pottage and Evans, 1994), a key aspect of competence being the ability of the workplace to be a 'learning organization' (Pedler *et al.*, 1991; Senge, 1990) and be continuously open to change, listening to users and valuing its front-line staff.

This chapter highlights external influences to current workplace practice in the public and voluntary social care sectors over the past 20 years and provides examples – the Investors in People (IiP) programme, The Macpherson Report and the work of the Audit Commission – to explore different ways in which competence can manifest itself through workplaces.

External influences: a summary

During the 1980s criticisms of the efficiency and effectiveness of the state surfaced because of the questioning of the economic viability of public services and the values and principles underpinning them. The state became more of a 'regulator not provider' (Jones and Tucker, 2000, p. 8). There was an emphasis on the need for better management and accountability, a lessening of power held by the trade unions and a growth of the 'for-profit' sector. Research evidence also challenged the notion that all was well in public services. A number of publications (Audit Commission, 1986; DoH, 1985) questioned the competence of social care decisions and economies. Anti-oppressive practices developed, and an increased representation of women and black people in the workforce challenged many existing social care practices (Association of Black Social Workers and Allied Professions, 1983; Wilson and Mitchell, 1981). A competent workplace was increasingly seen as one that did not discriminate on grounds of gender, 'race', sexuality or disability.

Scandals and crises in social care hastened change. Public inquiries into child deaths and child sexual abuse shocked the social work profession into action and change (London Borough of Brent, 1985; London Borough of Greenwich, 1987). An increased professionalization of workers occurred, and vocational qualifications in England, Scotland and Wales were developed. These centred on the assessment of individuals' workplace practice, using explicit, measurable criteria. Managers could also be assessed for their competence under the Management Charter

Initiative. Childminders, foster carers and others integral to, but not employees of, some public services were also encouraged to gain professional skills and qualifications. A diversity of professional qualifications and awarding bodies developed, and it has been argued that these bodies were actively attempting to break down the power of the higher education sector, particularly in health and social care.

By the early 1990s legislation, regulation and accountability led the way with a more explicit contract culture in which voluntary and private agencies formally agreed to provide services on behalf of local authorities (Jones and Tucker, 2000). Legislation in adult and children's services set new guidelines and standards for practice. Local authorities, for example, were now required to give 'due consideration' to 'race', culture, language and religion when providing services. User consultation and participation were encouraged and the planning, monitoring and evaluation of services emphasized. User involvement was accelerated by the growth of self-help user movements (Beresford, 1999; Beresford and Croft, 1993). Young people became better represented and their views more central than before (Fletcher, 1993; Morris, 1998a; Shaw, C., 1998). A competent workplace was therefore one that paid attention to the needs of different groups and listened to users. Registration and inspection became functions of local authorities, covering their own services as well as the voluntary and private ones (Davies, 2000).

The growth of professionalization and managerialism continued. Total Quality Management, National Occupational Standards, the Business Excellence Model, British Standards and IiP became common indicators of workplace competence. Given the proliferation of standards from which to choose, there has been an attempt to develop a framework that sets a 'standard for standards' in social care (Darvill, 1998).

Scandals still, however, drove government's reactions to services and the tightening up of standards in public care. These included the 'pindown' inquiry into abuse in children's homes in Staffordshire (Levy and Kahan, 1991) and the Warner Report into the training of residential care workers (Warner, 1992). The publication *People Like Us* (DoH/Welsh Office, 1997) led to a more coherent approach to improving services for children who live away from home.

By the late 1990s New Labour and the 'Third Way' initiated additional radical changes to public services. Building on the previous government's work, there is now a substantial government control of the National Curriculum and a focus on literacy and numeracy, as well as on measurable academic outcomes, for children as a way of assessing the success of schools. With the Quality Protects initiative, the government required local authorities to set out yearly plans for meeting specific targets for children in public care (DoH, 1998b), for example to increase the number of qualifications achieved by 'looked-after' school leavers and decrease the number of placement moves that children experience during one year. The receipt of grants depends on how well authorities demonstrate that they will meet these targets in their action plans. At the time of writing, an initiative to encourage local authorities to attend to services for black and 'minority ethnic' groups is underway (Thompson, 2000).

The Disability Rights Commission 1999 will work to eliminate discrimination against disabled people. It opened for business in April 2000 and will operate in a way similar to that of the Equal Opportunities Commission and the Commission for Racial Equality, setting and monitoring standards, providing information and advice, investigating complaints and undertaking research.

The mission embodied in the government's *Modernising Social Services* document (DoH, 1998c) is that of *Promoting independence, Improving protection and Raising standards*. Government initiatives such as 'best value' and benchmarking involve establishing a measure of an authority's current performance and situation on services they offer, against which they can measure their progress and compare themselves with similar authorities (Wright, 1999). Local authority managers are being encouraged to become more literate with regard to the economics of the services of which they are part and to use research and other evidence in their practice (Atherton, 1999; Stein *et al.*, 1999).

The current government is also determined to improve the National Health Service. Their White Paper, published at the end of 1997, demonstrates a commitment to take a lead in setting standards and requires local NHS Trusts to implement good governance (DoH, 1997).

So have these developments changed the nature of workplaces? The next sections will use the examples of IiP, the Macpherson Report and the Audit Commission to highlight how competence in the workplace may be evaluated, planned and expanded.

Investors in People: valuing staff

IiP is a framework of standards covering the training and development of staff, organizations being externally assessed using a national framework of standards. IiP is based on four principles – commitment, planning, action and evaluation – each with a number of indicators. For example, an indicator of an organization's commitment would be:

> The organization has considered what employees at all levels will contribute to the success of the organization and has communicated this effectively.

An indicator of planning might thus be:

A written plan identifies the organization's training and development needs, and specifies what actions will be taken to meet these needs. (Investors in People Report, 1999)

An IiP assessor provides a diagnostic report to an organization aiming for the standard, setting out what the organization has already achieved in relation to the indicators and what still needs to be done. This forms a plan of action. After six months or a year, an independent assessor returns to see how the organization now meets the indicators and writes a final report recommending (or not) IiP status. If endorsed by the Recognition Panel, the organization receives a copy of the report, a framed certificate, a plaque and the use of the IiP logo on all its literature. A formal presentation ceremony can be held if desired and attracts local publicity. IiP emphasizes the role of learning and development in the workplace and can be applied to any workplace setting. In a survey of social service departments' use of a range of social care standards, IiP was rated as flexible, ensuring continuity and consistency, and straightforward to implement. The standards also enabled benchmarking comparisons to be made with other organizations. Some criticisms were that the system had to be adapted to fit the context of social services, did not focus on competence in service delivery or user involvement and was time consuming (Darvill, 1998).

Day nurseries, schools and hospitals providing services to children and families have sought IiP approval. IiP is coordinated locally through the local Chamber of Commerce. Taking part in the process can provide staff groups with an opportunity to focus on their own training needs as well as fostering a sense of corporate identity and involvement. A people-centred organization is likely to be more effective in its work with children and families.

The Macpherson Report: acknowledging institutional racism

Institutional racism is the process by which systems, policies and procedures, which may not necessarily be designed to discriminate *intentionally*, in *effect* result in poorer outcomes and life chances for particular ethnic groups. In the UK attention has focused on skin colour racism, but other racisms, such as those based on religion, dress and culture, are not excluded (Bhavnani and Phoenix, 1994). Considerable evidence of institutional racism in children's services exists and has been well documented over the years. The evidence highlights a low take-up of services by some groups and an over-representation in the system by others. It covers also a lack of attention to human rights and needs (Butt, 1994; Butt and Mirza, 1996;

Chand, 2000; Humphreys *et al.*, 1999 and see Chapter 5). Lord Macpherson, in the report of the inquiry into the death of the African-Caribbean teenager Stephen Lawrence, publicly highlighted institutional racism in an unprecedented way (Macpherson, 1999). This report is important as it highlights the hidden nature of discrimination, which can influence and affect all workplaces, considerably advantaging some people and severely disadvantaging others.

A survey by Family Rights Group into services for black and 'minority ethnic' children in 52 local authorities found:

> There was a very stark contrast between those respondents who demonstrated good practice and those who didn't. This contrast was not linked to local authority size or ethnicity but more to the amount of responsibility taken by management and political members. (Family Rights Group, 2000, p. 79)

Not keeping records of the ethnicity of children and families receiving (or not receiving) services means that there is a lack of tangible evidence with which to plan. Differences between groups can be denied or ignored. There is a pressure at the time of writing to alter the Race Relations Act 1976 to include public services and institutional racism. Workplace practice has to alter as the process of racial discrimination embedded in public services becomes more open to scrutiny and can thus be challenged by service users. A competent workplace should be representative of the population it serves, should explicitly challenge racial discrimination at every level and should be actively inclusive of black people, whether service users or other community members.

The Audit Commission: a watchdog on quality

The Audit Commission aims to bring about an improvement in economy, efficiency and effectiveness among local authorities and National Health Service bodies in England and Wales through value for money studies and the audit process. In 1994 they published a review of child health and social services provision (Audit Commission, 1994). This followed from the Children Act 1989, the NHS and Community Care Act 1990 and the 1990 GP Contract, which provided a new framework for supporting children and families. The Commission broke new ground by scanning across agency boundaries between community child health and social services, examining actions taken in order to work collaboratively to meet the needs of children and families.

The report produced evidence on what was and what was not working and provided guidelines for managers and practitioners on the better co-ordination of services for children in order to ensure effective and best value provision. For example, the report described how services for disabled children were fragmented between different agencies, the children's needs being marginalized as a result. One of their recommendations was to have a focal point for the joint assessment, delivery and review of the care of disabled children, such as in a child development centre. They advocated that all children should have access to a child development centre, providing a single point of entry for all services. These kinds of recommendation can have a major influence on the workplace. A child development centre that works in an interdisciplinary way and consistently puts the needs of children and parents first demands particular skills and expertise from all personnel – listening and respecting different perspectives, negotiating multi-disciplinary solutions to problems and sharing resources. This example illustrates how an external monitoring body can provide an assessment that is focused on efficiency and value for money outcomes rather than personnel or staff development matters.

Conclusion

A number of messages can be drawn from the above. First, different types of external influence, as illustrated by the three examples, can be effective in different ways. Second, workplaces and the people in them do not exist in isolation: they are part of wider society and influenced by prevailing legislation, values and priorities. For example, repealing Section 28 of the Local Government Act will show a commitment towards ending the discrimination against lesbian and gay parents and their children. The parents of disabled children now have a greater expectation that their children will go to a local school. Both require workplaces to examine their policies, practice and culture, and ensure that they promote inclusion.

Third, central and local government can set standards for workplace competence and expect compliance. The 'best value' initiative, for example, expects local authorities to plan, monitor and review their performance using a number of criteria. A day nursery will be just as accountable for providing evidence of effective consultation with parents as will the whole social services department.

Fourth, the values, goals and principles that are being encouraged – for example, children's and parents' rights, justice, equality, empowerment, communication and lifelong learning – are all worthwhile skills for anyone to develop. In the age of regulation, standards and 'economy, efficiency and effectiveness', it is important to remember that children and families work is human services work, and that interpersonal skills are the core skills of the business.

Fifth, a competent workplace recognizes the fear of change. There can be resistance to sharing power and a fear of taking responsibility for one's own actions and those of other people, as well as of making mistakes. Many of the external influences have met with resistance and criticisms for their motives and methods. The pace of change can leave many children's services practitioners reeling. Change is good, but it needs to be managed appropriately. Too little can lead to complacency, too much to overload and inefficiency.

Lastly organizations owe it to the people they serve to keep in mind their key overall objective of improving the quality of life of children and families.

20

An Ecological Perspective on Child Abuse

Gordon Jack

The word 'ecology' is usually used to refer to the mutual interdependence of plants, animals, people and their physical environments. There is growing scientific knowledge and public awareness about these processes of interaction, with increasing concern about the impact of human activities, such as deforestation and fossil fuel emissions, on global climate changes and the depletion of the protective ozone layer around the earth. These environmental changes, in their turn, have potentially serious consequences for plant, animal and human life.

This ecological perspective can also be applied to the study of child development in general and child abuse in particular (Belsky, 1993; Bronfenbrenner, 1979). The child, the child's family and the environments in which they live influence one another in a constant process of reciprocal interaction. Within the ecological model, child abuse is understood to be a product of the characteristics of the environments in which it occurs rather than simply being the result of the actions of certain individuals. In other words the behaviour of individuals can only be fully understood by taking into account the influence of the environment in which they live. This means that child development and child abuse are the product of the various stresses and supports, or risk and protective factors, that exist in the child's environment. Where the effects of the risk factors present outweigh those of the protective factors, there is an increased likelihood that the child's development will be impaired or even that he or she will experience some form of abuse. Conversely, if the right combination of protective factors exists, the outcomes for the child may be positive, even in the face of a generally negative environment.

Definitions of what constitutes 'child abuse' of different kinds depend upon who is doing the defining and for what purpose. For example, a national inquiry into the prevention of child abuse in the UK used a fairly broad definition that included 'anything which individuals, institutions or processes do or fail to do which directly or indirectly harms children or damages their prospects of safe and healthy development into adulthood' (DoH, 1996a). By this definition a substantial proportion of children could be said to be at risk of suffering abuse. However, even using the more restrictive official definitions of abuse currently in use in the UK (physical abuse, neglect, emotional abuse and sexual abuse), it is estimated that approximately one million children a year are at risk. When this figure is coupled with the three million or so children living in poverty in the UK at the present time, it can be seen that child abuse, however it is defined, is a serious and widespread social problem, requiring urgent and large-scale attention.

Unfortunately, the child protection system that has been set up in the UK, to deal with child abuse and neglect, is not well suited to dealing with the problems of a large majority of these children and their families. It has been developed in response to a number of high-profile child abuse deaths and is dominated by a preoccupation with investigation and surveillance. It deals with only a small minority of the total number of incidents of abuse and neglect that are estimated to occur each year, and it also tends to fail to provide any helpful services to meet the often considerable needs of most of the children and families investigated. By basing the existing system on the most extreme cases, in which children have tragically died at the hands of their carers, the pattern of responses developed has often proved to be inappropriate for the vast majority of cases, in which children's lives are not at risk but their health and development are, nevertheless, being undermined.

The child protection system has also failed to adopt an ecological perspective, which emphasizes the influence on individual behaviour of the social, economic and community circumstances in which child abuse and neglect arise. Instead, it has highlighted parental inadequacies and family pathology as explanations, thereby contributing to the problems of parents drawn into the child protection system more often than it helps to alleviate them. Recent years have seen an attempt to re-balance the official responses provided to children and families in which abuse and neglect may be a risk. The role of family support services is now being emphasized more, and an ecological approach has been incorporated into the assessment framework to be used by all social workers. There is still, however, far too little real understanding of the impact of environments on children and families and the preventative implications of adopting a fully developed ecological perspective (Jack, 1997, 1998, forthcoming).

This chapter will focus on the effects of these social, economic and community influences on children's development and family functioning. A range of examples will be used to illustrate both the direct influences that environments can have upon children and their more indirect influences, through their effects on parents.

Environmental influences on parents and children

The main environmental influences on children and families can be divided into three broad categories:

- poverty and inequality
- social support and social capital
- societal and cultural factors.

Each of these areas of influence will be examined in some detail, before going on to consider the implications for the development of ecologically informed policy and practice that aims to prevent child abuse and neglect, and improve the life chances of all children.

Poverty and inequality

Anybody who attempts to understand the causes of child abuse and neglect will be struck by the fact that the rate varies, often significantly, between different geographical locations. Further investigation reveals that a considerable amount of the variation in the incidence of child abuse, particularly in the rates of physical abuse and neglect, can be directly attributed to socio-economic factors.

This association between socio-economic circumstances and child abuse, is illustrated in a large number of research studies. In one study, conducted in Cleveland, Ohio, four community-level factors accounted for almost half of the variation in recorded cases of neglect and abuse of children. The most significant single factor was the level of impoverishment of the community, one of the other factors being proximity to neighbouring areas of concentrated poverty (Coulton *et al.*, 1995). Another study, carried out in Glasgow, found that the community level of male unemployment accounted for two-thirds of the variation in rates of physical abuse and neglect across the city (Graham *et al.*, 1998). A third study, this time undertaken in Chicago, which used a measure combining nine socio-economic and demographic factors, was able to account for 79 per cent of the variation in the rate of child abuse and neglect. The poorest areas of Chicago were found to have a child maltreatment rate four times higher than that of the most affluent areas (Garbarino and Kostelny, 1993).

It is clear from studies undertaken by other researchers that an important factor influencing the rate of child abuse (and a wide range of other health-related outcomes) is the degree of inequality that exists within a particular society or community, the degree of inequality, rather than the overall level of prosperity of a society, being the crucial factor. It is the individual's, or family's, position in their society, relative to other members of that society, that is responsible for a significant variation in outcome for child development and child abuse (Wilkinson, 1996). This means that raising the general level of prosperity of a particular country or community is likely to have little impact on the rate of child abuse and neglect if the degree of income inequality is significant and remains unchanged. This is particularly worrying for the UK, which has experienced a steeply rising level of income inequality in recent years. For example, the proportion of children living below the official poverty line rose from only one in 10, at the end of the 1970s, to over one in three by the end of the 1990s, putting the UK at the head of the child poverty league in the EU (*Guardian*, 28 April 1997). Minority ethnic families and families headed by lone parents (mainly women) have been particularly affected by this growing impoverishment.

Inequality of this nature has not only a negative effect on individual development and behaviour, but also a corrosive effect on the way in which individuals and families interact with each other within their wider communities. This is the subject of the next section.

Social support and social capital

Social support consists of the practical help, emotional support and advice and information available to individuals through their relationships with relatives, friends, neighbours, work colleagues and professional or voluntary helpers. These networks of relationships vary in the number of people included, the frequency of their contact and the reliability and usefulness of the support that they can provide. Such relationships are also a potential source of stress and conflict, and the ecological perspective requires that we assess the overall balance of support and stress carried by these interactions (Jack, 1997).

Numerous research studies have demonstrated that supportive social relationships, especially those provided by relatives and close friends or neighbours, have a positive effect on parental well-being, family functioning, parent–child interaction and the development of children (Dunst and Trivette, 1990). Conversely, social isolation is consistently associated with poorer health (Blaxter, 1990) and an increased risk of child abuse and neglect (Coohey, 1996). The absence of practical assistance with child care has negative effects on parents in any context, and the perception that social support will be available, if needed, in times of acute stress is beneficial for parents living in disadvantaged circumstances (Hashima and Amato, 1994). Areas with a lower level of social interactions between neighbours and friends tend to be associated with a higher rate of physical abuse and neglect, even after other factors, such as poverty and resident composition, are taken into account (Garbarino and Kostelny, 1993;

Vinson *et al.*, 1996). It also seems likely that such 'socially impoverished' environments will be more open to exploitation by the perpetrators of child sexual abuse outside the family context (Gallagher, B., 1998).

To a significant extent, parents' social networks tend to reflect their position in the social structure of the society in which they live (Cochran, 1993). This means that family environments that potentially represent the greatest risk to children's well-being, and which are therefore in greatest need of the protective influence of social support, are likely to be those with access to more restricted, less reliable and less satisfying social relationships (Fischer, 1982; Thompson, 1995).

Evidence is emerging, from around the world, that a significant proportion of the link between inequality and child abuse is caused by a link between inequality and the level of social cohesion or social capital of a society or a community (Jack and Jordan, 1999; Kawachi *et al.*, 1997; Wilkinson, 1996). More economically divided societies, such as Britain, New Zealand and the USA, show lower social cohesion (levels of trust/density of group membership) and a higher level of both health inequality and child maltreatment. Conversely, more egalitarian societies, such as Japan and Sweden, show no comparable health and social inequality. No other factors so far investigated can adequately explain these findings (Wilkinson, 1996).

Societal and cultural factors

Societal and cultural attitudes and beliefs, as well as the organizations and services that flow from them, also influence the level of child abuse, as we have already seen in relation to the emergence of the child protection system in the UK. In societies where the physical punishment of children is either rare, or legally prohibited, the child physical abuse rate tends to be significantly lower than in countries where corporal punishment is sanctioned. In the same way societies that view children as being the property of their parents, and in which the state is prepared to intrude into the 'private' sphere of family life only in extreme cases, will find it very difficult to prevent child abuse. In contrast societies that place a strong emphasis on children's rights, as citizens, and view their upbringing as a shared responsibility between parents, the communities in which they live and the state, are likely to experience a much lower level of all kinds of child abuse (Belsky, 1993).

Since British society currently resembles the first rather than the second of these models, there is little prospect of significantly reducing, for example, the sexual abuse of children in the UK until the imbalance of power that exists between adults and children, in general, and between men and women, in particular, is effectively challenged (Pringle, K., 1998a). In the meantime, however, families and communities, and the professional and voluntary services that work with them, must continue to do what they can to promote the welfare of children and reduce their risks of suffering 'significant harm'. So what does an ecological perspective tell us about the strategies that are most likely to be effective in these endeavours? This is the subject of the next section.

Community-level prevention of child abuse and neglect

It should be clear, from what has been said above, that strategies aiming to reduce the incidence of child abuse will have to address the needs of children, parents, families and communities simultaneously. This requires that agencies working in this field collaborate closely with each other, and with local people, to develop integrated, systemic approaches that aim both to improve the quality of life for all children and to reduce the risk of child abuse. We can divide the existing and emerging preventive and early intervention strategies into three broad categories – home visiting, centre based and community building. These approaches are not mutually exclusive, and all three will be necessary in some areas or individual situations.

The main types of early intervention and family support programme now promoted by the government are home-visiting schemes and family centres (see Macdonald and Roberts, 1995, for a comprehensive review). The Child Development Programme, for example, uses specially trained health visitors to provide advice to families on childcare and childrearing issues, as well as focusing on mothers' own health and well-being. Although not specifically designed to prevent child abuse, an evaluative study found that the rate of reported physical abuse was halved among the intervention families, and child protection registrations overall were reduced by 40 per cent (Barker *et al.*, 1992). Similar positive results have emerged from a number of ecologically based home-visiting schemes in the USA (see, for example, Olds *et al.*, 1994), one authoritative review concluding that 'extended home visitation can prevent physical abuse and neglect among disadvantaged families' (MacMillan *et al.*, 1994, p. 835).

Evaluations of family centres have also demonstrated their ability to provide effective social support and childcare to disadvantaged parents, as well as safe play space and social stimulation for their children. The best centres also provide opportunities for their users to develop and contribute their own skills for the benefit of others. Their impact on rates of child abuse is, however, more difficult to ascertain, and, in common with most family support programmes, they can have difficulty successfully engaging some parents, particularly fathers, in their activities (Ruxton, 1992; Smith, 1992).

However, services of this nature, which primarily target individual children and families, do little to affect the community-level factors that the ecological perspective has revealed are so important in influencing the rate of child abuse and neglect. What is called for, in addition to home-visiting and centre-based services, are community development strategies that aim to develop or extend the capacity of local neighbourhoods and communities to provide safe and supportive environments for both child and adult residents alike.

One example of a successful community development project, specifically aimed at reducing child abuse, was developed on the Canklow Estate in Rotherham. The local authority funded a small team of community social workers to develop and maintain the informal and formal social support networks available to local families. The team helped to either establish or support a wide range of local groups, including pre-school playgroups, youth clubs, women's groups and adult education classes, all of which extended the support networks of individuals and the social capital of the community. An evaluation of the project after a five-year period demonstrated a very positive impact on local children. For children at risk of abuse, there was a marked reduction in the number of children 'looked after' by the local authority away from home, formally supervised by social workers in their own homes and placed on the child protection register (Eastham, 1990; Holman, 1993).

Communities that Care provides another example of an approach that attempts to build community capacity, through education, youth work and support for families. Originally developed in the USA, this model is currently being tested in both the UK and the Netherlands. It involves assisting communities to assess their own strengths and weaknesses, in a systematic and standardized way, and to use existing research evidence to develop effective strategies to reduce risk and enhance the prevention of harm to children (see Little and Mount, 1999). There are now a number of useful guides available to assist practitioners who want to work in partnership with residents of communities in this way, helping them to assess their strengths and weaknesses, including the level and type of resources that already exist. Locally agreed priorities and acceptable strategies for tackling problems can then be developed, in collaboration with the appropriate health, education and welfare agencies, in both the voluntary and the statutory sectors (DoH, 1993a; Hawtin *et al.*, 1994).

This approach also characterizes some government initiatives, such as Sure Start and the New Deal for Communities, aimed at improving the circumstances of families living in disadvantaged communities. Both of these programmes are essentially ecological in their perspective, adopting a multi-faceted approach that attempts to address the needs of children, parents and communities in an integrated way. An evaluation of their impact is built into these programmes, which should help to determine how effective they are in reducing child abuse and the disadvantaged circumstances that undermine so many children's lives. However, without significant progress in eradicating child poverty, reducing income inequality and effectively tackling the power imbalance that continues to exist between men and women, and adults and children, any gains that schemes of this kind can make are likely to be limited.

Conclusion

The ecological perspective presented here has a number of important lessons for anyone interested in the origins and prevention of child abuse. It should be clear that no single solution to these problems exists. The causes of child abuse are many and varied, and require coordinated attention to the needs of children and parents, as well as the communities and societies in which they live. When tested against this framework, the shortcomings of the existing child protection system in the UK are all too apparent. Insufficient attention has in the past been paid to the major influence that environmental factors and structural inequality have upon the lives of children and their families. Official responses have tended to place too narrow an emphasis on the apparent shortcomings of individual parents without recognizing the effects of the environment on parenting behaviour.

Although the early signs of a wider understanding and application of an ecological perspective are now emerging, there is clearly still a reluctance to undertake the more fundamental review of society, and of the structural inequalities that exist within it along the divisions of gender, race, age, disability and income, that would be required fully to implement an ecological approach.

Part IV

Working with Children and Families

21

Children's Health at School

Berry Mayall

To what extent is health prioritized in primary schools?

Policy pronouncements on the relationship between education and health had a new emphasis during the 1990s. The notion of the health-promoting school has gained currency through the 1988 Education Reform Act and through the UK version of the European Network of Health Promoting Schools (Hamilton and Saunders, 1997). Health education, or health promotion, is identified as an essential component (albeit not a core curriculum topic) for schools.

What, then, is the material context for these initiatives? What is the condition of our primary schools? The quality of buildings varies widely. As a 1993 survey in England and Wales (the CHIPS study)[1] showed (Mayall *et al.*, 1996), only two-fifths of teachers rated their building as good, and for the 30 per cent of schools built before 1903, this percentage dropped to a fifth. Half the teachers rated the toilets and the playground good, but only a quarter rated playground equipment good; again, newer buildings attracted a higher score. Children experienced overcrowding both in class and in the playground as being unpleasant, and it led to accidents at break-times. According to the Audit Commission the backlog of maintenance work had risen by 60 per cent between 1989 and 1996 (NUT, 1997).

Nutritional standards for school meals, a fixed meal price and the requirement on local education authorities to provide a school meal were abandoned under the 1980 Education Act, and compulsory competitive tendering was introduced in 1988 (Sharp, 1993). The overall effect has been to lower the take-up rate and to cause adult concern that children, faced with a choice in the cafeteria, choose bad food.

Children's opportunity for physical activity has been reduced by two pincer movements. Some schools have shortened or abandoned playtimes (Blatchford, 1999), and some have reduced curriculum sports time, the pressure on schools to achieve a high test score in core subjects (English, Maths and Science) being an important factor.

School provision for the care of children who have a medical condition, have an accident or fall ill varies widely and has low priority. Thus in the CHIPS survey, fewer than a fifth of schools had a sole-use sick room or one shared only with the school nurse, 37% had nowhere for children to rest when they were unwell, and 12% had no room (not even one shared with another use) available for the school health service, so that the nurse or doctor had to work in whatever space could be found on the day. The proportions of schools with staff trained (on minimal criteria) to care for illness and accident varied widely, 13% having no one. The school health service was also patchy, 5% of schools having no school nurse visit, 20% two or three visits per year, and 17% weekly visits. Furthermore, 'a fundamental flaw with the existing School Health Service is that it does not allow for a clear NHS input into schools by way of the provision of "hands on" care for pupils where needed' (House of Commons Health Committee, 1997, para 87, p. xxviii).

These features of children's work environments forcibly suggest that the opportunity for maintaining, restoring and promoting their health is accorded a low priority in education policy and practice.

Why are schools unhealthy?

One kind of explanation must lie in the long tradition of divided responsibilities between the health and education services. The history of official unwillingness to recognize links between the two starts with compulsory state education (1870s), with battles over the responsibility for dealing with an unpalatable truth: that starving sick children would have to be fed and cured, otherwise education expenditure would be wasted (Hurt, 1979). Currently, with a third of children living in poverty (Bradshaw, 1997), some schools provide breakfast, but the Department for Education and Employment (DfEE) expects schools with a large proportion of poor children to compete in academic excellence with schools serving wealthier populations. A reluctance to grant adequate resources for health in schools has continued, with ups and downs, to this day (Harris, 1995; Mayall, 1996), and children's ability to maintain their health has varied accordingly.

These divided responsibilities reflect the notion that bodies and minds are separable and thus the appropriate province of separate ministries. Although the ministries have begun to collaborate, education policy today centres essentially on the curriculum, top priority being given to numeracy, literacy and science. The physical conditions in which children work are accorded much lower priority: it seems that they are not regarded as impacting on children's well-being and willingness to learn. Similarly, what children eat at midday is not regarded as the responsibility of the education authority or the school. Indeed, by devolving decisions about the material and nutritional character of the school to the school, governments have divested themselves of responsibility. A key topic here is the unsatisfactory and unclear division of responsibility for health and safety as between school (under the Local Management of Schools) and Local Education Authority; governors and headteachers must take measures to ensure health and safety but, obviously, only to the limit of their responsibilities (Stock, 1994). In one school, for example, the Head saw no point in improving the interior of classrooms (her responsibility) until the local authority (responsible for the buildings) had repaired rotten structures (Mayall *et al.*, 1996).

These policies tie into basic beliefs, commonly held by educationalists at all levels, that children are to be conceptualized as objects of adult teaching, as immature and lacking in competence, and as lacking knowledge relevant to the school curriculum (Alderson, 2000). Schoolchildren are defined not as social actors but, significantly, as 'pupils'. The formal social order of the school is controlled by teachers, whose work is controlled by education policies.

Recent policy initiatives further serve to shift the emphasis away from state and school responsibility by identifying parents as being responsible for education. Under the banner of 'parental involvement in schools', parents are asked to fund schools and, through home–school agreements, to agree formally to work for the school, for example to guarantee specific bedtimes for their children, to oversee homework and to attend meetings as required. This shift also serves to reduce the social status of children. At home children are to be objects of parental control in the interests of narrowly defined school achievement, rather than social actors. Evidence suggests that children disapprove of these school interventions into the home, these interlocking adult controls (Edwards *et al.*, 2000).

What do children bring from home to school?

When children start school they are competent in many areas of self-care at home. They dress themselves, ask for or take food when they are hungry, use the toilet as needed, rest, play and learn at will. When they feel ill they lie down; when they need care they ask for their mothers' help. They monitor and adjust their own health status, in conjunction with parental (mainly mothers') care. These competencies are encouraged by mothers – who happily share the responsibility for healthcare with their children. Children discuss and negotiate decisions with other children and parents (Mayall, 1994; Newson and Newson, 1978).

Children's agency within a caring environment at home contrasts with what they encounter at school. School typically demands that children subordinate their embodied selves to the curriculum and to the social order of the school. They are not understood as competent, or as morally reliable. They have to ask permission – sometimes refused – to go to the toilet; they can get a drink only at break – if a water fountain is working; they can eat, rest, learn and play only when adults say so. Sickness bids may be met with disbelief or with temporizing – 'get on with your work and see how you go'. When children stay off school for any reason, their own explanation will not suffice: only a parental note or phone call will do (Mayall, 1994; Mayall *et al.*, 1996).

These adult controls of the physical are matched by their control of the social. It is uncommon for children to participate in discussing and revising the organization of the school day, codes of conduct or the management and improvement of difficult behaviour, or to participate in improving the school building and grounds. Children say that, at school, you have no control and no choice (except at break); teacher authority is absolute; teachers do not recognize children's wishes to care for themselves and often suspect their statements, requests and motives;[2] and children are scathing about the physical environment, especially uncared-for buildings, bleak playgrounds where there is nothing to do, the toilets and school food (Titman, 1994).

What would a healthy school look like?

A healthy school would be one in which children acted as participants in the continuous process of improving the learning, social and physical environment. This approach differs from that proposed in some of the health promotion literature, in which damaging assumptions about children's immaturity, lack of knowledge and self-esteem colour the discourse, where the complementary assumption is that the central activity is staff work on children to 'support' them, to 'build pupil self-esteem' and to 'stimulate' children, and where the principal desired outcomes are changes in 'pupils' attitudes, knowledge, self-esteem and behaviour' (Hamilton and Saunders, 1997, pp. 9, 19).

In order to reconceptualize children as participants, adults must reconsider their general notions of children; an active recognition of children's knowledge, competencies and experiences is relevant to the planning and improvement of schools. Also required is a recognition of the power imbalance between children and adults, especially at school. This is hard, not only because adult authoritarianism is rife in schools, but also because in general, in every social context, children are subordinate to adults. Children themselves make this point forcibly: they regard childhood as a condition or status subordinated to adulthood, and experience this at home, in school, in shops and on buses. Notably, children define 'free time' as time out of immediate adult control and therefore value it (Mayall, 2001).

Rethinking child–adult relationships needs careful, democratic and continuous negotiation. An open recognition of the power imbalance is a prerequisite for moving on. A recognition of children's rights to express their views and have them taken into account is the next step; then the task becomes that of negotiating the best way forward to take account of both children's and adults' rights and wishes. Neill's (1976) point that, as Head at Summerhill School and *in loco parentis*, he was responsible, in the last resort, for some decisions is recognized and accepted by children as being integral to the protection and provision responsibilities of adults towards children. The work of reconstructing one school on democratic principles has been described by its staff and children (Highfield School, 1997).

Respect for children's participation rights must be matched with complementary understandings of the embodied character of children's experience. The current government has begun to allocate substantial funds to the long-neglected task of upgrading school buildings and play-grounds (DfEE, 1998); this provides an opportunity for all the agencies concerned to consult with children as well as staff and parents.

Although staff time may be saved when democratic procedures are in place – because behaviour and academic achievement improve and are managed by the children and staff jointly – evidence from schools working to promote children's health indicates that extra staff time resources are usually needed to work up collaborative programmes (Hamilton and Saunders, 1997), and whilst Highfield benefited from a particularly dynamic and clear-sighted Head, some schools may be less lucky.

The input of welfare and health-related services to schools needs higher priority in the planning and provision of services. The CHIPS study showed a reduction over recent years in the services offered by social services and health services (visits to the school, the availability of specialist advice, referral to specialists) (Mayall *et al.*, 1996). The National Health Service should provide 'hands on' care for children as needed (House of Commons Health Committee, 1997). These services are vital to help the work of school staff, children and parents. Staff and children may need help with managing conditions (such as asthma, diabetes and epilepsy); staff may need advice on how to care for and teach children with an impairment and how to provide a healthy working and playing environment for the children. (In Sweden, the school nurse advises on ergonomics!) Children should have access to a confidential health and welfare service at school; indeed, school is the ideal environment since they cannot easily go to GPs and social services departments on their own (Mayall and Storey, 1998). In addition parents are entitled to know that their children are being looked after at school, in sickness as well as health. This is an increasingly important issue when mothers are being urged to go out to work without payment for time off to care for children.

More broadly, the complex issue of appropriate divisions of responsibility between school, health service, parents and children for the care and cure of children needs re-thinking to take account of the prevalence of medical conditions, the integration of special needs children in mainstream schools, the pressure on mothers to go out to work and the dawning recognition that children are competent health carers.

Discussion

A first theme in this chapter is the splitting of minds and bodies, which takes place at the theoretical, policy and practical levels. We have all been taught to do it through long-established Western traditions whereby the mind is understood as 'disembodied' and mind is superior to body (see, for example, Turner, 1992). Only recently has a sociology of the emotions addressed the complexities of the interlinkage between body and mind through the mediating influence of emotion (Williams and Bendelow, 1998). The traditional split has been highly significant in the structuring, financing and running of schools; the well-being of children compared with that of other workers has been grossly neglected. The perceived function of schools – to address children's minds – may in part be identified as a contrast to the perceived messy intersections of bodies, feelings and relationships of life at home. But we may add that the lowly social status of children, compared with that of other workers, may also account for the low level of resources allocated to their well-being at school.

A second theme here concerns the neglect, even rejection, of children's rights in the education system (Lansdown and Newell, 1994). Health services and social services have been quicker to recognize these rights, perhaps because consent concerns interventions that may critically affect children's well-being in the here and now, so children can readily be understood to have relevant knowledge and views. In contrast education commonly looks to the children's future and devalues present experience; furthermore, the education service aims to serve societal needs, which some self-styled experts regard as lying outside children's knowledge or competence. These (as I believe untenable) points were made by a minister asked about the discrepancy regarding children's participation between an education Bill (for the Education Act 1993) and the Children Act 1989:

> The answer is that the (Children) Act ranges much more widely on welfare issues, interpersonal relations and the child's existence in a social environment, whereas the Bill deals with more strictly educational matters. It is at least arguable that there is a difference between taking full account of a young person's attitudes and

responses in a social and welfare context and asking the child to make a judgment, utter an opinion or give a view on his or her educational requirements (Hansard, quoted in Hill and Aldgate, 1996, p. 96)

Third, this chapter raises the issue of the division of responsibility for children at school between the state education service, parents and children. The present division in the UK allocates insufficient responsibility to the first; it illogically asks mothers to work for the school as well as go out to work; and it views children not as participants in the education enterprise but as objects of adult intervention. In Finland, in contrast, the high level of state responsibility for education ensures critical practical effects: all children get a free school meal, all buildings are of a common – high – standard, and safe children's routes to school are provided. Almost all parents work, and they can do so in the knowledge that their children are educated, protected and provided for by the state. Children themselves take responsibility for their journey to school, for homework and for how they spend time after school until the family meet at home (Alanen, 2001). This chapter has argued for some movement towards this socialist model, in the interlinked interests of children's rights and the construction of healthy schools.

Notes

1 The Children's Health in Primary Schools study (CHIPS) was funded by the ESRC (1993–95) (Ref. no. ROOO 23 4476).
2 These issues are explored in the author's most recent study *Negotiating Childhoods* (ref. no. L129 25 1032), funded under the ESRC Children 5–16 Programme (1997–99).

22

Theories of Child Development

Wendy Stainton Rogers

This chapter examines the main theories that have been offered to explain
how children develop. It also looks, briefly, at some of the criticisms that
have been made about developmental theorizing and at some of its consequences for how children are treated.

Nature versus nurture

Our modern, present-day theories of child development have their roots in
seventeenth- and eighteenth-century philosophy, usually being traced
back to the work of John Locke (1632–1704) and Jean-Jacques Rousseau
(1712–78), although both drew on earlier thinking.

Prior to Modernism, Christianity tended to view the child as being
innately 'sinful'. Locke challenged this. He argued that, at birth, a child is
like a *tabula rasa* – a blank slate – that is 'written on' by his or her experience. Children, he suggested, are born with different degrees of intelligence
and different temperaments, but he rejected the idea (which stemmed from
Plato) that they are born with any innate knowledge or morality. Locke
believed that it is the parents and others who, in the way in which they
bring up and educate the child, mould their characters – for good or evil.
Locke thus saw nurture as being the most important influence on development. The assertion of the Jesuit, Francis Xavier (1506–52) 'Give me a
child until he is seven, and anyone may have him afterwards' describes a
similar view, as later did that of the behaviourist John B. Watson: 'Give me
a dozen healthy infants and my own world to bring them up in, and I will
guarantee to turn each one of them into any kind of man you please.'

Rousseau, in contrast, saw nature as the key factor in a child's development. He viewed children as 'noble savages', possessing a natural sense of
right and wrong. As far as he was concerned children are born inherently

good and with the ability to reason and make moral decisions. Rousseau also believed that children are fundamentally different from adults. He is often credited with the first truly developmental account of childhood, including two key elements of our modern developmental theories: the idea of maturation, and the notion that development progresses in stages. Current theories stressing the role of nature have also been much influenced by Charles Darwin's (1809–82) theory of evolution, brought up to date by more recent discoveries, most notably the working of genetics and the biochemistry through which genetically encoded information passes on characteristics from one generation to another.

This nurture/nature debate has been woven through developmental theorizing throughout its history and is still very much alive today. One of psychology's 'big debates', for example, has been whether intelligence is mainly a matter of genetics (nature) or experience and education (nurture). There continue to be major arguments about how far development is a natural process that 'just happens' (that is, it is a biological process) and how far can it be controlled and influenced by experience (that is, it is a process of socialization and learning). The kinds of question raised cover the extent to which people are the product of their genetic inheritance – is their personality determined from the moment of conception?; is character, intelligence, even sexuality, 'bred in the bone'? Or are these mainly the product of experiences in childhood? Does upbringing determine what kind of adult a child becomes? Do serious troubles and traumas in childhood lead to mental health problems in adulthood? We can think of developmental theories, therefore, as comprising three main kinds: those which stress the role of nature; those which stress the role of nurture; and those which view development as an interplay between nurture and nature (often called interactional theories). We will look at each of these in turn.

Theories that stress the role of nature

Following on from the ideas of Rousseau have been a number of psychological theories that stress the role of biology – nature – in determining how children develop. The best known of these is Piaget's (1950) theory of cognitive development, which we will examine in this section.

Piaget's theory of development

Piaget was mainly interested in the way in which children's thinking abilities develop. Psychologists call these the child's cognitive abilities. So Piaget is called a *cognitive developmental theorist*. Piaget's theory views biology as being crucially important. In today's terminology he would see cognitive development as operating primarily as a 'wired-in' program (rather like a computer program) that runs its course, hardly influenced at all by nurture. One stage of development follows another, just as a computer program goes through a sequence of predefined steps.

What defines Piaget's theory is *how* he saw those steps as progressing. He proposed that cognition does not just get gradually better – children do not simply become more and more cognitively competent, bit by bit, as they grow up. Rather, he argued that children undergo a series of *transformations* in *how* they think. In other words he suggested that children are not just cognitively less able than adults, but also that they actually think in a fundamentally different way. To use a phrase coined by Piaget's followers, the child is a 'cognitive alien' – cognitively speaking, a different kind of being.

Piaget's view is that the development of human thinking progresses in a similar transformational way, passing through distinct, separate stages. Piaget described four main stages of cognitive development, the child undergoing a major transformation in passing from one to another. These are:

Stage 1   Sensori-motor thought
Stage 2   Pre-operational thought
Stage 3   Concrete operational thought
Stage 4   Formal operational thought

Stage 1: Sensori-motor thought (birth to two years)

According to Piaget the first two years of life are a time when children's thinking is very basic. Below about two years old children cannot think in any abstract way: they cannot manipulate symbols in their mind. Their thinking is limited to making links between the inputs from their senses (what they hear, see, taste and so on) and movements (such as picking up something in their hands). This is what sensori-motor means. The newborn baby's sensori-motor reactions are all instinctive, although some last only a few days.

Later (by about 15 months of age) children have generally developed the ability to take exploratory actions. When these produce interesting results (like a plate of biscuits being brought into reach by pulling the tablecloth) the child will subsequently use this action intentionally. What has gone on is a lot of learning. As anyone who has looked after a child of this age will know, this can include some quite sophisticated behaviour, such as the 'I throw it on the floor and you pick it up' game! Nevertheless, until language develops, it is learning of a very simple kind, associations being made between some kind of event or feeling and the child responding to these in fairly simple ways.

Stage 2: Pre-operational thought (2–7 years)

At the age of two, or just before, the first proper abstract thought becomes possible: the child becomes able to use mental imagery. This major transition is reflected in the acquisition of language, imaginative play and the ability to remember things long after the event.

But for all the competence of children of this age, Piaget argues that they lack the ability to think logically (in 'operations', he called it – hence the term pre-operational thought). To illustrate this he claimed that they could not give the correct answer to such questions as 'Are there more flowers, or more red flowers?' Later children begin to reason by 'rules of thumb' (Piaget called this intuitive thought), which can focus on one, but only one, aspect of a situation. So children think that there are more white beads in the row below because they concentrate on the length of the row:

○ ○ ○ ○ ○   White beads

●●●●●   Black beads

Stage 3: Concrete operational thought (7–11 years)

A crucial leap in intelligence occurs at about the age of seven. From intuitive thought children make the jump to logical reasoning. To Piaget this means that they become able to move ideas about mentally, to carry out operations upon them. A good example of this is a trade-off between different aspects of things. Children can, for example, take into account both the height and width of a beaker containing liquid in order to determine the volume of the liquid. A child at this stage (but not before) 'knows' that when we pour liquid from a tall, thin beaker into a short, fat one, the amount of liquid has not changed. Before concrete operational thought children will say that there is more liquid in the tall beaker, but once children reach the concrete operational stage, they will say that the amount of liquid is the same. However, pre-adolescents still do not reason like adults because their logic is limited to imagery of the 'real' (that is, experienced) world. This is what Piaget means by concrete.

Stage 4: Formal operational thought (age 11 to adulthood)

One of the fascinations of science fiction is that it allows us to speculate about alternative worlds. What would a person be like if he or she were brought up by aliens? How different would society be if our gender only became apparent once we reached adolescence? What would it be like to live in a four-dimensional house? The ability to think out such ideas is what Piaget means by the last great transformation, the acquisition of the ability to think hypothetically and outside direct experience, to play out 'what if' possibilities in our minds. This includes more 'intellectual' thought, for example playing chess or solving complex mathematical problems. While some children gain this mastery earlier, it usually takes until about age 11 to get to grips with abstract ideas.

In Piagetian theory each successive cognitive stage is an integration and consolidation of what has gone before. Later stages do not replace earlier ones (as a computer chip can be replaced). Rather, the mode of knowing is completely reconstructed as new knowledge and more sophisticated ways of thinking become available.

Theories that stress influence of nurture

In this section we will examine two main kinds of theory: learning theories (including both classical and social learning theories), which were devised by psychologists, and theories of cultural influence, devised by anthropologists.

Learning theory

Classical learning theory is based on the work of psychologists such as B.F. Skinner (1905–90), called Behaviourists because they focus on behaviour as the objective aspect of human functioning that we can study, as opposed to experience, which is individual and 'private', and thus, they say, cannot be studied.

Underpinning this theoretical perspective is the notion of behaviour modification. It is used, for example, to control disruptive pupils by giving them praise and attention for good behaviour and 'time out' (ignoring them) as a punishment for bad behaviour. It is also used in penal institutions and some mental hospitals to control behaviour. Patients are given a set of rules, the desired behaviour being rewarded by tokens. These gain value as rewards as they can be exchanged for sweets, cigarettes or favours (such as watching television).

Developing skill at sport is another common application of learning theory. Nobody can, for example, instantly become a tennis ace, but most people can become reasonably competent if they are willing to devote the time to building up their skills, starting with the most basic and gradually refining them. People who play sport professionally now use video-recording to help them to fine-tune their skills. By watching a recording of their performance they can get feedback about what they are doing wrong and what they are doing right. This feedback is crucial to enable them to improve.

Fundamental to learning theory are the notions of rewards and punishments, based on the idea that behaviour followed by a reward tends to become more common, behaviour that is punished becoming less so.

Social learning theory

The example of sports players using video-recordings to improve their performance gives an important clue to the limited applicability of conditioning to human learning. While there are some very basic responses that can work according to simple conditioning, people generally learn because they have an awareness and insight into what they are doing. Consequently, psychologists have developed more complex theories of social learning.

Social learning theories recognize that, for human beings, learning almost always takes place within a complex social environment, where rewards and punishments work at a psychological level. Rewards may, for example, include feelings of achievement and self-esteem, whereas punishments may take the form of feelings of stupidity or being humiliated.

Theories that view child development as an interplay between nurture and nature

In this section we will look at theorization concerning development based on the interplay between 'nature' (that is, the biological basis of behaviour) and 'nurture' (that is, the influence of the social and cultural environment). This has been neatly encapsulated by Richards:

> throughout development there is an essential tension between the biological and the social. The infant and his [sic] social world are in constant interaction; just as the biological infant structures and modifies his social environment, so he is socially structured by it and his biology is modified. (Richards, 1974, p. 1)

This kind of theory proposes that 'the whole may be more than the sum of its parts', that with something as complex as human behaviour and experience, the causative influences are likely to be multi-factorial, co-actional and complex. The best known interactional theory is undoubtedly Freud's theory of psychosexual development. We will look at this next, along with two important theories that were developed from it: Bowlby's attachment theory and Erikson's theory of psychosocial development.

Freud's model of psychosexual development

Freud also saw development as passing through stages, although progress through the stages is in his theory seen as being fundamentally influenced by nurture. In Freudian theory what matters is how the individual resolves the internal, psychic conflicts to be faced at each stage.

The first element of Freud's psychodynamic theory is that babies are born irrational and 'savage' – instinctively acting for self-gratification alone. Freud called this component of personality the *Id* – a part of us that remains for life, our 'base, animal nature', selfish, savage, irrational and uncivilized. According to Freud babies come into the world all Id, but they are soon expected to go beyond satisfying their own needs and to respond to the demands of others (for example, by smiling and paying attention).

From such small beginnings comes the baby's thinking and perceiving self, which Freud called the *Ego*. With the Ego babies can learn. Most importantly they learn to wait for gratification and to choose one form of gratification over another. In simple terms it is the 'reasoning self', and it runs a kind of psychic economy that satisfies the demands of the Id with the minimum of pain and cost. The child's parents or other carers set the rules about feeding, or bedtime, or potty training, and the baby's Ego does its best to work within these rules to gain satisfaction for the Id.

Then, as the child matures, the third psychic 'character' – the *Super-ego* – comes into play. This is formed when children acquire insight into and then *internalize* the social rules and cultural mores of the community, society and culture in which they are raised. The Super-ego is the child's 'conscience', acting in dynamic opposition to the Id – 'doing what is right' is always having to be balanced against 'doing what I want'. This ongoing 'battle' is managed by the Ego and continues throughout life.

Freud's theory of development can be understood by analogy – development as dragon-slaying. In this analogy the child is, from birth, faced with a sequence of hazards to be overcome – psychic 'dragons' that have to be slain – in order to attain the prize of fully functioning, healthy adulthood. These 'dragons' are powerful feelings experienced by the Id – feelings that are not only frightening and dangerous, but also unacceptable to the Super-ego. Therefore the Ego must find ways to conquer them.

Freud's theory thus views development as a biologically grounded process that is modified by experience and socialization. Development is a matter of *working* through (as opposed to going through) a series of predetermined stages as an individual matures from infancy to adulthood, the outcome being determined by the success (or lack of it) with which the individual tackles the challenges that the stage presents. If the individual fails at any point, he or she will remain entrapped, unable fully to progress further.

Freud claimed that the sexual instinct acts as a 'driver' throughout life, starting in infancy. It is important to recognize that by 'sexual' he meant a much wider definition than we would usually interpret it as having today, something more like sensual pleasure. He hypothesized that the site of this sensual pleasure shifts sequentially as the child develops, moving the child through a series of psychosexual stages.

The oral stage is the first stage that the infant experiences. The mouth is the site of sensuous pleasure, which infants gain through sucking and chewing. The anal stage describes the time that children reach at about one year old, when the anus becomes the site of their sensuous pleasure, which they gain through the physical sensations of excretion. The 'dragon' to be fought here is toilet training, and, if it is not accomplished properly, an 'anal personality' can develop – an obsession with neatness, stubbornness and holding on to possessions. The phallic stage is linked to a child at around three to four years old, when the child's genitals become the site of sensuous pleasure – which is achieved through masturbation. This, according to psychodynamic theory, is a very active phase, and differs for boys and girls. Two main things happen, according to Freud:

- Boys notice that they have a penis and girls do not; girls notice that boys have a penis but they do not.
- The focus on genital pleasure stimulates sexual attraction to the parent of the opposite sex: boys became attracted to their mothers, girls to their fathers.

These experiences have a different significance for boys and girls: their impact is different, and they resolve them in different ways.

The latency stage describes the period at which children move into a period of latency, during which sensual pleasure assumes much less importance. Last is the genital stage, when physiological changes at puberty lead to a re-awakening of sexual desire. This is initially *homo-erotic* (that is, sexual attraction to people of the same gender), but, via more 'dragon-slaying', it is soon 'normalized' into *heteroeroticism* (that is, sexual attraction to people of the other gender).

Once again, Freud theorizes different processes for males and females. Young men find this transition easier, since, as at the phallic stage, their attention is focused on the penis. Young women, however, have a much more difficult time as they must make the transition from gaining sensual pleasure from the clitoris (in masturbation) to achieving it through the vagina (in sexual intercourse). Freud thought that a girl has little aware-ness of her vagina until puberty, and that the redirection of her sexual energy to the vagina is therefore a difficult hurdle for her. If she cannot overcome it, and remains *fixated* on clitoral orgasm (from childhood masturbation), Freud believed that a woman remains immature.

Bowlby's attachment theory

Possibly one of the most famous post-Freudian developments of psycho-analytic theory is that of attachment theory, and of these John Bowlby's work on maternal deprivation is probably the best known. Bowlby (1969, 1980) developed attachment theory by combining ideas from psycho-analysis with those from the study of how animals behave in their natural environments (ethology). From ethology he drew on the concept of *imprinting*. This is a process that happens to some newborn animals, such as ducks. What happens is that, just after they have hatched, they form an immediate, irreversible and strong attachment to whatever moving object they see. This is usually their mother, but an ethologist, Konrad Lorenz, demonstrated that imprinting will 'work' even when a human is substi-tuted for the mother duck. The imprinted duck chicks then follow the object of their imprinting wherever it goes, right throughout their early life: you have probably seen a mother duck walking along with a string of chicks behind her.

Bowlby adopted this concept of imprinting into a theory about human behaviour. He speculated that infant humans, like ducks, might have a sensitive period soon after birth during which they would normally become imprinted on their mother. This he called *bonding*. According to his theory humans need to bond with their mothers if they are to grow up in a healthy, well-adjusted manner. His theory thus had the following main components:

1 There is a sensitive period between birth and about five years of age which is crucial for bonding.

2 Attachment develops out of the interaction between the infant and mother – behaviours such as the baby crying and smiling trigger the mother to respond.

3 It is normally the mother who thus becomes the child's *primary attach-ment figure*. The bond between mother and child is unique and power-fully important for the child's development. Another person can take this place, but only if he or she has constant contact during the child's sensitive period for attachment.

4 Once bonding has occurred, the child will remain attached.

5 If bonding does not happen or is disrupted during the sensitive period, it cannot happen later. The child will not have a primary attachment figure and this will lead to failure in the normal process of development.

Bowlby gathered support for his model by observing the consequences of depriving a child of maternal contact (that is, maternal deprivation) during the sensitive period. Bowlby looked at what happened, for example, to children who had spent a long period of infancy in hospital or institutions and found that they were much more prone to emotional and psychological problems in later life. The child cut off from contact with the mother becomes frozen and withdrawn. To protect itself from the pain of separation, it shuts off its feelings and turns inside upon itself. Bowlby drew on psychoanalytic theory to suggest that the child subjected to maternal deprivation has particular problems in relation to the acquisition of the Super-ego. Such individuals, he argued, grow up emotionally cold and without a conscience. It is relatively easy to see how this follows on from Freudian theory – how such an outcome could be seen to arise from 'dragons' that the child has failed to slay in infancy and which therefore lurk around causing mischief.

Bowlby's version of attachment theory – that children need their mothers constantly present and that *only* their mothers will do – is now seen as being too strong. Critics such as Michael Rutter (1981) point out that the children whom Bowlby studied were severely deprived of almost all human contact and not just contact with their mothers. They argue that children form a number of attachments (with, for example, their fathers and grandparents, and carers such as childminders), but they still agree that, in order to develop normally, attachment is crucial. Children need to develop long-lasting and close relationships with their carers. They do not just need the physical necessities of life such as food and shelter: they also need human warmth and emotional nurture if they are to grow up as functioning human beings.

The best known proponent of attachment theory in relation to working with children and young people, especially in residential settings, is possibly Winnicott. Winnicott (see, for example, 1958) developed ideas especially concerning the impact of loss. He suggested that if children suffer the loss of the person who loves and cares for them (that is, their primary attachment figure or figures), they will experience potent feelings of abandonment. This, Winnicott argued, can have very harmful consequences for the child's psychic development, especially the sense of identity and self-respect.

Erikson's model of psychosocial development

More recent psychodynamic models stress the Ego, playing down the biological drives and incorporating the notion of social forces. One of the best known of these is Erikson's (1963) model, which additionally widens the process of development to cover the whole life span (Table 22.1).

Like Freud, Erikson saw development as mastering a series of challenges. Unlike Freud, however, he saw the challenges going well beyond the age of the genital stage. Erikson stressed the importance of adolescence as being particularly important in forming a sense of identity, followed by phases in adulthood that focus on acquiring intimacy, developing skills and competence, the capacity for mature love, to care for others and ultimately to attain 'wisdom'. There is thus far less focus on sexuality and far more on the creative, adaptive and social aspects of personal growth. Furthermore, he stresses that the challenges offer positive as well as negative opportunities. It is not just a matter of all the dreadful things that can happen if one stage is not coped with properly: each one offers the individual the potential for personal fulfilment.

While Erikson, like Freud, defined development as a series of stages, he did not see them as a simple set of discrete 'boxes' from which the individual jumps one to another as each challenge is met, overcome and done with. Rather, the labels he gave each stage define the challenge that is focal and crucial at a particular age. Even when they have been resolved, the tensions still remain throughout life.

Conclusion

However, while developmental theorizing may be useful in helping us, as adults, to get a better understanding of children's understanding and experience of the world, it is important that we do not get beguiled by them into concentrating upon just what children lack, what they cannot do. Critics of developmental theorizing – especially developmental psychology – argue that we need to counteract such enchantment by drawing on theories that look at issues of power. They therefore require us to acknowledge the extent to which children's 'incompetence' may be a matter of powerlessness, which may be less a matter of their immaturity than of the way in which adults deny children power, all in the name of 'doing what is in their best interests'. Maybe, they suggest, it is often not their interests we are serving, but ours.

Table 22.1 Erikson's model of psychosocial development

Stages of life – the challenge to be mastered	What is gained if the challenge is resolved	Age	Equivalent Freudian stage
Basic trust versus mistrust			
This derives from the relationship between the new baby and his or her mother (or other caretaker). If the mothers provide love, affection and consistent meeting of needs, the infant learns to trust the surrounding world, but inconsistent treatment or insufficient nurture contribute to a developing sense of mistrust	Hope	Infancy	Oral
Autonomy versus shame and doubt			
This challenge is to resolve the tension between asserting autonomy and the shame and doubt that is fostered by continued, forced, dependence and conformity. If parents (or other caretakers) allow the child more and more freedom and opportunities for independence, autonomy is gained. But if the child is over-protected and expected to be too conforming, the outcome will be a sense of shame and doubt	Will-power	Early childhood	Anal
Initiative versus guilt			
The tension here is between the rewards of initiating for yourself – working with purpose towards a goal you choose – and the potential for guilt by having your initiatives thwarted or ridiculed. Where children are encouraged to show initiative, they flourish; where they are made to feel bad about it, they become guilt ridden and may learn to 'put on a front', hiding their true self	Purpose	Age of play	Phallic
Industry versus inferiority			
Here children reach a stage at which they are capable of working hard and developing competence across a range of skills. When rewarded and supported they develop a pride in their own ability and the capacity for industry, but when not rewarded or unsupported, they develop feelings of inferiority	Competence	Primary school	Latency

(cont'd)

Table 22.1 Erikson's model of psychosocial development (cont'd)

Stages of life – the challenge to be mastered	What is gained if the challenge is resolved	Age	Equivalent Freudian stage
Identity versus identity confusion This is often a time of upheaval and confusion. The conflict at this stage has been termed the 'identity crisis', in which there is a strong need to define 'who I am' at the same time as dealing with a confusion of different 'pulls' from all sorts of direction. A successful resolution is an ability to define the self and the capacity to understand and abide by the standards and mores of society. Unresolved, adolescents remain confused, and become 'totalistic' – convinced that they, and only they, know what is right, rejecting and rebelling against all other values	Fidelity	Adolescence	Genital
Intimacy versus isolation The resolution of the identity crisis enables the individual to seek deep, intimate relationships, including love that goes beyond sexual desire. Thus this stage presents opportunities to form close relationships based upon mutual sharing. If not the individual emerges as isolated and cut off from love	Love	Young adulthood	
Generativity versus stagnation The focus here is on concern for the next generation and the society in which that generation will grow up. If individuals accept the responsibility of generativity, they develop the capacity to care – to take responsibility for the well-being of others. A rejection of the generativity challenge means the individual cares only for him- or herself, leading to stagnation, a sense of hopelessness and meaninglessness that may constitute a 'mid-life' crisis	Care	Middle adulthood	
Ego integrity versus despair This final stage of life involves a reflection on the accomplishments of previous years. Ego integrity develops when individuals are satisfied with what they have achieved, but if they see their life as a series of unattained goals or opportunities that were missed, they will develop a sense of despair	Wisdom	Maturity	

23

Working with Disabled Children

Ruth Marchant

Everyone working with children should be working with disabled children for at least some of the time because 3–5 per cent of children are disabled (DoH, 1998a; OPCS, 1986). If you have worked with more than 20 children over time, you should have worked with at least one who is disabled. Yet because of the way in which services are organized in the UK, it is possible to work in many settings and meet no disabled children. Whatever your experience, this chapter is designed to enable you to reflect on some of the current issues and debates and their implications for practice with all children, both disabled and non-disabled.

The social context of childhood disability

We live in a society that makes disabled children very vulnerable, one that has very ambivalent feelings about disabled children. We live in a society in which disabled children are often excluded from the mainstream of life, where it is often not very safe to be disabled and where disabled children are often oppressed.

The impact of this oppression can range from others merely feeling uncomfortable around disabled people to an intolerance of such magnitude that people may lose their lives (Middleton, 1996). Disabled children and adults often experience discrimination in health care (Rutter and Seyman, 1999) and face a far higher risk than other people of having their lives 'abbreviated' in different ways (see Wolfensberger, 1990). On an everyday basis one of the impacts of this oppression is the social exclusion of disabled children:

> It is clear that as a society we do not want to include disabled children. We do our best to prevent their birth. If this fails we seek to normalize them. If this fails we render them invisible by an elaborate system of segregation. (Middleton, 1996, p. 36)

Many disabled children have experiences of being excluded. Exclusion can be direct and explicit or implicit and subtle. Children can be excluded by the things that people do and do not do. Acts of omission are fairly common in children's everyday lives: disabled children may not be asked around to play at other children's houses, they may experience being left out by other children in the park and playground, and they may not be included in outings or gatherings. Acts of omission also happen within services. Policies may be written as if all children are non-disabled, buildings built as if all children can walk, communication carried out as if all children can talk, literature produced as if all children can see and procedures in place assuming that disabled children do not share any needs with other children.

Disabled children also face powerful processes of devaluation. These can be expressed in apparently 'unthinking' day-to-day comments. It sometimes seems as if being disabled makes a child a piece of public property; confidentiality and respect for privacy may be seen as irrelevant. The following are questions that have been asked and comments that have been made over the heads of children, not 20 years ago, but in the last couple of years. Some were from strangers, others from professionals:

Is he a Down's syndrome?

Is she spastic?

Is he autistic?

Does she talk?

Is he yours?

Will he get better?

Was she born like that?

Does he always do that?

Can't you keep her still?

Is he dangerous?

Is there a cure for it?

Have you claimed compensation?

Will she die young?

Have you tried a dairy-free diet?

Can't you keep him quiet?

What a shame

Such a pity

It's so sad

His poor parents

Such a tragedy

Poor little thing

She should never have been born

It is also important to remember that there are more disabled children in groups already socially disadvantaged. Whatever system is used to classify disability, there are twice the number of disabled children in social class V households as in those of social class I, and there is a strong relationship between childhood disability and poverty household income (Dobson and Middleton, 1999; DoH, 1998a).

Disabled children face major barriers to being included as equal members of society. The strength of these processes means that it is not possible to work with disabled children in a 'neutral' way.

What do we mean by disabled?

Definitions of disability are neither absolute nor static over time. Both our definitions and the language we use to talk about disability change in line with our understanding. Definitions and language are important because they construct our understanding. There are different ways of defining and understanding disability. Within the disabled people's movement, and within some services and professional groups, there has been a move from an individual to a social model of disability.

The social model of disability uses the term 'disability' not to refer to impairment (functional limitations) but rather to describe the effects of prejudice and discrimination, the social factors that create barriers, deny opportunities and thereby dis-able people (Morris, 1998a; Oliver, 1999). Children's impairments can of course create genuine difficulties in their lives, but many of the problems faced by disabled children are not caused by their conditions or impairments but by societal values, service structures or adult behaviour.

The social model contrasts with the individual model of disability, which:

locates the 'problem' of disability within the individual and sees the cause as functional limitations or psychological losses assumed to arise from disability. (Oliver, 1999, p. 33)

The medical model is the most common example of an individual model of disability and continues to dominate thinking and practice.

There are ongoing debates about which children should be considered disabled, about for example whether deaf children constitute a linguistic minority rather than being disabled. Other controversial issues include children who are either 'temporarily' or 'potentially' disabled, for example children with cancer, or those with HIV or AIDs.

There is no single 'correct' definition: the definition of disability used within the Children Act 1989 describes substantial and permanent disability, but different services use different definitions. Within the disabled people's movement the emphasis is on whether individuals define themselves as disabled, but this is not so easy for children, especially young children or those with learning disabilities.

Services for disabled children

Services for disabled children are often fragmented between different agencies. Young disabled children often come sequentially to the attention of health, then education and then social services workers. Different perspectives, values and professional languages can complicate working together across agency and discipline boundaries. It is important to remember that disabled children are likely to be in touch with a range of services whose work should ideally be complementary or at least should not conflict.

In the past disabled children have often been excluded from or marginalized within services. Many services have been developed with only non-disabled children in mind, or conversely with only disabled children in mind. While this is beginning to change, and services are increasingly aiming to become more 'inclusive', relationships between the families of disabled children and social services are often dominated by arrangements to separate children from their families through the provision of respite care (Morris, 1998b). Consequently, certain patterns and standards of care become established for disabled children that would not be tolerated for other children: a child may, for example, find him- or herself sleeping in four different places every week: residential school, home, link family and respite care unit.

All parents and children need breaks from each other, but natural breaks (playing out, visiting friends, joining in organized activities and staying with relatives) may be unavailable to disabled children.

Defining the purpose of any service as 'respite' can create a confusing situation. The child's experience of the service can become incidental since its defined purpose is to give the child's parents a break. A social model perspective is helpful in identifying children's real needs, which often means seeking ways in which to overcome disabling barriers that prevent them accessing the social and leisure opportunities available to their non-disabled peers.

What do disabled children need?

A disabled child's care needs might be more complex, take more time or continue for more of childhood, but basic care remains a right of all children.

It is important to begin with what all children have in common. The basic needs of disabled children are no different from those of any other child:

> Professionals working with children need not and should not start from a different position when the children are disabled. (Middleton, 1999, p. 92)

While disabled children's basic needs are the same as those of all children, impairments may create additional needs. Disabled children are likely to face additional disabling barriers that inhibit or prevent their inclusion in society. All children, for example, need friends. Some disabled children may have impairments that affect their ability to make friends, and many disabled children face particular barriers in establishing and maintaining friendships.

However, recognizing disabled children as children first does not imply any denial of a child's particular needs:

> Ensuring equality of opportunity does not mean that all children are treated the same. It does mean understanding and working sensitively and knowledgeably with diversity. (DoH/DfEE/Home Office, 2000, paragraph 1.43)

To work well with disabled children means finding a balance between recognizing their humanity as children first and then ensuring that their particular needs are met. A balance must be struck. Approaching disabled children as if they are 'just like other children' can be as harmful as assuming that they only have needs arising from their impairments.

Be clear about who you are working with and why

It seems that disabled children and their families may be particularly vulnerable to professional confusion about 'who is the client'. The history of social work with disabled children has often been a history of work with the parents of disabled children. Working in partnership with parents is important, but so too is working in partnership with children. Where views and needs conflict, clarity becomes crucial.

Some families describe dealing with service providers as being the most difficult aspect of caring for their disabled children (DoH, 1998a). From talking with families it seems that some of the difficulties arise because of a lack of clarity about the roles and responsibilities of professionals and services. It appears that the parents of disabled children are assigned multiple and sometimes contradictory roles by professionals. Twigg and Atkin (1993) describe the range of ways in which professionals in social and health care systems conceptualize and respond to parents: they are perceived, simultaneously, as resources for the statutory services, co-workers and service recipients in their own right, while their children may or may not also be perceived as service recipients. This can create an ambiguous and confused relationship.

It may be important to learn about the probable effects of an impairment or condition before meeting a child and his or her family. Cross (1998) reports a disabled teenager as saying:

> I wish they knew more about disability, I mean, it's sort of embarrassing to have to explain yourself. (p. 102)

Learning about a child's condition does not mean becoming an expert: it means knowing enough to fulfil your responsibilities towards the child and his or her family.

There are organizations of and for people with almost all impairments and conditions, and for parents; these are often good sources of accessible and up-to-date information. It is important, however, to remember that all children experience their condition differently. Thus the best source of information will usually be the child and the family.

Disabled children are likely to have already been assessed, and it makes sense to use information already gathered, having obtained consent as appropriate. Parents find it hard to tell their story again and again. Both children and family members often assume that agencies will share information with each other and may be surprised to find that they do not. Parents and children can be asked who they think has the most relevant knowledge – many have reported thinking the wrong professionals were consulted (Russell, P., personal communication, 1999).

Integrated inter-agency assessment processes are in place in some areas and being developed in others (Khan and Russell, 1999; McConahie, 1997; Russell, 1995).

Recognize the importance of the child's identity and self-esteem

Recognizing disability as a positive identity is not easy in our society. As they grow up, disabled children will receive negative messages about being disabled and need a positive internal model of disabled identity to counteract negative stereotypes. Children can internalize the messages they receive about what it means to have an impairment.

There are strong parallels with issues for black children growing up in a racist society, but there are also key differences. In terms of family context, black children usually have black families who can provide a positive role model whereas disabled children often have non-disabled parents. Many disabled children rarely meet disabled adults and may assume that they will somehow grow out of their impairments with age. This is a sensible assumption if one meets many disabled children and no disabled adults.

A child's impairment is an integral part of their identity, not something separate or incidental. It is of course not the only aspect of their identity, but it should always be considered. It has been noticed that disabled children are often defined within a one-dimensional identity that is largely 'degendered, asexual, culturally unspecific and classless' (Priestley, 1998, p. 220). All aspects of a child's identity should be recognized, although different aspects will assume greater or lesser significance at different developmental stages.

For example, the cultural identity of disabled children should be recognized. Prejudices about race and disability can compound each other. There is evidence that families from minority ethnic groups caring for a severely disabled child are even more disadvantaged than white families in a similar situation (Chamba *et al.*, 1999).

Disabled adults have an important role to play in the lives of disabled children and their families, and the disabled people's movement is paying increasing attention to children's issues (see Cross, 1998; Morris, 1998c; Shakespeare and Watson, 1998):

> I learn more from them [disabled adults] than I can learn from anybody, about what their childhoods were like. (Parent, quoted in Beresford, 1994)

Working protectively with disabled children

Disabled children are particularly vulnerable and face an increased risk of abuse in many settings (Westcott and Jones, 1999). They ought to be over-represented in our child protection systems, yet research suggests that they may be significantly under-represented (Morris, 1998a, 1999a). The mistaken assumption that disability protects from abuse contributes to the vulnerability of disabled children.

The increased vulnerability of disabled children to abuse results from social attitudes and the special treatment of disabled children; disabled children tend, for example, to be more isolated, to be more dependent and to have less control over their lives and their bodies, and may be less likely to be heard or believed. Disabled children are often in the care of many more adults than other children; they are more likely to spend time in institutional settings, and the usual safeguards may not be in place (DoH/Welsh Office, 1997; Morris, 1995).

Another factor in the vulnerability of disabled children is the denial of the sexuality of disabled people. This has until recently been a taboo subject. Disabled children can grow up thinking that somehow sex is not for them, which can again increase their vulnerability.

Disabled children and challenging behaviour

Disabled children are more likely to be perceived as having challenging behaviour. The context of their lives may affect others' expectations: disabled young people can sometimes 'get away with less' than others. It is useful to remind ourselves that most children and young people do not behave well all the time, do not do what they are told immediately and without arguing, do not always go along with all adult suggestions and do not always eat sensibly, get ready for school without protest or go to bed and get up again when asked.

That said, it seems that children with learning disabilities, autism or language delay do face an increased risk of developing challenging behaviour. Physical and sensory impairments are also known to increase this likelihood. However, the increased likelihood of developing chal- lenging behaviour is not necessarily a direct result of these impairments but may be related to other factors.

Communicating with disabled children

Communication is a basic human need, good communication probably being the single most important protective factor in the lives of disabled children. Good communication means child-centred, respon- sive communication.

People who are generally good at communicating with children are also likely to be good at communicating with disabled children, but they may need encouragement and support to adapt their skills and try out new approaches. General listening, communication and play skills are usually more useful than attempting to become competent in a wide range of communication methods.

A broad and flexible definition of communication is important when working with children whose impairments affect their communication. We often act as if talking were the 'best' or the only valid way to communicate, yet we know that this is rarely the case for any child. Total communication means tuning in on all channels, attending for example to speech, sign, symbols, body language, facial expression, gesture, behaviour, art, photographs, objects of reference, games, drawing and playing. For a brief summary of the most commonly used alternative/augmentative communication methods, see Marchant and Martyn (1999).

Recent work suggests innovative ways of engaging with and consulting disabled children (Beecher, 1998; Beresford, 1997; Griffiths *et al.*, 1999; Kirkbride, 1999; Marchant *et al.*, 1999; Morris, 1998c, 1999b; Prewett 1999; Russell, 1998; Sanderson, 1997; Ward, 1997).

Conclusion

This chapter has been strongly influenced by consultation with disabled children and young people, and by the parents of disabled children through various routes, and I am grateful for individuals' consent to use their words and their ideas.

It is an exciting time to be working with disabled children: knowledge and resources are developing rapidly and our understanding of what it means to be disabled is being challenged. The basic needs of disabled children and their families are no different from those of any other child and family:

> Everybody's got something different about them, and some things are just more different than others. But we're all – I don't know – different in different ways. (Disabled girl of 12, quoted in Cavet, 1998, p. 91)

24

Involving Children and Families in Decision-making about Health

Chris Thurston and Jenny Church

It is now acknowledged that a more holistic approach is required to meet the needs of the sick child and that parents should be closely involved in the care of their child (Moules and Ramsay, 1998). Nursing practices have emerged which place greater emphasis on communication, negotiation and partnership (Casey, 1988; Smith, 1995). Health care professionals have recognized that partnership is only possible when children and parents are fully informed and involved in decision-making and have, largely, accepted that children and families have knowledge about themselves and their individual needs that is an essential element in the process of planning and providing care.

Children, like adults, react to illness and hospitalization in different ways according to such things as previous experience and understanding. They may think that they are to blame for their illness or that they are being punished (Campbell and Glasper, 1995). They may be influenced by media representations of illness, accidents and hospitals. Children have vivid imaginations and a fear of the unknown can often make them more anxious. This demonstrates the importance of preparing children for hospital and offering them clear, honest explanation. Information helps children to feel more in control and cope with their illness and hospitalization. Distressing experiences in hospital can leave children with long-lasting negative attitudes towards health care workers.

Partnerships in care

The notion of working with children and families, and accepting them into the decision-making process, would have been seen as totally inappropriate as little as 30 years ago, when parents were seen as amateurs getting in the way of the professional carers (Darbyshire, 1994). Now parents are more likely to be seen as a welcome addition to the team caring for their child because children clearly need their parents in times of stress for emotional support and for the knowledge and experience that the parents have accumulated in caring for their own child (Moules and Ramsay, 1998). Parents may also act as an advocate for the child during decision-making (Swanwick, 1995), but this role may be complicated by their own wishes and feelings about the issue and their own experiences relating to health care workers. Other ways in which health professionals can acknowledge that working in partnership with families in health care is the appropriate way to support children include open visiting on children's wards, facilities for resident parents and encouraging parents to continue to care for their child's daily needs (DoH, 1996b).

Hutchfield (1999) describes how parental involvement varies. Parents will be involved in their child's care through offering emotional support, and they may participate in the child's nursing care, if they wish, with the teaching and support of staff. The key ingredient needed to achieve a partnership between child, parents and health care workers must be the negotiation of patterns of care based on mutual decision-making and trust.

This approach was recognized within the Partnership Model of Care devised by Casey (1988) and is still seen as a valuable basis for work with children today. The philosophy underpinning this model is that the care of children, well or sick, is best carried out by their families, with the support of health care professionals when necessary. A shared plan of care should be negotiated to ascertain who will carry out the different aspects of care: the parents, the child or the nurse (Fradd, 1996). In this way the child's care in hospital is undertaken in an environment of cooperation and consideration of the needs of the child and the family.

The most important aspect of this family-centred care is the question of who makes decisions about the interventions required for the child. For the parent, moving from the normal everyday parent–child relationship to a parent–sick child role, there will be difficulties in assuming different roles and responsibilities (Palmer, 1993). Taylor (1999) explores the complexities of parental responsibility in relation to decision-making and consent. As someone who experienced being the parent of a seriously ill child, she describes how in everyday life parents constantly make decisions for their children, but medical treatment can overwhelm these decision-making abilities. She found that her ability to consider all the options and make a rational decision was impaired, and she was offered and gratefully accepted the support and guidance of the consultant, who she felt was acting in her child's best interest.

Families need to receive clear information on how to support their child and how they themselves can be supported in both the decision-making process and the day-to-day care of their child. In her study of mothers' experiences of being with their children on the intensive care unit, Noyes (1999) describes how mothers viewed participation in care as a positive way of coping. They highlighted how important it was to listen, talk and do things for their children, and the support in this role by nurses was described as a major influence on their ability to cope.

Health care professionals are therefore often seen as supportive. It has, however, to be acknowledged that they are also the gate-keepers to the resources, information and services that the child and family may require, and that they have the power to offer or withhold any of these aspects. Professional communication is by far the greatest source of consumer complaint, the rate of dissatisfaction being cited as high as 70 per cent in the mothers of children with a variety of illnesses (Davies, 1993). Mothers wanted honesty and encouragement, and they asked that their child be treated as an individual and that the family as a whole rather than just the child's illness, be considered.

Many children's wards continue to develop philosophies of care that articulate family-centred care and partnership; in practice, however, the emphasis remains mainly on partnership with parents rather than children and parents. Many health care staff have not yet fully acknowledged children's rights to participate in the assessment and management of their health care needs.

Children's rights in health care

Health care staff and parents may have been over-cautious in their assessment of children's ability to understand and to contribute their opinions and feelings. The UNCRC (1989), ratified by the UK in 1991, acknowledges the child's right to autonomy under Article 12, but the UK's First Report to the UN (DoH, 1994) sought to defend the retention of emphasis on parents rather than children as decision-makers in relation to health care.

One study in the USA recorded children's reflections on health care (Fleitas, 1997). One child commented, 'Please don't talk about me when you come into my room! Talk to me. I'm seven years old so I can understand.' Davis-Jones (1998) argued that to turn these rights into reality requires children to be offered the opportunity of expressing themselves in ways that are appropriate to their age and communication skills. She has produced a resource pack of children's drawing and writing on health care that records their experiences, fears and misconceptions, and offers praise, criticism and advice to those who provide health care. Many children demonstrated concern about what would happen to them, their concerns about not knowing what would happen being as great as any fear of pain.

It takes time to listen not only to what children say, but also to the messages behind their questions and words (Doyle and Maslin-Prothero,

1999). Children may say one thing but mean another, and they may say what they think the nurse, parent or doctor wants to hear. A child faced with the need for medical treatment should be given every opportunity to understand the implications of the treatment, the alternatives available, the implications of not having the treatment, the side effects, the prognosis and the probable recovery period (Lansdown, 1995).

Nurses are those most closely involved in the child's care, and it is normally they who set the agenda for recognizing autonomy in individual children. Fulton (1996) maintains that nurses need to assess their own values and beliefs, and she proposes three priorities to be addressed: giving children a voice in the provision of their services; upholding children's rights to give or withhold consent to treatment; and ensuring vigorous attention to children's pain control. She proposes that these elements can be achieved through education and a change in attitude without incurring extra expenditure. Children who endure unpleasant procedures need help in retaining a sense of control and are especially sensitive to situations that erode this control. Here is another quote from a child from the Fleitas study (1997):

> What I object to is: 'No, you can't go to the canteen; no, you can't go to the school-room; no, I've just made your bed, so you can't lie down.' (p. 200)

This example of lack of respect for children's autonomy only serves to undermine their self-esteem and confidence, and does not enable children to develop their decision-making skills.

The way in which children respond to the opportunity to be involved in decision-making will depend on the attitudes of the family and of health care staff. Parents often have realistic expectations of their child's ability, but children need to know that their views and opinions will be respected by nurses and doctors as well (Alderson and Montgomery, 1996). This can commence with small-scale decisions such as a child requiring insulin injections choosing the site of the injection, or a child requiring a wound dressing deciding what time of day to have this done or being given the choice of which nurse should carry out the procedure.

Children and consent

Consent is a legal requirement for medical treatments, and some argue that it is necessary before all, including the most minor treatments or interventions (Barrow, 1999). Parents have the right, responsibility and power to give consent for their children under 16, but the increasing recognition of children's rights raises the issue of children's involvement in consent to treatment.

There are three components underpinning the concept of consent: information, competence and lack of coercion (Orr, 1999). By giving clear information that the child can understand and using communication skills appropriate to the child's stage of development, health care staff can facilitate informed consent from a child. Questions should be encouraged and answered honestly. Nurses and doctors are held in high esteem by children and parents as having ultimate knowledge and expertise, but they should not allow this to impinge on a child's and family's confidence to form their own opinion. Doyle and Maslin-Prothero (1999) view the health care staff as informants keeping the child up to date with the treatment and progress. They see the health care professional as a communicator who is able to translate the medical and technical language into the child's language and able to negotiate with the child in a time frame to suit the child rather than the health care team. Assessing how well children have understood what they have been told is another essential element of communication in the decision-making process (Orr, 1999).

The second component, competence, is a complex issue. If children's competence is to be respected, the law must give those who are able to do so the right to give or withhold consent (Moules and Ramsay, 1998). Prior to 1986 children under 16 were not deemed competent in the law to give consent to medical treatment. Following the 1985 'Gillick' decision in the courts, the right to consent and confidentiality was given to those under 16 who sought contraceptive advice. Since this decision the concept of 'Gillick competence' has been used to apply to individuals under 16 who have sufficient knowledge and understanding to give consent to treatment. The ability of a child to make competent decisions varies depending on the situation. Alderson (1993) interviewed 120 children undergoing planned orthopaedic surgery who had all previously undergone several operations. She discussed with them the age at which they felt children could make decisions about non-life-saving surgery. One boy responded, 'I would like to see the age limits scrapped and maturity brought in. As you grow up your age has a stereotype. I'm trying to escape from that stereotype.' (p. 48)

Relevant experience of illness, treatment or disability is far more salient than age for acquiring competence (Alderson and Montgomery, 1996). Children with chronic conditions such as cystic fibrosis often have an in-depth knowledge of their condition, and their long-term relationships with medical staff often increase their recognition as competent.

The third component of consent is coercion. This applies to all kinds of decision made by parents and health care professionals on behalf of children. Gaining the trust, cooperation and consent of children and young people with emotional and behavioural problems and mental illness poses particular challenges. They may be suffering with many internal conflicts and be caught up in a cycle of coercive situations with their parents and families, or they may have been the victims of abuse.

An emphasis on communication on the part of health professionals is essential in order to avoid treatment or management becoming coercive (Shaw, M., 1998). Recent over-rulings in the law courts of young people's appeals against treatment have reserved decision-making rights for parents, doctors and the courts. Shield and Baum (1994) have suggested that this leads to a situation in which children and young people whose competence is in question are found to be rational and able to give consent only if they accept the advice of a doctor, but they are seen as incompetent if they reject that advice.

Alderson and Montgomery (1996) recommend the use of a code of practice setting out the basic principles of children's rights to receive clear and detailed information, to express their views and to grant or withhold consent to treatment, provided that the child is considered competent by health care staff acting in good faith and subject to the supervisory role of the courts.

Upholding children's right to be involved in decision-making requires a change in attitudes. A new pragmatic approach is needed towards how we view childhood and children. The emphasis on protecting the child from responsibility and maintaining dependence has to be questioned. All health care workers need to examine their own values and beliefs and how these have emerged within their own social and cultural environment, and thus begin to develop an understanding of change in society. Most health care professionals would say that their first priority is the health and welfare of patients; it follows then that they should value the contributions that the child and family can make to a greater understanding of their individual well-being.

25

Men Working in Childcare

Martin Robb

Men, as workers within childcare services, have become a focus for wider concerns about changing gender roles, the expansion of childcare provision and the response to evidence of institutional abuse. This chapter explores some of the issues raised by the presence of men in childcare work, drawing on recent research studies, including a pilot study undertaken by the author into the experiences and attitudes of a group of male nursery workers.

Research on men working in childcare

There is a small but growing body of research on men working in childcare in Britain. Ruxton (1992) surveyed 77 family centres run by NCH Action for Children and found that, although male workers were still relatively rare, there was a substantial amount of support among female staff for employing more men. Penn and McQuail's (1997) research among trainee nursery nurses discovered that gendered perceptions of childcare work were deeply embedded in childcare training. More recently, the Thomas Coram Research Unit conducted the first nationwide study comparing the experiences of men and women working in childcare, concluding that the implications of a mixed gender workforce need to be the subject of wider debate (Cameron *et al.*, 1999). Beyond the UK, Jensen (1995) has reported on the issues raised by employing an equal number of women and men in some Swedish day-care centres, while Murray's (1996) study of day care in California reported the ways in which gender inequality is reproduced by current employment practices. My own pilot study (reported below) involved interviewing a small number of randomly selected male workers, all of whom had current or recent experience of working in nurseries in England.

The debate about men in childcare

This growing body of empirical research in this area has been comple-
mented by a vigorous debate in the academic and professional literature.
Some studies have argued for increasing men's participation in childcare
work on grounds of equality of opportunity and as a way of breaking
down conventional gender roles (Burgess and Ruxton, 1996; EC Childcare Network, 1994). Ruxton (1992, p. 16) claims that 'encouraging male
involvement in childcare is in the main a positive step towards gender
equality and in the interests of children'.

Others, however, have taken a less optimistic view. Pringle (1992) argues
that the role of gender and particularly of masculinity in child abuse has
been overlooked. He challenges the assumptions both that children need
male role models and that 'caring' men cannot also be abusive. In a reply to
Pringle, Carter (1993) claims that he risks reinforcing essentialist discourses
surrounding sexuality and that his argument overlooks the contribution of
wider social and institutional factors in abuse cases. Also in response to
Pringle, Ruxton (1994) has argued that abuse committed by women (albeit
far rarer than that by men) represents a challenge to such a position.

Cameron *et al.* characterize the debate in Britain and the USA concerning
men and childcare as being polarized between discourses of risk and equality:

> The contradictions are plain: on the one hand, valuing and encouraging men
> workers so as to improve gender equality, and on the other suspecting their
> involvement in something damaging to children. (Cameron *et al.*, 1999, p. 17)

This fundamental tension is present not only in academic and professional discussions of the issue, but also in representations of men as carers
for children in the mass media (Robb, unpublished observations). My
own research set out to explore the ways in which conflicting discourses
about men and childcare were reflected in the experiences and attitudes of
male childcare workers. The research was informed by Connell's (1995)
work on masculinity, especially his emphasis on *masculinities* as plural
and dynamic, rather than on masculinity as a fixed and immutable
essence. Starting from this theoretical position, I was interested in investigating not only how prevailing discourses shaped men's experience as
childcare workers, but also how these same discourses helped to construct
their sense of themselves as men and as workers.

Participants in the pilot study

In the following descriptions, the names have been changed; the information was correct at the time of the interviews.

Darren is white, 17 years old and working in a private nursery. He is working towards NVQ Level 2 in Child Care.

Kevin is white, 22 years old and works as a supervisor in a play area in a pub/restaurant, although he has recent experience of working in a nursery. He is a qualified nursery nurse and has a City and Guilds in Community Care.

Joseph is black, 31 years old, visually impaired and was born in Nigeria. He works in a private nursery and has NVQ Level 2 in Child Care.

Niko is white, 22 years old, and was born in England of Greek parents. He has an NVQ Level 3 in Child Care and works in the nursery school section of a private combined school and nursery.

Pete is white, 57 years old and joint owner-manager with his wife of a private nursery. He previously worked as a teacher and head teacher in primary schools.

The remaining sections of this chapter summarize the findings of the study and compare them with evidence from other recent research.

Experiences and attitudes

The interviewees were asked about the attitudes of children, other workers and parents to them as male workers. All of the men felt that the children in their care treated them in much the same way as female workers, some expressing the view that many children seemed to prefer a male worker. Describing the attitudes of female co-workers, some felt uncomfortable about being the only male worker in the team:

> At the beginning it was a bit awkward for me, not for the girls but for me. It was a bit awkward because I was the only man here. (Niko)

In their research study, Cameron *et al.* (1999, p. 70) found that both male and female workers highlighted the staffroom as a site of 'gendered discussions'. This was borne out in my own research by Joseph, who claimed that female workers changed the subject of their conversation when he entered the room. Kevin recalled quite negative reactions from his time at college, where he was the only male trainee in his group:

> We did have a talk from an NSPCC worker and as soon as he left the room – it was about child abuse – one of the girls turned round to me and said 'Oh, is that why you're doing the course, to get at children?'... On the Family and Community Care

...I was the only one in a sea of about seventeen females by the time the course started, it started to – the water started to get a bit murky like. (Kevin)

The study carried out by Cameron *et al.* (1999) found that women workers generally believed the jobs to be divided equally, whereas men felt that they were often expected to do practical jobs around the building. This view was only shared to a limited extent by the men who were interviewed:

Well I've been asked to change a light bulb now and again... No, but no, I always end up doing the same as what the females do. (Kevin)

Cameron *et al.* (1999) found a general level of support among parents using childcare centres for employing male workers, particularly as role models for boys. In my own study Darren's sense that many parents value the presence of a male worker was echoed by Kevin, who reported that this positive response often followed initial surprise:

But they come round to it and they sort of say, 'Oh, we would love a male looking after our child', and somebody the other day told me that, she said 'I'd have preferred a male nanny than a female nanny'... she has got a little boy. (Kevin)

However, in relation to intimate physical care – such as nappy-changing – parents appear to be more cautious. Ruxton (1992) reports the male family centre staff whom he interviewed as feeling inhibited about physical contact with the children in their care, while the parents interviewed by Cameron *et al.* (1999) advocated a close supervision of male workers involved in intimate care. In her research in US childcare centres, Murray (1996) noticed a definite division of labour in this area, men being routinely excluded from activities that might lead to parental accusations, as well as male workers voluntarily refraining from such duties. Of the five workers I interviewed, three had experienced difficulties, including outright parental hostility:

They had come in, apparently the father had come in with his child, saw me in the nursery and asked if I was allowed to change nappies, and when he got the answer 'yes' promptly walked out again with his child. (Kevin)

Pete operated a self-imposed restriction in this area:

One thing I won't do, and that's changing a nappy. I do it to protect myself if you like... I'm sure the parents all trust me. But I think it's something which personally I'm quite happy to do, but I don't think it's wise. (Pete)

Joseph related an incident in which a mother complained that he had touched her daughter inappropriately when changing her, as a result of which his involvement in nappy-changing was restricted. It is interesting that the justification given by management for this restriction was Joseph's visual impairment rather than his gender. At other times, however, it appears that Joseph's gender was used as a cover for hostility to aspects of his ethnic and cultural identity. Ruxton quotes a black male worker for whom ethnicity is the key factor structuring his sense of identity in the workplace – 'I first of all notice that I'm black and then I notice that I'm male' – while in the same study a project leader described the experience of a male student who was black and gay, who initially felt excluded and unable to challenge racist and homophobic comments (Ruxton, 1992, pp. 24, 43). Such experiences point to a need for childcare centres to have clear policies to challenge racism and harassment (Lane, 1999).

These experiences reflect the complex and contradictory nature of current attitudes towards men working in childcare. On the one hand many children, parents and female workers appear to welcome men's involvement, while at the same time anxieties about the risk of abuse and about men's motivation lurk in the background, having the power to shape men's experience in the workplace. These anxieties are especially powerful when they intersect with racist and other discriminatory attitudes. Some of the men's responses, such as Pete's characterization of himself as a father-figure, suggest a tension within the men themselves between discourses of equality and more traditional ideas about men's roles.

Reasons for working in childcare

Cameron and colleagues found that, for both male and female workers, early familial experience of caring for younger children was an important influence on their decision to work in childcare: 'Several workers referred to always having children around, to caring for their siblings, to babysitting and to taking an interest in neighbours' children' (Cameron *et al.*, 1999, p. 59). When asked how they came to be working in childcare, experiences of caring for younger relatives were also mentioned by the younger interviewees in my study, including Darren:

> I've got loads of cousins and younger cousins and things, just enjoyed when they come round, looking after them and things.

An early experience of a caring role within the family is more usually associated with girls and has been seen as a key element in girls' socialization for conventional roles as mothers and carers (Chodorow, 1978).

This early sense of themselves as being capable of caring for children was associated by some of the men with being the child of a lone mother, or with a strong female influence in their upbringing:

> I suppose with being brought up by two women I've not been sort of taught how to go and mend a car or how to lay bricks or anything like that, so it wouldn't have occurred to me to go and do a job like that anyway, whereas I've always been taught how to care for people so it was just the natural thing to go into really. (Kevin)

For almost all of the men, a love of children and enjoyment of working with them was the main motive for entering this area of work. Niko's answer was typical:

> There's not really a way to explain what got me into it, it's just something which I've got inside which I like to work with children. (Niko)

In contrast, Pete described how he and his wife came to be running their nursery in terms of the practical options available towards the end of a teaching career, and in relation to the business opportunities offered by the nursery voucher scheme then being introduced. Pete, however, also mentioned not wishing to join the school inspectorate because it would have taken him away from direct contact with children. Joseph was also quite pragmatic, describing childcare as a second choice after computing, forced on him after the diagnosis of a visual impairment, although he later mentioned a desire to prepare himself for his role as a parent as being important.

If the interviewees' reasons for working in this area were a mixture of the affective and the pragmatic, their description of the parts of the work that they most enjoyed reinforced conventional ideas of men's role in relation to children. Some clearly preferred the educational aspects of their role, while others expressed an enthusiasm for physical play. This reflects wider conventions: men have traditionally been employed as teachers but not as nursery nurses, while within families fathers have tended to gravitate towards play rather than routine care.

These findings are borne out both in the study by Cameron *et al.* (1999), who found that men were more likely to enter childcare work for philosophical reasons, and by Murray, who recounts that all of the men she interviewed 'framed their contributions as intellectual and academic in nature', concluding that the ways in which they conceived their role 'are very gendered in that they emphasize intellectual (masculinized) contributions over emotional (feminized) ones'(Murray, 1996, p. 374).

The future aspirations of men working in childcare also seem to reflect quite conventional views. Among the workers they interviewed Cameron *et al.* (1999) found that the men were more overtly ambitious. Niko and Kevin both nurtured the ambition to manage their own nurseries, Kevin expressing a frustration at being managed by others (or perhaps by women):

> I would like to see myself with my own day nursery, running my own day nursery and being in charge for a change. (Kevin)

According to Ruxton, although men in childcare tend to be less qualified than women, 'they tend to be propelled into management or policy positions' (Ruxton, 1992, p. 35). Murray claims that when men enter childcare, 'what they find is a hierarchical structure that promotes their interests', and in her own research she found that men were frequently valued simply for being men (Murray, 1996, p. 375).

Men's role in childcare work

The need to provide male role models is often put forward to support arguments for increasing men's involvement in childcare. When asked whether men brought anything special to childcare work, there was a shared sense among the men I interviewed of the importance of male role models for young children, especially boys. There was, however, less clarity about what precisely this meant. It was sometimes expressed in terms of providing an alternative model of masculinity:

> Having a male in there, so that children grow up thinking that it's not only mummy that looks after baby, that daddy can do it as well... or a male can do it as well. (Kevin)

More than one interviewee expressed the view that this kind of role model was particularly important for children with non-resident fathers:

> My father wasn't around – I was never taught how to mend a car or anything that the male does. I was never taught a male's role, whereas a male in a day nursery, okay they wouldn't be mending a car or anything like that, but there was a male role model there for little girls and little boys, to see what the difference is in a man and a female. (Kevin)

This more conventional view of gender 'differences' was echoed by Niko: 'I think the child always needs a bit of male influence around the place.' In some answers, there was a sense that an all-female staff team was somehow deficient:

> I think the children get more out of having a male and a female role model than not, because some of the nurseries I've been in you get children from the age of

three months upwards left five days a week about five to eight until quarter past six with just a bunch of women and not their parents. (Kevin)

Kevin's choice of words here ('just a bunch of women') echoed his earlier remarks about finding himself in a 'sea' of women at college ('the water started to get a bit murky') and can be construed as revealing more than a trace of misogyny. This ambivalence about the precise nature of the role of men is echoed by Ruxton (1992), who found widespread support for male role models to challenge stereotypes but also some confusion about exactly what kinds of behaviour should be modelled.

Murray believes that men's roles in childcare, like those of women, tend to replicate their role in families: she found that 'men in child care perceive themselves as extending the emotional labour of men in families', while it was 'not uncommon to hear women workers attributing the benefits of having male co-workers to the masculine roles they play within the family' (Murray, 1996, p. 373). The study by Cameron *et al.* also found a confused picture, leading them to ask:

> What roles should be modelled?... For example, are men workers to challenge stereotypes of men in roles in families, replacing the absent, distant or discipli- narian father figure with a man who is more physically and emotionally involved in caring for children – more like a woman cares, in fact? Are they to replicate men's roles, and be a strong, 'firm', caring figure to demonstrate 'balance' with women? Or are they to compensate for 'deficient' fathers, by introducing to children new ways of trusting and believing adults? (Cameron *et al.*, 1999, p. 88)

This tension mirrors wider societal uncertainty. As mentioned earlier, writers such as Burgess and Ruxton (1996), as well as organizations such as the EC Childcare Network (1990), have argued that increasing the number of men in childcare work will provide an alternative model of masculinity for children and thus help to break down gender stereotypes. Others, notably Pringle (1995, 1998b), have seen the argument for more male role models as part of a wider backlash against lone mothers and attempts to reinstate men's authority within the family in relation to children.

Conclusion

The evidence from recent research studies and my own pilot study suggests that the contradictory discourses about men and childcare that circulate in society have practical implications for the experience of male childcare workers. Men's experience of working in childcare appears, from this evidence, to be structured in a variety of ways by wider thinking about their presence in this field of work. At the same time the attitudes of male childcare workers themselves exhibit many of the same tensions, if the views expressed by the sample interviewed in this study are at all representative. For example, some of the answers given by the men interviewed demonstrate that working in childcare, and expressing aspects of an alternative, caring male self-identity, do not preclude elements of a more conventional, even misogynist, masculinity. Not only is it evident that all men are not the same (neither all potential abusers nor all models of an alternative, caring masculinity), but it is also apparent that men (like women) are not the same 'all through'.

The examples quoted in this chapter show men working in childcare negotiating and actively constructing their identities as men and as workers, drawing on a range of often contradictory discourses about gender and the care of children. This would tend to confirm the post-structuralist view of subjectivity as a site of disunity and conflict (Weedon, 1992) and of masculinities (the ways in which men articulate and live out their identities as men) as diverse and often contradictory, even within the same individual (Connell, 1995).

I believe that the findings reported here raise important questions about the place of men in childcare work that deserve to be explored further. By illustrating the ways in which male childcare workers' experience is shaped by wider social attitudes, recent research studies point to the need for a more open debate and for clearer guidelines to ensure equality in the workplace. By showing that male workers are themselves caught up in the same contradictory discourses about men's role in relation to children, this pilot study perhaps suggests a way forward from the currently polarized debate about this issue, as well as raising questions for further research.

26

Perspectives on Parenting

Dorit Braun

Perhaps the most important question when considering the role of parents, and ways of meeting their needs, is to ask whom we are talking about. In much of the literature and practice, parent usually means mother. This is frequently justified on the grounds that mothers do the majority of child-care. However, if we examine the people around children who contribute in various ways to their development and well-being, it is clear that fathers as well as mothers matter, and that there are many other people involved – grandparents, aunts and uncles, godparents, family friends, older siblings, neighbours, childminders and so on.

A more helpful framework for thinking about 'parenting' is to regard it as a function, or a set of tasks, and then to look at the range of people who contribute to those tasks. This perspective also allows us to recognize that children themselves make a contribution – not just to their own development, but also to that of their peers and siblings.

The context: changes in families

The past 20–25 years have seen a significant change in the ways in which family life is lived. At the current rate it is estimated that one in four children will experience the divorce of their parents by the time they are 16, and over half of all divorces occur in the first 10 years of marriage. One in four families with dependent children are headed by a lone parent. Over half the divorced parents of children will remarry, forming a step-family. Estimates suggest that at least 50 per cent of remarriages that form a stepfamily also end in divorce, and that a quarter of stepfamilies break down in the first year (Family Policy Studies Centre, 2000).

At the same time, many parents do not marry: by 1998 almost 38 per cent of births occurred outside marriage – four out of five of these births being registered jointly by both parents, and three-quarters of these being registered as their sharing the same home (Office for National Statistics,

1999). Children whose parents are not married when they are born are more likely to experience the separation of their parents before they are 10 than are the children of married parents (Clarke, 1997).

Official statistics show that there are around 12.5 million dependent children, of whom 2.5 million are living in stepfamilies, and that around 300,000 children are born into a stepfamily (National Children's Bureau, 2000). Statistics do not count the thousands of young people aged 16 and over who are involved in stepfamily life, or the children and young people in stepfamilies where the step-couple are not married. Many children live in more than one household, living with one parent and having regular contact visits with the other. Statistics suggest that most children live with their mother following divorce or separation, but that nearly half of children from separated families see their non-resident father at least once a week; however, another third of children see their non-resident father at most once or twice a year (Social Policy Research Unit, 1997). Grandparents can be especially important to children at times of family change; in one survey 78 per cent of children said that grandparents were key people in their lives (Ghate, 1997).

Other changes in society have also had an impact on family life. In 1995/96 a third of all children were living in poverty – three times as many as in 1975 (Institute for Fiscal Studies, 1999). A changing pattern of work means that, in some households, no one is in paid employment, while in 62 per cent of married couples with children, both parents are in paid employment (Ferri and Smith, 1996). Working hours make a difference to how much involvement parents can have with their children: over one quarter of fathers work more than 50 hours a week, and nearly 1 in 10 work more than 60 hours a week (Warin *et al.*, 1999).

The past 25 years have seen an increased interest in parenting, culminating in a consultation paper published by the government in 1998 on *Supporting Families* (Home Office, 1998). Governments have been nervous about intervening in family life and about telling people how to be good parents, but they have accepted that the social cost and the individual cost to children of bad parenting is unacceptable. This increased interest has in some ways served further to isolate and privatize parenting. The moral panics about the impact of divorce, separation and lone parenting, as well as the increased public understanding of child abuse and of what children need, make parents question their own ability to parent effectively, question the ways in which they were parented – thus introducing a complex dynamic into relationships with grandparents – and sometimes feel ashamed and embarrassed about finding it difficult to be a parent, especially as their children get older.

Does family structure matter?

A recent review of research evidence of the impact of divorce and separation on children reviewed evidence from more than 200 research reports (Rodgers and Prior, 1998). This shows that parental separation must be seen as a process beginning before and continuing after the separation – it is not a single event. Short-term distress at the time of separation is common but usually fades with time, and long-term adverse outcomes apply to only a minority of children. However, the review of research shows that this minority of children of separated families are twice as likely than their peers from intact families to:

- live in poor housing;
- be poorer as adults;
- have behavioural problems;
- perform less well in school;
- need medical treatment;
- leave school and home when young;
- become sexually active or pregnant, or parent, at an early age;
- have depressive symptoms, and a high level of smoking, drinking and drug use during adolescence and adulthood.

The review challenges some popular views about outcomes for children. The age at which separation occurs is not important in itself, boys are not more adversely affected than girls, and the absence of a parent figure is not the most influential feature of separation for children's development. Outcomes for children are affected by:

- finances: hardship can limit educational achievement;
- family conflict, which can contribute to behavioural problems;
- parent's abilities to recover from the distress of separation, which affects children's ability to adjust;
- multiple changes in family structure which increase the probability of a poor outcome for children;
- quality contact with the non-resident parent, which can improve the outcome for children.

There is political and ideological disagreement about the cause and impact of family change, and about whether or not the state should intervene to reduce the rate of divorce and separation. The evidence of a rising divorce rate suggesting that hand-wringing and collective dismay do not reduce the likelihood of divorce, although they may well make it harder for adults and children experiencing divorce to seek help and support. The real issue for the future is less about what structure works best but about how children and adults can be supported through this change to minimize distress and disruption, and how conflict can be reduced in these situations, since it is the conflict that is most damaging to children. This more practical perspective accepts that the family exists in many shapes and sizes, that society cannot dictate 'acceptable' and 'unacceptable' family forms, and that children, whatever their family structure and background, are entitled to high-quality nurture, care and education. What does this entail? How can it be provided? And by whom?

'Good enough' parenting

Bettelheim (1995) has argued that perfection is not within the grasp of ordinary human beings and that 'good enough' is a more realistic ambition. This term has been widely accepted by practitioners as being more realistic, although few define the precise difference between perfect and 'good enough'.

There are many debates about what constitutes good enough parenting. Much of the literature in the past about the needs of children came from a white, eurocentric and middle-class view of childhood (Kemps, 1997). Research identifies a range of tasks for parents/carers, which are summarized in the review *Confident Parents, Confident Children* (see Pugh *et al.*, 1994):

- The basic tasks for parents and carers are to: provide basic physical care, affection and security, stimulate innate potential, provide guidance and control, and teach responsibility and independence.

- The qualities needed by parents and carers are identified as: warm and affectionate behaviour, clear limit-setting, speed in recognizing needs, an acceptance of faults, predictability and consistency, respect for the individual and a recognition of the child's good qualities.

- The building blocks of parenting are identified as: bonding and attachment, empathy, self-awareness, touch, discipline or setting clear limits, unconditional love, honesty and respect, and developmental knowledge.

- Children also need a sense of their own identity and history. The questions surrounding identity and history are particularly complex for children of mixed heritage parents and for children who have experienced the separation and re-partnering of one or more of their parents.

Research suggests that parenting is a two-way process and that children are independent social actors rather than empty vessels (Prout, 1999). Children make an impact on their parents and carers; each child has a unique personality and a unique place and position within his or her family context. The relationship between each parent and each child will be different, and some children do present a far greater challenge to parents and carers than others. There is as yet very little research on or understanding of the vulnerability or resilience of individual children – most research has focused on parenting styles and their impact, again perhaps making it harder still for parents with challenging children to seek and find support.

It is clear from the tasks identified above that many people can contribute to the nurture, care and education of children and young people. The focus on parenting, however, often prevents us noticing, let alone valuing and supporting, those contributions. It is clear that if we are to liberate parents from the idea that they have to do this alone, we must also start to acknowledge the contributions that other people make to the work of parenting. It is also clear from the tasks and qualities identified above that parenting is a complex and challenging task, requiring a combination of knowledge, attitudes, skills and qualities that few people can have all of the time and that many people find difficult to have a lot of the time, especially if their own experience of childhood was problematic. The idea that parents and carers need support should not be seen as strange – a stranger idea is that parents and carers do *not* need support. But what kind of support? When and why might support be needed? How should it be provided? By whom?

What kind of support?

Those working in parenting education and support have long argued that support should build people's confidence and self-esteem, as well as providing knowledge, understanding, information and skills. A useful definition can be found in *Confident Parents, Confident Children* (Pugh *et al.*, 1994). Support includes parenting groups and courses, information leaflets and books, practical support such as babysitting or befriending, helplines and one-to-one conversations between a range of professionals and parents. The value of the latter kind of support is rarely discussed or identified, but it can make very good use of scarce professional time and, if done well, can make parents and carers feel heard and understood; if not done, however, it can make them feel ignored and unimportant (Braun, 1993).

Support at key transitions

Those involved in parenting education and support have argued for a life cycle approach to the provision of parenting support and have also argued for the need for universal support (see Pugh *et al.*, 1994). A framework based on key transitions is helpful for thinking about the needs of children and parents/carers at particular times, provided that care is taken to consider the different possibilities for children and adults at different stages. A universal framework means that information and support can be seen as everyone's entitlement, thus taking away the stigma of asking for it.

Key transitions for parenting education and support are identified below. What is interesting is that practice is much better developed to provide support to the parents and carers of younger children – probably because they are easier to reach, and also because they often have an enthusiasm to learn about parenting.

- *The transition to parenthood*
  Many, although not all, people prepare for childbirth, but very few prepare for parenthood. Research indicates that between 10 and 15 per cent of women suffer from postnatal depression, suggesting particular support needs for mothers and others in the family (One Plus One, 1999). Other research indicates that the arrival of a new baby in a step-family is a particularly difficult and challenging time (Ferri and Smith, 1998). Little effort has been made to understand or meet the needs of different people during the transition to parenthood – mother, father, grandparents, other siblings, ex-partners, half-siblings and stepsiblings, aunts, uncles... a new baby changes everything for everyone, yet most of the emphasis goes on preparing women for this change. Two recent programmes have looked at couple support during this key transition, one focusing on training for health visitors (One Plus One), the other providing couple support and education (PIPPIN). Very few programmes look to support the whole family, although it is now clear that grandparents are of critical importance in providing support to very young parents (see Family Policy Studies Centre, 2000).

- *The transition to full-time education*
  Infant and primary schools place a high value on helping parents to help their children settle into a new school. For many parents and carers this marks a time when their young child is getting older and will from now on be subject to many influences beyond the family and household. This can feel like an enormous challenge and loss to the adults and the children – it is not just, nor simply, an exciting time. Many schools and nurseries organize home visits when a child is about to start full-time education, parents are often invited to attend sessions at the school or nursery, and many playgroups and family centres provide innovative programmes to bridge the transition for both adults and children.

- *The transition to secondary education*
  In recent years more attention has, as a consequence of the idea of parental choice of school, focused on this stage. Secondary schools now pay considerable attention to introducing the school to prospective parents and children, to induction days for children who will be starting the new school, and to the home–school relationship. Again, the impact on parents and families of a child starting secondary school is rarely acknowledged or discussed. This change, like many others, is assumed to be all positive. Yet for families it may mean a child learning to use public transport, an earlier start to the day, different children starting the day at different times and being in different places. The child may be attending a large institution that the parents themselves experienced as being difficult and alien, or one of which they have no experience, if, for example, they have moved to Britain from another country. Their child may experience bullying if this has not already been experienced. Most of this work is done by teachers, and few other agencies are involved, but teachers lack the time and training to deal with the complexity of concerns facing adults and children when starting secondary school.

The missing transitions

As challenging are the key intervention points and places for the provision of parenting education and support:

- *Being bullied, including racial and sexual harassment*
  This is all too frequent an experience and leaves both the child or young person and his or her parents and carers feeling powerless. It can cause a crisis of confidence as both parent and child recognize the inability of the parent to protect the child from bullying. It can also lead to feelings of guilt and inadequacy if one's own child is the bully.

- *Sexual awakening/identity*
  Parents and carers are their children's first and foremost educators about sex and sexuality, yet few have the support, information or understanding to do this well. It can be especially challenging in a stepfamily, when children become aware of their parents as sexual beings or when a child or parent is gay or lesbian.

- *The separation or divorce of one's parents*
  As identified above, at the time of separation the adults are likely to be distracted and distressed, and likely to need support themselves. Recent efforts to extend the support offered by organizations such as Relate, and by mediation services, have started to meet this need, but the needs of children at such a time are much harder to satisfy. Again, there is a

need for children to receive information and support from the people around them, and there is a role here for teachers, youth workers and school counselling services.

- *The remarriage or re-partnering of one or both of one's parents*
The review of research discussed above identified that support is required at the time of the formation of a new family. This can be an especially hard time for children, as they have not had a choice about a new family being formed and may still have a fantasy about their original family getting back together, the conflict between the needs of parent and children being very hard to reconcile. Teachers and youth workers cannot 'put the family back together', but they can acknowledge the pain, grief and confusion felt by children and young people, and this in itself can make a big difference. Work undertaken by Parentline Plus with children and young people to explore their support needs when families change has demonstrated that although children and young people very clearly want to talk about the issues, the adults around them find this very difficult. The evidence from children and young people was that they wanted support and information from their peers, and in everyday settings, such as schools and youth clubs (Smith, 2000).

- *Moving home or country*
For any child, moving home can be a momentous change, just as it can be for their parents and carers. A change of address ought to become a commonplace trigger for any service provider to consider the support needs of children, young people and their carers.

Challenges for parenting education and support

Universal services for all who parent

Universal support is a good starting point, but it is not enough. Some groups do find themselves, or feel themselves to be, excluded from universal support, thus requiring targeted support. Such groups may include fathers, especially those not living with their children, refugee families, families living in bed-and-breakfast accommodation, families in which there has been a history of domestic violence, and ethnic minority families. This is not to argue that the needs of such families cannot be met by universal services – universal services should indeed make an effort to meet the needs of all families – but rather to argue that the circumstances in which these families live make it more likely that they will feel excluded from universal services, that they will find it difficult to share all their experiences in a group where few people will be familiar with these experiences, and that they may gain less from groups in which few people share their experiences.

Other families do have more specialist needs for support. Recent initiatives include the provision of parenting education for the parents and carers of young offenders, the new parenting orders making this compulsory for some. Early evidence suggests that parents welcome the compulsory nature of the parenting course, feeling initial resentment but then suggesting that it has been very helpful and that compulsion would have been the only way to get them there (Lord Warner, 1999). Others who may need specialist support include:

- the parents and carers of children with disabilities;
- parents and carers with disabilities;
- the parents and carers of children with mental health problems;
- families in which there has been a history of abuse.

Such support has been recognized by the Children Act and by the Quality Protects guidance, and is dealt with in other chapters of this book. It is, however, important to recognize that many parents and carers will want to access specialist support via universal services.

Reaching people who are parenting

When one considers all the people who have a role in parenting, and one looks at the key transition points for children and young people, it is evident that there are not always obvious routes and places to reach people to provide information and support. Schools play a key role because they are a universal service, but schools need time and resources to provide additional support. Moreover, at times of particular stress, such as divorce or non-attendance at school, parents may not see school as their ally. For these reasons Parentline Plus has opted to put considerable effort into working with the media to provide information in ways that can reach millions of people and are easily accessible and understandable. To successfully change the notion that parenting is hard, and that many different people are involved, requires a culture shift, and such shifts need significant media attention and interest.

The children: devils, angels or our future?

Perhaps the biggest challenge facing those keen to support parents and parenting is that of how children are regarded and understood. Parentline Plus has set itself strategic aims that include:

- changing the debate about whether parents need support to one of what kind of support works best for different people providing parenting work;
- changing the debate about children as monsters and demons needing to be controlled to one of the different ways in which children and young people can participate in community and social life.

As long as most policy initiatives are aimed at curbing and controlling children and young people, those who are parenting are almost bound to feel beleaguered and criticized. As the debate starts to move into new territory, we can all begin to work together to support children, young people and families. We can start to recognize at a policy and practice level that improved, sensitive and appropriate services for children and young people help their parents, and we can look to the training and support needs of those working with children as well as at the opportunities to increase support to parents and carers.

27

Developing Partnership Practice

John Pinkerton

The starting point for this chapter is the general acceptance that partnership should be a defining characteristic of work with children and their families. Despite this there appears to be considerable difficulty in establishing partnerships between those who provide childcare services and those who receive them. This undoubtedly reflects an imbalance of power that is deeply etched into the social and political structures of British society, based on inequalities of class, gender, age and race, and the nature of the state. It is suggested here, however, that these structural constraints on partnership can be understood and challenged by attending to the values, knowledge and skills of the individuals working within such structures. To help to understand and promote partnership, this chapter sets out an approach for developing and evaluating partnership practice through the exploration of personal values and the consideration of the necessary knowledge, methods, techniques and skills.

The policy space for partnership practice

A rather awkward mixture of concern to advance public accountability through user empowerment along with a belief in consumerism as a means of quality control has directed aspects of social policy over the past 20 years. The aim has been to encourage consumer satisfaction and service efficiency through a range of checks and balances between those who manage and deliver services and those who use and are affected by them. Current trends are focused on increasing acceptance by individuals of their responsibility for their own circumstances while at the same time increasing direct public involvement in the planning, organization and delivery of services under the banner of partnership.

A commitment to partnership practice has been reflected in all areas of public policy and is particularly clear in relation to personal social services (Croft and Beresford, 1997). In child welfare the Children Act 1989 (Ryan, 1994), and the associated legislation in both Scotland and Northern Ireland (Tisdall *et al.*, 1998), provides a legal mandate for partnership with children and parents. The legislation emphasizes the importance of children's wishes and feelings, and recognizes the central place of parental responsibility in ensuring children's quality of life. Court-sanctioned intervention in family life is restricted to situations in which children are at risk of significant harm and partnership with parents is unachievable. In all three British jurisdictions the overall thrust of policy is towards the provision of well-coordinated comprehensive family support. Services are targeted at families most in need, with the aim of assisting parents to become independent and confident in undertaking their responsibilities towards their children. This requires that workers delivering the services develop the necessary knowledge, values and skills to work in partnership (Family Rights Group, 1991; Pinkerton and Houston, 1996).

This 'promotional' position within the UK is in line with an emerging international consensus about principles underpinning children's services. It is seen as the preferred middle ground on the social policy continuum that emerged during the twentieth century. At one end of that continuum lies a 'state-ist' position, which is now generally regarded to have proved itself intrusive, inefficient and ineffective. The 'state-ist' approach to welfare is associated in its fullest form with the countries of the Soviet bloc prior to their collapse and in a less ambitious form with the pre-1980s British welfare state. At the other end of the continuum is an authoritarian 'minimalist' position, in which the state leaves social care, including that of children, to whatever families and private charity may, or may not, be able to provide. That harsh reliance on the vagaries of informal social care is exemplified in the South American dictatorships and in a much less extreme form in the attempted roll-back of the state in Britain during the 1980s and early 1990s.

The new international consensus aimed at promoting the capacities of children and their families is usefully expressed in the UNCRC. Article 12 states the child's right to express an opinion, and to have that opinion taken into account, in any matter or procedure affecting the child. The direct participation of children is central to the development and delivery of services. At the same time, and this can be easily overlooked, the Convention asserts in its preamble the fundamental position of the family as 'the natural environment for the growth and well-being of all its members and particularly children'. As such it should be afforded 'the necessary protection and assistance so that it can fully assume its responsibilities' (CRDU, 1994, p. 313). Providing that support to families requires working in partnership with parents.

Difficulties with partnership

Despite the level of commitment in principle to partnership, there continues to be confusion about what exactly is meant by the term and in particular about how to turn it into the routine characteristic of the relationship between those who provide and those who use children's services. The *Concise Oxford English Dictionary* defines partner as 'one who shares or takes part with another'. *The Dictionary of Social Work* describes partnership as 'a working relationship between care professional and service user in which the latter has some influence in deciding what is to be done and how' and notes that 'no genuine partnership can be formed unless there is some distribution of power – even if not equal distribution of power – between the partners' (Thomas and Pierson, 1995, p. 262). What these definitions make clear is that the pursuit and management of power is central to partnership (Harris, 1997) and that this is expressed through a certain type of relationship. At the core of partnership lies a purposeful relationship in which two or more parties engage because they share a goal and recognize that it is only through pooling their resources and agreeing on how best to work together that the goal can be met.

Much of the problem with partnership working lies in the absence, confusion or difficulty of achieving agreement over what constitutes the shared goal of the worker and the family. In addition those employed to work with children and families seem to have great difficulty in accepting that what they bring to any partnership can only be a contribution, often a minor one, to the wider and deeper pool of resources that go to ensure that children live their lives to the full. It has also been noted that while many professionals have a commitment to partnership, 'this is not easily translated into practice, particularly when it means relinquishing power and status' (Calder, 1995, p. 751).

Calder's comment was made in the context of child protection work in which the relationship between worker, parent and child is often circumscribed by legal requirements and a perception that the worker's role is to protect children from their parents. In such situations the power and status imbalance is crucially linked to the worker being advantaged as a representative of the state, but it is also informed by the parents being disadvantaged by factors such as class, gender, race and age. Child protection work brings into particularly sharp relief the difficulties there can be for partnership, but they are not peculiar to it. Discussion with pre-school staff, health visitors or teachers will also show that it is power relations, an inability to appreciate what it is that the other person has to offer and a lack of agreement over goals that frustrate partnership working with parents and children in those areas too.

Partnership in practice

Child protection is now an area in which there has been considerable work carried out on partnership. While it does raise its own particular issues, and in some cases ensuring the safety of children requires forms of legally sanctioned intervention that preclude partnership working, work in this area does usefully highlight some general aspects of partnership. Thoburn *et al.* (1995) provide a useful review of literature in this area as part of research into family involvement in the child protection process. The research was one of the 20 studies commissioned by the DoH in relation to child protection (DoH, 1995). Thoburn *et al.* provide a wide range of recommendations in their conclusion. A number of these are set out below, having been selected because they clearly demonstrate that what is involved in partnership is ensuring an effective working relationship through giving attention to basic requirements such as written information, practical arrangements and emotional support:

- Parents should receive standard leaflets and other suitably recorded information, as well as personal explanation from a social worker, to help them in understanding social services duties and responsibilities.

- It should be made clear to family members whom they can call on to accompany them to case conferences and other meetings, and to provide support before, during and after such events.

- Parents and older children and their supporters need to be well prepared for meetings, including being involved in a discussion beforehand of any written reports that are going to be considered.

- Resources need to be provided that will facilitate attendance at meetings, including childcare, transport, trained interpreters and appropriate aids for people with disabilities.

- When family members are from a race or culture different from the majority of those in attendance at a meeting, particular care is needed to explain the proceedings, and use should be made of translators and interpreters.

Thoburn *et al.* also stress that the agency needs to be wholehearted in its support of workers who attempt to involve parents and children in the work. This is also a point stressed by Marsh and Fisher (1992) in a study concerned with developing partnership within social services generally. They suggest a number of useful questions to test how committed an agency is to partnership:

- Are there any written policy statements in support of partnership?
- Are service users directly involved in drawing up agency policy?
- Do service users' views have a direct impact on staff training?
- Is there clear written information about services available to users in relevant styles and languages?
- Does the agency encourage service users to define their own needs, and are these expressed needs taken seriously?
- Where a need is not met, or a service imposed, are users provided with an explanation by the agency?
- While a service is being provided, are written agreements part of routine agency requirements?

Partnership as personal practice

As partnership is about ensuring a certain type of relationship, there is an onus on anyone wanting to work in this way with children and families to be aware of what it is he or she is bringing to the relationship. One crucial aspect of this is a person's values. Individuals need to identify their personal values and prejudices and consider whether they actually have a value base consistent with working in partnership. A simple exercise for exploring this is to complete the sentence 'I believe that...' with statements such as those listed below:

- the state has the right to ultimate responsibility for every child;
- parents have rights through responsibilities in regard to their children;
- the best interests of the child must always be the primary consideration;
- all children have the right to be brought up within their own families;
- each child is a unique human being;
- parents are individuals with their own needs and rights;
- staff are unique individuals with emotional needs as well as being workers with rights and responsibilities;
- children, parents and staff all have the right to mutual respect;
- honesty and effort deserves recognition and praise.

These value statements highlight the rights not only of children and parents, but also of the state and the workers delivering services. Such rights are increasingly formalized in law and in agency procedures, but that should not distract from the need to also express them within personal belief systems. When an individual considers whether such statements sit easily with her or his personal beliefs about working with children and families, and in particular when the exercise is done with a specific family in mind, it generally becomes apparent that beliefs tend to be contingent on circumstances. It is also found that values which may be regarded as of equal importance when considered in the abstract compete against one another in practice (Pinkerton and McLoughlin, 1996).

Dealing with such inconsistencies and conflicts requires judgments about the relevance of and relative weighting to give particular beliefs. This requires a degree of understanding of and involvement with the specifics of a situation that can only be achieved through the open style of working found in partnerships. Once someone is aware of the inconsistencies and conflicts in their own value system, it is much harder to take a closed, once-and-for-all view of any person or situation. It also becomes apparent that values must be directly linked to knowledge. To make judgments based on the specifics of a situation in which partnership is being pursued requires a knowledge of both need and services.

In relation to need it is necessary to have a psychological and sociological knowledge base that provides an understanding of the dynamic interaction within social systems and how these play out for individuals within the context of established patterns of human growth and development. This knowledge provides working hypotheses about the needs of individual family members, which can be explored with them in order to discount or confirm their accuracy. To test a hypothesis effectively also requires another type of knowledge – a knowledge of the particular history, characteristics and aspirations of the individuals involved. To gather that knowledge it is important to avoid 'typification', often encouraged by agency procedures, in which relationships with those looking for or receiving a service are defined by routine responses that place the service users into set, typical categories (Marsh and Fisher, 1992). This may be sufficient in certain situations and is necessary to a degree in order to ensure consistency of service, but needs boxed in this way are needs only partially understood.

Workers also have to bring to the partnership their knowledge of services. They should themselves know, or know how to access easily, the detail of what services their agency has to offer, the conditions in which they can be offered, what can be required as of right by service users and what is at the discretion of the agency. They also need to know the procedures for both becoming and ceasing to be involved with particular services. In addition they must be able to identify what mechanisms are available for complaint or representation with regard to the infringement of service users' rights. A knowledge of services also means understanding the context of the service – how it fits with the strategic aims of their agency, legal rights and obligations and social policy goals.

It is crucial to be clear on the mandate for working with families on particular goals: 'These goals may be agreed with the user because they are what the user wishes to work on, or they may be agreed with the client as a result of some external authority placing them on the client's agenda via legal proceedings' (Marsh and Fisher, 1992, p. 18). That second mandate provides a difficult basis for partnership working but can be 'reframed' through making a connection between the legally mandated goal and one which the user wants to work on (for example, the removal of a child to a foster placement, the legally mandated goal, and work on the child's challenging behaviour, the parental goal). Another approach is 'making a deal', whereby access to a resource wanted by the parent (a place in a nursery) or freeing themselves of involvement with the agency (coming off the child protection register) is dependent on working on the externally mandated goal.

Partnership through negotiation

In order to work in partnership it is also necessary to have understood and mastered techniques for managing the relationship through which the process of matching needs and services, and working towards an agreed outcome, is achieved. That requires a knowledge of how to negotiate. Negotiation is integral to partnership practice in that it permits both partners to signal their needs and wishes to the other so that both can search for a common goal and find the means of pooling their resources to work together in achieving the desired outcome. The process of negotiating can be thought of as comprising four steps. These are not rigidly bounded, movement back and forward being likely to occur.

- *Step One:* the potential for negotiation has to be established through information-gathering on and the assessment of what the potential partners will be bringing as a shared goal and as resources to pool.

- *Step Two:* a negotiating strategy needs to be planned that builds on the strengths of the partners and can overcome the barriers to working together.

- *Step Three:* the goals and means of intervention have to be negotiated, agreed and then implemented by the partners.

- *Step Four:* the intervention has to be evaluated by the partners through exchanging information and opinion on what has or has not been achieved, leading to an agreed closure or to a return to the information-gathering and assessment of the first step in order to start the process over again.

These steps are more or less easily followed according to the particular goal being pursued and the specifics of the situation. Providing a place for a child in a playgroup, for example, may be easily negotiated where it is a matter of clarifying and agreeing cost and practical arrangements with a working parent. Negotiating a placement at the same playgroup may, however, prove very demanding when social services wish to use the placement as part of a child protection plan to which angry parents are resistant. It is worth repeating that partnership cannot always be achieved and may not be appropriate to every situation.

Success in moving through the four steps will depend, at least in part, on the communication skills of the person working with the family. One key skill is the ability to maintain a focus and where necessary refocus on the desired outcome. This can be difficult because there may be more than one aspect to the outcome, and there may be differing degrees of commitment among family members to the various goals being pursued. Accurate, timely and clear information giving is very important here. This can be achieved verbally, by using written information, through video and audiotapes or by a combination of methods. It is crucial to check that the information being given is being received and understood. The use of written agreements can be a very important technique in achieving that clarity (Aldgate, 1989).

At the start of working on a partnership, but also while an intervention is being implemented, there is a need to ask the types of question that will allow people to explore what it is they really want and what they are able and willing to do to achieve it. Such questioning may well need to be blended with openly confronting opinions and behaviours that are unhelpful to clarifying and pursuing the agreed goals. Confronting needs to be balanced with positively reinforcing those opinions and behaviours which have been helpful to the process. It is also useful to be able to rehearse alternatives to the opinions and behaviours that are blocking progress. These more difficult aspects of communication are likely to be managed with greater success where time has been given to building a relationship based on active listening and empathy.

Relationships and the work involved in implementing an intervention have to be paced. Whatever the pressure to deliver quickly, the working through of all four stages should be attended to. The time this will take is proportionate to how difficult it will be to get an agreement about goals and the complexity of the desired outcome. There is almost always a tendency to rush closure, and it is important to resist that because closure represents a platform for moving on that needs to have been clearly secured.

Learning from the service user

While it is essential that anyone working with a family has the skills to justify their involvement, it is important not to see that as making them the more important partner. It is worth recalling the earlier point that partnerships are about pooling resources and that the worker needs what the family has to bring just as much as the family needs the worker's knowledge and skills. The worker has to be able to appreciate, clearly identify and positively reinforce what it is that family members are bringing as resources to the partnership. One of the things they will uniquely bring is a perspective on how effective the worker's personal partnership practice is – is it working for them; if so how and why; and if not, why not?

In acknowledgement of that unique perspective, it is appropriate to end this discussion of partnership with two sets of advice that parents suggested (Pinkerton *et al.*, 1997, Appendix B, section 3) would be helpful to someone wanting to work in partnership. You should make sure you:

- check that our understanding of what is happening is the same as yours
- check that we are all working for the same goal
- use everyday language we can understand
- show openness and honesty
- be realistic about how well you really know us
- be prepared to share something of yourself with us
- be realistic in your expectations of us
- be prepared to reach a compromise
- make decisions together with us
- deliver on what you say you'll do.

Watch out that you do not:

- forget that we are meant to be working together
- be vague
- stick too rigidly to rules and regulations
- come across as threatening
- avoid taking responsibility for your words and deeds
- write reports on us before you really know us
- put us 'under a microscope'
- make judgements of us based on assumptions and hearsay
- expect more of us than you would of anyone else in our situation
- exclude us from making or sharing with you the key decisions.

If the staff providing services to families constantly remind themselves of these 'dos' and 'don'ts', if they self-critically reflect on the values, knowledge and skills underpinning their practice, including acknowledging the constraints of social structural inequality, the very real difficulties in achieving partnership in practice will not disappear, but challenging opportunities for more ethical and more effective partnership practice with families can be created.

References

Abrahams, C. (1994) *Hidden Victims: Children and Domestic Violence*, London, NCH Action for Children.

Ackroyd, S. (1995) British public services, *International Journal of Public Service Management*, **8**(2): 19–32.

Adoption Law Review (1990) Discussion paper, No. 2, para. 134.

Alanen, L. (1994) Gender and generation: feminism and the 'child question', in Qvortrup, J., Bardy, M., Sgritta, G. and Wintersberger, H. (eds) *Childhood Matters. Social Theory, Practice and Politics*, Aldershot, Avebury Press.

Alanen, L. (2001) Childhood as a generational condition, in Alanen, L. and Mayall, B. (eds) *Conceptualizing Child–Adult Relations*, London, Falmer.

Alderson, P. (1993) *Children's Consent to Surgery*, Buckingham, Open University Press.

Alderson, P. (2000) *Young Children's Rights: Exploring Beliefs, Principles and Practice*, London, Jessica Kingsley.

Alderson, P. and Montgomery, J. (1996) *Health Care Choices: Making Decisions with Children*, Institute for Public Policy Research, London.

Aldgate, J. (ed.) (1989) *Using Written Agreements with Children and Families*, London, Family Rights Group.

Allen, N. (1998) *Making Sense of the Children Act. A Guide for the Social and Welfare Services*, Chichester, John Wiley & Sons.

Amin, K. and Oppenheim, C. (1992) *Poverty in Black and White: Deprivation and Ethnic Minorities*, London, CPAG.

Aries, P. (1962) *Centuries of Childhood*, Harmondsworth, Penguin.

Armstrong, C., Hill, M. and Secker, J. (1999) Young people's perceptions of mental health, *Children and Society*, **13**: 1–13.

Armstrong, D. (1995) The rise of surveillance medicine, *Sociology of Health and Illness*, **17**(3): 393–404.

Article 12 (1999) *Respect! A Report into how well Article 12 of the UN Convention of the Rights of the Child is Put into Practice in the UK*, Nottingham.

Ashley, J. (1999) Parental responsibility – a new deal or a costly exercise? March, *Family Law*, 175.

Ashworth, K. and Walker, K. (1994) 'Reeboks, a Game Boy and a cat': things children own, in Middleton, S., Ashworth, K. and Walker, R. (eds) *Family Fortunes: Pressures on Parents and Children in the 1990s*, London, Child Poverty Action Group.

Association of Black Social Workers and Allied Professions (1983) *Black Children in Care – Evidence to the House of Commons Social Services Committee*, London, ABSWAP.

Atherton, C. (1999) *Towards evidence-based services for children and families*, Theorising Social Work Research Seminar, http://www.nisw.org.uk/tswr/atherton.html

Atkinson, A.B. (1998) *Emu, Macro-economics and Children*, Innocenti Occasional Papers, Economic and Social Policy Series, No. 68, Florence, UNICEF.

Audit Commission (1986) *Making a Reality of Community Care*, London, HMSO.

Audit Commission (1994) *Seen but not Heard: Co-ordinating Community Child Health and Social Services for Children in Need*, London, Audit Commission.

Audit Commission (1999) *Children in Mind*, London, Audit Commission.

Baker, A. and Duncan, S.P. (1985) Child sexual abuse: a study of prevalence in Great Britain, *Child Abuse and Neglect*, pp. 457–67.

Barker, W.E., Anderson, R.M. and Chalmers, C. (1992) *Child Protection: The Impact of the Child Development Programme, Evaluation Document No. 14*, Bristol, Early Childhood Development Unit, Department of Social Work, University of Bristol.

Barnardo's (1998) *Children are Unbeatable*, Ilford, Barnado's.

Barn, R. (1993) *Black Children in the Public Care System: Child Care Policy and Practice*, London, Batford.

Barrow, C. (1999) Consent in practice, *Paediatric Nursing*, **11**(8): 39–40.

Barton, C. and Douglas, G. (1995) *Law and Parenthood*, London, Butterworth.

Beck, U. (1997) Democratization of the family, *Childhood*, **4**(2): 151–68.

Becker, H. (1963) *Outsiders*, New York, Free Press.

Beecher, W. (1998) *Having a Say! Disabled Children and Effective Partnership. Section 2: Practice Initiatives and Selected Annotated References*, London, Council for Disabled Children.

Belsky, J. (1993) Etiology of child maltreatment: a developmental-ecological analysis, *Psychological Bulletin*, **114**: 413–34.

Beresford, B. (1994) *Positively Parents: Caring for a Severely Disabled Child*, York, Social Policy Research Unit.

Beresford, B. (1997) *Personal Accounts: Involving Disabled Children in Research*, York, Social Policy Research Unit.

Beresford, P. (1999) *Service Users' Knowledges and Social Work Theory: Conflict or Collaboration?*, Theorising Social Work Research, http://www.nisw.org.uk/tswr/ beresford.html

Beresford, P. and Croft, S. (1993) *Citizen Involvement*, London, BASW.

Berridge, D. (1997) *Foster Care: A Research Review*, London, Stationery Office.

Berridge, D. (1999) Working with fostered children and their families, in Hill, M. (ed.) *Effective Ways of Working with Children and their Families*, London, Jessica Kingsley.

Bettleheim, B. (1995) *A Good Enough Parent? The Guide to Bringing up your Child*, London, Thames and Hudson.

Bhavnani, K. and Phoenix, A. (1994) *Shifting Identities, Shifting Racisms*, London, Sage.

Bifulco, A. and Moran, P. (1998) *Wednesday's Child: Research into Women's Experience of Neglect and Abuse in Childhood and Adult Depression*, London, Routledge.

Blatchford, P. (1999) The state of play in schools, in Woodhead, M. (ed.) *Making Sense of Social Development*, London, Routledge/Open University.

Blaxter, M. (1990) *Health and Lifestyles*, London, Routledge.

Blaxter, M. and Paterson, E. (1982) *Mothers and Daughters. A Three-generational Study of Health Attittudes and Behaviour*, London, Heineman Educational.

Bluebond-Langer, M. (1978) *The Private Worlds of Dying Children*, Princeton, NJ, Princeton University Press.

Blumberg, R. *et al.* (eds) (1995) *Engendering Wealth and Well-being*, Boulder, CO, Westview Press.

Blyth, E. (1990) Assisted reproduction: What's in it for children? *Children's Society*, **4**(2): 167, 182.

Bohn, D. (1990) Domestic violence and pregnancy: implications for practice, *Journal of Nurse Midwifery*, **35**: 19–21.

Borland, M., Pearson, C., Hill, M., Tisdall, K. and Bloomfield, I. (1998) *Education and Care Away from Home*, Edinburgh, Scottish Council for Research in Education.

Bowker, L., Arbitell, M. and McFerron, J. (1988) On the relationship between wife beating and child abuse, in Yllo, K. and Bograd, M. (eds) *Feminist Perspectives on Wife Abuse*, London, Sage.

Bowlby, J. (1969) *Attachment and Loss*. Vol. 1: *Attachment*, London, Hogarth Press.
Bowlby, J. (1980) *Attachment and Loss*. Vol. 3: *Loss*, London, Hogarth Press.
Bradshaw, J. (1990) *Child Poverty and Deprivation in the UK*, London, National Children's Bureau.
Bradshaw, J.R. (1997) Family policy and family poverty, *Policy Studies*, **17**(2): 93–106.
Branchflower, G. (1999) Parental responsibility and human rights, January, *Family Law*, **34**.
Braun, D. (1993) Parent Education Programmes, in *Enhancing Parenting Skills*; see also Combes, G. and Schonveld, A. (1992) *Life Will Never be the Same Again*, Health Education Authority; Braun, D. and Schonveld, A. (1993) *Approaching Parenthood, A Resource for Parent Education*, London, Health Education Authority.
Bronfenbrenner, U. (1979) *The Ecology of Human Development*, Cambridge, MA, Harvard University Press.
Brown, C. (1984) *Black and White Britain: The Third Policy Studies Institute Survey*, London, PSI/Heinemann.
Brown, S. (1998) *Understanding Youth and Crime: Listening to Youth?*, Buckingham, Open University Press.
Browne, J. (1995) Can social work empower?, in Hugman, R. and Smith, D. (eds) *Ethical Issues in Social Work*, London, Routledge.
Buckingham, D. (1996) *Moving Images: Understanding Children's Emotional Responses to Television*, Manchester, Manchester University Press.
Buckingham, D. (2000) *After the Death of Childhood: Growing Up in the Age of Electronic Media*, London, Polity Press.
Burgess, A. and Ruxton, S. (1996) *Men and their Children: Proposals for Public Policy*, London, Institute for Public Policy Research.
Burman, E. (1994) *Deconstructing Developmental Psychology*, London, Routledge.
Butler, J. (1993) *Bodies that Matter: On the Discursive Limits of 'Sex'*, New York, Routledge.
Butt J. (1994) *Same Service or Equal Service: the Second Report on Social Services Department's Development Implementation and Monitoring of Services for the Black and Minority Ethnic Community*, London, HMSO.
Butt, J. and Mirza, K. (1996) *Social Care and Black Communities*, London, REU.
Calder, M. (1995) Child protection balancing paternalism and partnership, *British Journal of Social Work*, **25**: 749–66.
Cameron, C., Moss, P. and Owen, C. (1999) *Men in the Nursery: Gender and Caring Work*, London, Paul Chapman.
Campbell, B. (1993) *Goliath: Britain's Dangerous Places*, London, Methuen.
Campbell, S. and Glasper, A.E. (1995) *Whaley and Wong's Children's Nursing*, London, Mosby.
Cannan, C. and Warren, C. (1997) *Social Action with Children and Families: A Community Development Approach to Child and Family Welfare*, London, Routledge.
Carlen, P. (1996) *Jigsaw – a Political Criminology of Youth Homelessness*, Buckingham, Open University Press.
Carter, P. (1993) The problem of men: a reply to Keith Pringle, CSP Issue 36, *Critical Social Policy*, (38): 100–5.
Casey, A. (1988) A partnership with child and family, *Senior Nurse*, **8**(4): 8–9.
Cavet, U. (1998) *People Don't Understand: Children, Young People and their Families Living with a Hidden Disability*, London, National Children's Bureau.
Chamba, R., Ahmad, W., Hirst, M., Lawton, D. and Beresford, B. (1999) *On the Edge: Minority Ethnic Families Caring for a Severely Disabled Child*, London, Policy Press.
Chand, A. (2000) The over-representation of black children in the child protection system: possible causes, consequences and solutions, *Child and Family Social Work*, **5**: 67–77.
CRDU (Children's Rights Development Unit) (1994) *UK Agenda for Children*, London, CRDU.

Children's Rights Office (1998) *A Report to the UK Government on Progress Towards Implementing the Convention on the Rights of the Child: a Summary of the Views and Concerns of those Working with Children*, London, Children's Rights Office.

Children's Society (1999) *Research for Change – Young People, Youth Justice and the Use of Custody on Teeside*, Stockton, Youth Justice North East.

Childright (1995) UN criticises UK rights of the child report, No. 114, University of Essex, The Children's Legal Centre.

Childright (1998) Summary of the government's guidance on home–school agreements, No. 152, University of Essex, The Children's Legal Centre.

Childright (1999) *President of family division in favour of gay adoption*, No. 161, University of Essex, The Children's Legal Centre.

Chodorow, N. (1978) *The Reproduction of Mothering*, Berkeley, CA, University of California Press.

Christensen, P.H. (1998) Difference and similarity: how children's competence is constituted in illness and its treatment, in Hutchby, I. and Moran-Ellis, J. (eds) *Children and Social Competence: Arenas of Action*, London, Falmer Press.

Church, J. (1984) *Violence Against Wives: Its Causes and Effects*, Christchurch, New Zealand, John Church.

Church, S. and Doyle, P. (1997) Eat your words! Helping children to choose food wisely, *Children UK*, Summer, p. 3.

Clark, M.M. (1997) Developments in primary education in Scotland, in Clark, M.M. and Munn, P. (eds) *Education in Scotland: Policy and Practice from Pre-school to Secondary*, London, Routledge.

Clarke, L. (1997) *Stability and Instability in Children's Family Lives: Longitudinal Evidence from Two British Data Sources*, London, Centre for Population Studies, London School of Hygiene and Tropical Medicine, University of London.

Cochran, M. (1993) Parenting and personal social networks, in Luster, T. and Okagaki, L. (eds) *Parenting: An Ecological Perspective*, Hillsdale, NJ, Lawrence Erlbaum Associates.

Cockett, M. and Tripp, J. (1994) *The Exeter Family Study: Family Breakdown and its Impact on Children*, Exeter, University of Exeter Press.

Cohen, S. (1972) *Folk Devils and Moral Panics: The Creation of the Mods and Rockers*, New York, St Martin's Press.

Cohen, S. (1973) *Folk Devils and Moral Panics: The Creation of Mods and Rockers*, London, Paladin.

Cohen, S. (1985) *Visions of Social Control*, Cambridge, Polity Press.

Colclough, L., Parton, N. and Anslow, M. (1999) Family support, in Parton, N. and Wattam, C. (eds) *Child Sexual Abuse: Responding to the Experiences of Children*, Chichester, John Wiley & Sons/NSPCC.

Colton, M., Drakeford, M., Roberts, S., Casas, F. and Williams, M. (1997) Child welfare and stigma principles into practice, *Childhood*, 4(3): 265–83.

Commission for Racial Equality (1987) *Living in Terror: A Report on Racial Violence and Harassment in Housing*, London, CRE.

Commission for Racial Equality (1988) *Learning in Terror: A Survey of Racial Harassment in Schools and Colleges*, London, CRE.

Commission for Racial Equality (1989) *Housing Policies in Tower Hamlets: An Investigation into the London Borough of Southwark*, London, CRE.

Commission for Racial Equality (1990) *Sorry It's Gone: Testing for Racial Discrimination in the Private Rented Housing Sector*, London, CRE.

Commission for Racial Equality (1995) *Black Children and Exclusion*, London, CRE.

Connell, R. (1995) *Masculinities*, Sydney, Allen & Unwin.

Connolly, P. (1998) *Racism, Gender Identities and Young Children: Social Relations in a Multi-ethnic, Inner-city Primary School*, London, Routledge.

Coohey, C. (1996) Child maltreatment: testing the social isolation hypothesis, *Child Abuse and Neglect*, **20**(3): 241–54.

Cooper, A., Hetherington, R. and Katz, I. (1997) *A Third Way? A European Perspective on the Child Protection/Family Support Debate*, London, NSPCC.

Corsaro, W.A. (1997) *The Sociology of Childhood*, Thousand Oaks, CA, Pine Forge Press.

Coulton, C.J., Korbin, J.E., Su, M. and Chow, J. (1995) Community level factors and child maltreatment rates, *Child Development*, **66**: 1262–76.

Croft, S. and Beresford, P. (1997) Service users' perspectives, in Davies, M. (ed.) *The Blackwell Companion to Social Work*, Oxford, Blackwell.

Crompton, M. (1980) *Respecting Children: Social Work with Young People*, London, Edward Arnold.

Cross, M. (1998) *Proud Child, Safer Child: A Handbook for Parents and Carers of Disabled Children*, London, Women's Press.

Cunningham-Burley, S. and MacLean, U. (1991) Dealing with children's illness: mothers' dilemmas, in Wyke, S. and Hewison, J. (eds) *Child Health Matters*, Milton Keynes, Open University Press.

Darbyshire, P. (1994) *Living with a Sick Child*, London, Chapman & Hall.

Darling, J. (1994) *Child-centred Education – and its Critics*, London, Paul Chapman.

Darling, J. (1999) Scottish primary education: philosophy and practice, in Bryce, T.G.K. and Humes, W. (eds) *Scottish Education*, Edinburgh, Edinburgh University Press.

Darvill, G. (1998) *Organisation, People and Standards*, London, NISW.

Dasgupta, P. and Weale, M. (1992) On measuring the quality of life, *World Development* **20**(1): 119–31.

Davies, C. (2000) Frameworks for regulation and accountability: threat or opportunity?, in Brechin, A., Brown, H. and Eby, M. (eds) *Critical Practice in Health and Social Care*, London, Sage/Open University.

Davies, H. (1993) *Counselling Parents of Children with Chronic Illness or Disability*, Leicester, BPS Books.

Davies, L. and Fitzpatrick, G. (2000) *The Euridem Project*, Children's Rights Alliance for England, for evidence of democracy in education in Sweden, Denmark, Germany and Holland, London, Children's Rights Office.

Davis, A. and Jones, L. (1997) Whose neighbourhood? Whose quality of life? Developing a new agenda for children's health in urban settings, *Health Education Journal*, **56**: 350–63.

Davis, H. and Bourhill, M. (1997) 'Crisis': The demonization of children and young people, in Scraton, P. (ed.) *'Childhood' in 'Crisis'?*, London, UCL Press.

Davis, K. (ed.) (1997) *Embodied Practices. Feminist Perspectives on the Body*, London, Sage.

Davis-Jones, C. (1998) *Pictures of Healthcare*, London, Action for Sick Children.

De Winter, M. (1997) *Children as Fellow Citizens: Participation and Commitment*, Abingdon, Radcliffe Medical Press.

Deech, R. (1992) *The Unmarried Father and Human Rights*, 4 JCL at p. 3. (Quoted in Fortin, J. (1998) *Children's Rights and the Developing Law*, London, Butterworth.)

Derricourt, N. (1983) Strategies for community care, in Loney, M. and Clarke, J. (eds) *Social Policy and Social Welfare*, Buckingham, Open University Press.

DfEE (Department for Education and Employment) (1998) *5.4 Billion Investment in Modernising Schools – Blunkett*, Press Release 544/98. London, DFEE.

DfEE (Department for Education and Employment) (1999a) *Social Inclusion: Pupil Support*, Circular 10/99, July.

DfEE (Department for Education and Employment) (1999b) *The Education of Children Looked After by Local Authorities*, June, HMSO.

DHSS (Department of Health and Social Security) (1968) Seebohm Report *Report of the Committee on Local Authority and Allied Personal Social Services*, Cmnd 3703, London, HMSO.

DHSS (Department of Health and Social Security) (1988) *Report of the Inquiry into Child Abuse in Cleveland*, London, HMSO.

Dingwall, R., Eckelaar, J. and Murray, T. (1983) *The Protection of Children: State Intervention and Family Life*, Oxford, Blackwell.

Dobash, R. and Dobash, R. (1984) The nature and antecedent of violent events, *British Journal of Criminology*, **24**: 269–88.

Dobie, T. and MacBeath, J. (1998) *Pupil Councils: A Case Study of Pupil Councils in Fife*, Glasgow, QIE, University of Strathclyde.

Dobson, B. and Middleton, S. (1999) *Paying to Care: The Cost of Childhood Disability*, York, York Publishing Services.

DoH (Department of Health) (1985) *Social Work Decisions in Child Care*, London, HMSO.

DoH (Department of Health) (1989) *An Introduction to the Children Act 1989*, para. 2.4, London, HMSO.

DoH (Department of Health) (1993a) *Population Needs Assessment: A Guide to Identifying Local Needs,* Bristol, School of Advanced Urban Studies, University of Bristol.

DoH (Department of Health) (1993b) *Households Below Average Income* 1979–1990/1, London, HMSO.

DoH (Department of Health) (1994) *The UK First Report to the UN Committee on the Rights of the Child*, London, HMSO.

DoH (Department of Health) (1995) *Child Protection: Messages from Research*, London, HMSO.

DoH (Department of Health) (1996a) *Childhood Matters: The Report of the National Commission of Inquiry into the Prevention of Child Abuse*, London, HMSO.

DoH (Department of Health) (1996b) *The Patient's Charter (Services for Children and Young People)*, London, HMSO.

DoH (Department of Health) (1997) *The New NHS*, London, HMSO.

DoH (Department of Health) (1998a) *Disabled Children: Directions for their Future Care*, London, DoH.

DoH (Department of Health) (1998b) *Quality Protects: Framework for Action*, London, DoH.

DoH (Department of Health) (1998c) *Modernising Social Services*, London, Stationery Office.

DoH (Department of Health) (1998d) *The Quality Protects Programme: Transforming Children's Services*, LDC(98)28, London, DoH.

DoH (Department of Health) (1998e) Press release 0424, 5 November.

DoH (Department of Health) (1999a) *The Government's Objectives for Children's Social Services*, London, HMSO.

DoH (Department of Health) (1999b) *Code of Practice*, London, HMSO.

DoH (Department of Health) (1999c) *Second Report to the UN Committee on the Rights of the Child by the United Kingdom*, London, HMSO.

DoH (Department of Health) (2000) *Protecting Children: Supporting Parents*, London, HMSO.

DoH (Department of Health)/DfEE (Department for Education and Employment) (1996) *Children's Services Planning: Guidance Inter-Agency Working*, London, DoH/DfEE.

DoH (Department of Health)/DfEE (Department for Education and Employment)/Home Office (2000) *Framework for the Assessment of Children in Need and their Families*, London, Stationery Office.

DoH (Department of Health)/Welsh Office (1997) *People like us – the Report of the Review of the Safeguards for Children Living Away from Home*, London, Stationery Office.

DoH (Department of Health)/Welsh Office (2000) *Lost in Care – The Report of the Tribunal of Inquiry into the Abuse of Children in Care in the Former County Council Areas of Gwynedd and Clwyd Since 1974* (The Waterhouse Report), London, Stationery Office.

Doyle, K.A. and Maslin-Prothero, S. (1999) Promoting children's rights: the role of the children's nurse, *Paediatric Nursing*, **11**(8): 23–5.

Dunst, C.J. and Trivette, C.M. (1990) Assessment of social support in early intervention programs, in Meisels, S.J. and Shonkoff, J.P. (eds) *Handbook of Early Childhood Intervention*, New York, Cambridge University Press.

Durham County Council (1999) *Investing in Children: Statement of Intent*, Durham, Durham County Council.

Durrant, J. (1999) *The Status of Swedish Children and Youth since the Passage of the 1979 Corporal Punishment Ban*, London, Save the Children.

Durrant, P. (1997) Mapping the future? A contribution from community social work in the community care field, in Cannan, C. and Warren, C. (eds) *Social Action With Children and Families: A Community Development Approach to Child and Family Welfare*, London, Routledge.

Dwivedi, K.N. and Varma, V.P. (eds) (1996) *Meeting the Needs of Ethnic Minority Children: A Handbook for Professionals*, London, Jessica Kingsley.

Dwork, D. (1987) *War is Good for Babies and Other Young Children. A History of the Infant and Child Welfare Movement in England, 1898–1918*, London, Tavistock.

Dyhouse, C. (1981) *Girls Growing up in Late Victorian and Edwardian England*, London, Routledge & Kegan Paul.

Early Years Trainers Anti Racist Network (EYTARN) (1998) *Planning for Excellence: Implementing the DFEE Guidance Requirements for the Equal Opportunity Strategy in Early Years Development Plans*, Wallasey, EYTARN.

Eastham, D. (1990) Plan it or suck it and see, in Darvill, G. and Smale, G. (eds) *Partners in Empowerment: Networks of Innovation in Social Work*, London, NISW.

EC Childcare Network (1990) *Men as Carers for Children: Report on an EC Childcare Network Technical Seminar*, Glasgow, May 18–19, Brussels, European Commission Network on Childcare.

EC Childcare Network (1994) *Men as Carers: Towards a Culture of Responsibility, Sharing and Reciprocity Between Women and Men in the Care and Upbringing of Children*, Brussels, European Commission Equal Opportunities Unit.

Edwards, L. and Griffiths, A. (1997) *Family Law*, Edinburgh, W. Green/Sweet & Maxwell. The Children' Hearing System at pp386–431.

Edwards, R., David, M. and Alldred, P. (2000) *Children's Understandings of Parental Involvement in Education: Research Briefing*, Swindon, Economic and Social Research Council.

Erikson, E. (1963) *Childhood and Society*, New York, Norton.

Erooga, M. and Masson, H. (1999) Working with abusers to protect children, in Parton, N. and Wattam, C. (eds) *Child Sexual Abuse: Responding to the Experiences of Children*, Chichester, John Wiley & Sons/NSPCC.

Esmail, A. and Everington, S. (1993) Racial discrimination against doctors from ethnic minorities, *British Medical Journal*, **306**: 691–2.

Euronet (1997) *The New Treaty on European Union: What's in it for Children?*, Brussels, European Press.

Euronet (1999) *A Children's Policy for 21st Century Europe: First Steps*, Brussels, European Press.

Eurostat (1993) *Statistics in Focus: Income Distribution and Poverty in the EU 12 – 1993*, Luxembourg, Office des Publications des Communautés Européennes.

Evans, D. (1994) Falling angels: the material construction of children as sexual citizens, *International Journal of Children's Rights*, **2**: 1–33.

Family Policy Studies Centre (2000) *Family Change: Guide to the Issues*, Family Briefing Paper 12, London, Family Policy Studies Centre.

Family Rights Group (1991) *The Children Act 1989: Working in Partnership with Families*, Reader, London, HMSO.

Family Rights Group (2000) *Family Rights Group Newsletter*, Spring, London, Family Rights Group.

Farmer, E. and Pollock, S. (1998) *Substitute Care for Sexually Abused and Abusing Children*, Chichester, John Wiley & Sons.

Fernando, S. (1989) *Race, Culture and Psychiatry*, London, Routledge.

Ferri, E. and Smith, K. (1996) *Parenting in the 90s*, London, Family Policy Studies Centre.

Ferri, E. and Smith, K. (1998) *Step-parenting in the 1990s*, London, Family Policy Studies Centre.

Finkelhor, D. (1984) *Child Sexual Abuse: New Theory and Research*, New York, Free Press.

Finkelhor, D. (1986) *Sexual Abuse: A Sourcebook on Child Sexual Abuse*, London, Sage.

Fischer, C. (1982) *To Dwell Among Friends: Personal Networks in Town and City*, Chicago, Chicago University Press.

Fisher, D. (1994) Adult sex offenders: who are they? why and how do they do it?, in Morrison, T., Erooga, M. and Beckett, R. (eds) *Sexual Offending Against Children: Assessment and Treatment of Male Offenders*, London, Routledge.

Fleitas, J.D. (1997) To tell the truth: children reflect on hospital care, *Comprehensive Pediatric Nursing*, **20**: 195–206.

Fletcher, B. (ed.) (1993) *Not Just a Name*, London, Who Cares? Trust/National Consumer Council.

Foley, P. (1998) Reconfiguring knowledge: a discourse analysis of antenatal care, unpublished PhD thesis, University of Bradford.

Fortin, J. (1998) *Children's Rights and the Developing Law*, London, Butterworth.

Fradd, E. (1996) The importance of negotiating a care plan, *Paediatric Nursing*, **8**(6): 6–9.

Frank, J. (1995) *Couldn't Care More: A Study of Young Carers and their Needs*, London, Children's Society.

Franklin, B. and Petley, J. (1996) Killing the age of innocence: newspaper reporting of the death of James Bulger, in Pilcher, J. and Wagg, S. (eds) *Thatcher's Children. Politics, Childhood and Society in the 1980s and 1990s*, London, Falmer Press.

Fraser, H. (1998) *Interchange 50, Early Intervention: Key Issues from Research*, Edinburgh, SOEID.

Freeman, C., Henderson, P. and Kettle, J. (1999) *Planning with Children for Better Communities*, Bristol, Policy Press.

Freeman, M. (1997) 'The new birth right: identity and the child of the reproduction revolution', *International Journal of Children's Rights*, **4**: 273–97.

Fulton, Y. (1996) Children's rights and the role of the nurse, *Paediatric Nursing*, **8**(10): 29–31.

Gallagher, B. (1998) *Grappling With Smoke: Investigating and Managing Organised Child Sexual Abuse: A Good Practice Guide*, London, NSPCC.

Gallagher, R. (1998) *Children and Young People's Voices on the Law, Legal Services, and Systems in Scotland*, Glasgow, Scottish Child Law Centre.

Garbarino, J. and Kostelny, K. (1993) Neighbourhood and community influences on parenting, in Luster, T. and Okagaki, L. (eds) *Parenting: An Ecological Perspective*, Hillsdale, NJ, Lawrence Erlbaum Associates.

Garbarino, J., Stott, F.M. and Faculty of the Erikson Institute (1992) *What Children Can Tell Us*, San Francisco, Jossey-Bass.

Garratt, A.M. and Ruta, D.A. (1999) The patient generated index, in Joyce, C., O'Boyle, C. and McGee, H. (eds) *Individual Quality of Life Approaches to Conceptualisation and Assessment*, Amsterdam, Harwood Academic Press.

Gatens, M. (1992) Power, bodies and difference, in Barrett, M. and Phillips, A. (eds) *Destabilising Theory. Contemporary Feminist Debates*, Cambridge, Polity Press.

Gerrard, N. (1997) Little girls lost, *Observer*, Review Section, 31 August.

Ghate, D. (1997) *Talking About my Generation: A Survey of 8–15 year olds Growing Up in the 1990s*, London, NSPCC.

Gielen, A., O'Campo, P., Faden, R., Kass, N. and Xue, X. (1994) Interpersonal conflict and physical violence during the childbearing year, *Social Science and Medicine*, **39**: 781–7.

Gittell, R. and Vidal, A. (1998) *Community Organizing Building Social Capital as a Development Strategy*, London, Sage.

Glover, J. (1995) The research programme of development ethics, in Nussbaum, M. and Glover, J. (eds) *Women Culture and Development: A Study of Human Capabilities* Oxford, Clarendon Press.

Goffman, E. (1963) *Stigma: Notes on the Management of Spoiled Identity*, Harmondsworth, Penguin.

Goldson, B. (1997a) 'Childhood': an introduction to historical and theoretical analyses, in Scraton, P. (ed.) *'Childhood' in 'Crisis'?*, London, UCL Press.

Goldson, B. (1997b) Children in trouble: state responses to juvenile crime, in Scraton, P. (ed.) *'Childhood' in 'Crisis'?*, London, UCL Press.

Goldson, B. (1998) Re-visiting the 'Bulger case': the governance of juvenile crime and the politics of punishment – enduring consequences for children in England and Wales, *Juvenile Justice Worldwide*, **1**(1): 21.

Goldson, B. (1999) Youth (In)justice: contemporary developments in policy and practice, in Goldson, B. (ed.) *Youth Justice: Contemporary Policy and Practice*, Aldershot, Ashgate.

Goldson, B. (ed.) (2000) *The New Youth Justice*, Lyme Regis, Russell House.

Gore, C. (1997) Learning on a Saturday, in Garratt, D., Roche, J. and Tucker S. (eds) *Changing Experiences of Youth*, London, Sage.

Graham, B., Tanner, G., Cheyne, B., Freeman, I., Rooney, M. and Lambie, A. (1998) Unemployment rates, single parent density, and indices of child poverty: their relationship to different categories of child abuse and neglect, *Child Abuse and Neglect*, **22**(2): 79–90.

Green, L. (1998) Caged by force, entrapped by discourse: a study of the construction and control of children and their sexualities in residential children's homes, unpublished PhD thesis, University of Huddersfield.

Green, L. (1999a) Sexuality, sexual abuse and children's homes: oppression or protection?, in The Violence Against Children Study Group (eds) *Children, Child Abuse and Child Protection: Placing Children Centrally*, Chichester, John Wiley & Sons.

Green, L. (1999b) *Getting the Balance Right: A Cross Comparative Analysis of the Balance Between Legal Intervention and Therapeutic Support Systems in Relation to Responses to Child Sexual Abuse in England, Belgium and the Netherlands*, a report prepared for the European Commission, Nov 1999, under the Daphne Initiative, Centre for Applied Childhood Studies, University of Huddersfield.

Gregg, P., Harkness, S. and Machin, S. (1999) Poor kids: trends in child poverty in Britain 1968–96, *Fiscal Studies*, **20**(2): 32.

Griffiths, J., Cunningham, G. and Dick, S. (1999) *Onwards and Upwards: Involving Disabled Children and Young People in Decision Making*, Edinburgh, Children in Scotland.

Grosz, E. (1994) *Volatile Bodies*, London, Routledge.

Gunter, B. (1998) *The Effects of Video Games on Children: The Myth Unmasked*, Sheffield, Sheffield Academic Press.

Hagell, A. and Newburn, T. (1994) *Persistent Young Offenders*, London, Policy Studies Institute.

Haines, K. and Drakeford, M. (1999) *Young People and Youth Justice*, London, Macmillan.

Hall, S., Critcher, C., Jefferson, T., Clarke, J. and Roberts, B. (1978) *Policing the Crisis: Mugging, the State and Law and Order*, London, Macmillan.

Hallett, H., Murray, C., Jamieson, J. and Veitch, W. (1998) *The Evaluation of Children's Hearings In Scotland*, Vols I and II, Edinburgh, Scottish Office Central Research Unit.

Hamilton, K. and Saunders, L. (1997) *The Health Promoting School: A Summary of the ENHPS Evaluation Project*, London, HEA.

Harding, S. (1996) Standpoint epistemology (a feminist version): how social disadvantage creates epistemic advantage, in Turner, S.P. (ed.) *Social Theory and Sociology*, Oxford, Blackwell.

Harris, B. (1995) *The Health of the Schoolchild: A History of the School Medical Service in England and Wales*, Buckingham, Open University Press.

Harris, R. (1997) Power, in Davies, M. (ed.) *The Blackwell Companion to Social Work*, Oxford, Blackwell.

Hashima, P.Y. and Amato, P.R. (1994) Poverty, social support and parental behaviour, *Child Development*, **65**: 394–403.

Hawtin, M., Hughes, G. and Percy-Smith, J. (1994) *Community Profiling: Auditing Social Needs,* Buckingham, Open University Press.

Hay, C. (1995) Mobilisation through interpellation: James Bulger, juvenile crime and the construction of a moral panic, *Social and Legal Studies*, **4**(2): 197–223.

Henderson, P. (1997) Community development and children: a contemporary agenda, in Cannan, C. and Warren, C. (eds) *Social Action With Children and Families: A Community Development Approach to Child and Family Welfare*, London, Routledge.

Henderson, S. (1997) *Service Provision to Women Experiencing Domestic Violence in Scotland*, Edinburgh, Scottish Office.

Hendrick, H. (1990) *Child Welfare England 1872–1989*, London, Routledge.

Hester, M. and Pearson, C. (1998) *From Periphery to Centre – Domestic Violence in Work with Abused Children*, Bristol, Policy Press.

Hester, M. and Radford, L. (1996) *Domestic Violence and Child Contact Arrangements in England and Denmark*, Bristol, Policy Press.

Hetherington, R. and Cooper, A. (1999) Negotiation, in Parton, N. and Wattam, C. (eds) *Child Sexual Abuse: Responding to the Experiences of Children*, Chichester, John Wiley & Sons/NSPCC.

Hetherington, R., Cooper, A. and Wilford, R. (1997) *Protecting Children: Messsages from Europe*, Dorset, Russell House.

Hewlett, S. (1993) *Child Neglect in Rich Nations*, New York, UNICEF.

Highfield School (1997) *Changing our School: Promoting Positive Behaviour*, Plymouth, Highfield School and London, Institute of Education.

Hill, M. and Aldgate, J. (1996) *Child Welfare Services: Developments in Law, Policy, Practice and Research*, London, Jessica Kingsley.

HMI (Her Majesty's Inspectorate) (1980) *Learning and Teaching in Primary 4 and Primary 7*, Edinburgh, SED.

HMI (Her Majesty's Inspectorate) (1999) *Standards and Quality in Scottish Schools 1995–1998*, Edinburgh, Scottish Office (http://www.scotland.gov.uk/library/documents-w5/sqs-01.htm).

Hodgkin and Newell (1998) *Implementation Handbook on the Convention on the Rights of the Child*, New York, UNICEF.

Holland, P. (1996) 'I've just seen a hole in the reality barrier!': children, childishness and the media in the ruins of the twentieth century, in Pilcher, J. and Wagg, S. (eds) *Thatcher's Children? Politics, Childhood and Society in the 1980s and 1990s*, London, Falmer Press.

Holman, B. (1993) Pulling together, *Guardian*, 20 January.

Holman, R. (1998) A modest proposal against inequality, in Demos, *The Good Life*, London, Demos.

Home Office (1988) *Statistical Bulletin 42: Criminal Proceedings for Offences Involving Violence Against Children*, London, Home Office.
Home Office (1998) *Supporting Families. A Consultation Document*, London, HMSO.
Home Office (1999) *Interdepartmental Working Group on Preventing Unsuitable People Working with Children and Abuse of Trust*, First Report, London, HMSO.
Horn, P. (1989) *The Edwardian and Victorian Schoolchild*, Gloucester, Alan Sutton.
House of Commons Health Committee (1997) *Health Services for Children and Young People in the Community: Home and School*, Third Report, London, Stationery Office.
House of Commons Health Committee (1998*) Children Looked After by Local Authorities*, Second Report, Vol.1, HC 319-1, London, HMSO.
Howarth, C., Kenway, P., Palmer, G. and Miorelli, R. (1999) *Monitoring Poverty and Social Exclusion*, York, Joseph Rowntree Foundation.
Howe, D. (1994) Modernity, Postmodernity and Social Work, *British Journal of Social Work*, **24**: 513–32.
Howells, J.H. (1974) *Remember Maria*, London, John H. Butterworth.
Howitt, D. (1992) *Child Abuse Errors: When Good Intentions go Wrong*, Hemel Hempstead, Harvester Wheatsheaf.
Howitt, D. and Owusu-Bempah, J. (1990) The pragmatics of institutional racism: beyond words, *Human Relations*, **43**: 885–9.
Howitt, D. and Owusu-Bempah, J. (1994) *The Racism of Psychology: Time for Change*, Hemel Hempstead, Harvester Wheatsheaf.
Howitt, D. and Owusu-Bempah, K. (1999) Education, psychology and the construction of black childhood, *Educational and Child Psychology*, **16**: 17–29.
Hughes, H. (1988) Psychological and behavioural correlates of family violence in child witnesses and victims, *American Journal of Orthopsychiatry*, **58**: 77–90.
Hughes, M. and Luke, D. (1998) Heterogeneity in adjustment among children of battered women, in Holden, G., Geffner, R. and Jouriles, E. (eds) *Children Exposed to Marital Violence*, Washington DC, American Psychological Association.
Humphreys, C. (1999a) The judicial alienation syndrome: failures in response to post-separation violence, *Family Law Journal* (June): 1–4.
Humphreys, C. (1999b) Avoidance and confrontation: social work practice in relation to domestic violence and child abuse, *Child and Family Social Work*, **4**(1): 77–88.
Humphreys, C., Athar, S. and Baldwin, N. (1999) Discrimination in child protection work: recurring themes in work with Asian families, *Child and Family Social Work*, **4**: 283–91.
Humphreys, C., Hester, M., Hague, G., Mullender, A., Abrahams, H. and Lowe, P. (2000) *From Good Intentions to Good Practice: Working with Families where there is Domestic Violence*, Bristol, Policy Press (in press).
Hurt, J.S. (1979) *Elementary Schooling and the Working Class 1860–1918*, London, Routledge & Kegan Paul.
Hutchby, I. and Moran-Ellis, J. (eds) (1998) *Children and Social Competence: Arenas of Action*, London, Falmer Press.
Hutchfield, K. (1999) Family centred care: a concept analysis, *Journal of Advanced Nursing*, **29**(5): 1178–87.
Hylton, C. (1997) *Black Families' Survival Strategies: Ways of Coping in UK Society*, York, Joseph Rowntree Foundation.
Iman, U. (1994) Asian children and domestic violence, in Mullender, A. and Morley, R. (eds) *Children Living with Domestic Violence: Putting Men's Abuse of Women on the Child Care Agenda*, London, Whiting & Birch.
INRA (Europe) (1998) *Europeans and Their Views on Child Sex Tourism*, Eurobarometer 49, European Commission, Brussels.
Institute for Fiscal Studies (1999) *Poor Kids: Trends in Child Poverty in Britain, 1968–96*.
International Save the Children Alliance (1999) *Children's Rights: Reality of Rhetoric?*, London, Save the Children Alliance.

Investors in People, UK website: http://www.iipuk.co.uk

Jack, G. (1997) An ecological approach to social work with children and families, *Child and Family Social Work*, **2**: 109–20.

Jack, G. (1998) The social ecology of parents and children: implications for the development of child welfare services in the UK, *International Journal of Child and Family Welfare*, **98**(1): 74–88.

Jack, G. (2001) Ecological influences on parenting and child development, *British Journal of Social Work* (in press).

Jack, G. and Jordan, B. (1999) Social capital and child welfare, *Children and Society*, **13**: 242–56.

Jackson, T. and Marks, N. (1998) Found wanting, in Demos, *The Good Life*, London, Demos.

Jaffe, P., Wolfe, D. and Wilson, S. (1990) *Children of Battered Women*, Newbury Park, CA, Sage.

James, A. and Prout, A. (1996) Strategies and structures: towards a new perspective on children's experiences of family life, in Brannen, J. and O'Brien, M. (eds) *Children in Families. Research and Policy*, London, Falmer Press.

James, A. and Prout, A. (eds) (1997) *Constructing and Reconstructing Childhood: Contemporary Issues in the Sociological Study of Childhood*, London, Falmer Press.

James. G. (1994) *Discussion report for ACPC Conference 1994: Study of Working Together 'Part 8' Reports*, ACPC Series Report No. 1, London, DoH.

Jeffs, T. and Smith, M.K. (1996) 'Getting the dirt-bags off the street': curfews and other solutions to juvenile crime', *Youth and Policy*, **53**: 1–14.

Jenks, C. (1996) *Childhood*, London, Routledge.

Jensen, J.J. (1995) *Men as Workers in Childcare Services*, Brussels, European Commission Equal Opportunities Unit.

Jobling, M. (1978) Child abuse: the historical and social context, in Carver, V. (ed.) *Child Abuse: A Study Text*, Milton Keynes, Open University.

John, M. (ed.) (1996) *Children in Charge: The Child's Right to a Fair Hearing*, London, Jessica Kingsley.

Johnstone, M., Munn, P. and Edwards, L. (1991) *Action Against Bullying: A Support Pack for Schools*, Edinburgh, Scottish Council for Research in Education.

Jones, J.M. (1972) *Prejudice and Racism*, Reading, MA, Addison-Wesley.

Jones, L. and Tucker, S. (2000) Exploring continuity and change, in Brechin, A., Brown, H. and Eby, M. (eds) *Critical Practice in Health and Social Care*, London, Sage/Open University.

Joseph Rowntree Foundation (1999) *Small Fortunes*, London, Joseph Rowntree Foundation.

Kawachi, I., Kennedy, B.P., Lochner, K. and Prothrow-Smith, D. (1997) Social capital, income inequality and mortality, *American Journal of Public Health*, **87**: 1491–8.

Kelly, L. (1996) When women protection is the best kind of child protection: children, domestic violence and child abuse, *Administration*, **44**(2): 118–35.

Kelly, L., Regan, L. and Burton, S. (1991) *An Exploratory Study of the Prevalence of Sexual Abuse in a Sample of 16–21 Year Olds*, London, Child and Woman Abuse Studies Unit, University of North London.

Kemps, C. (1997) Approaches to working with ethnicity and cultural differences, in Dwivedi, K.N. (ed.) *Enhancing Parenting Skills. A Guide for Professionals Working with Parents*, Chichester, John Wiley & Sons.

Khan, J. and Russell, P. (1999) *Quality Protects: First Analysis of Management Action Plans with Reference to Disabled Children and Families*, London, Council for Disabled Children.

Kilbrandon, C.S. (1964) *Report of the Committee on Children and Young Persons, Scotland* (The Kilbrandon Report), Cmnd 2306, Edinburgh, HMSO.

Kirkbride, L. (1999) *I'll Go First: The Planning and Review Toolkit for Use with Children with Disabilities*, London, Children's Society.

Kirkwood, A. (1993) *The Leicestershire Inquiry 1992*, Leicester, Leicestershire County Council.

Kitzinger, J. (1997) Who are you kidding? Children, power and the struggle against sexual abuse, in James, A. and Prout, A. (eds) *Constructing and Reconstructing Childhood*, London, Falmer Press.

Kline, S. (1993) *Out of the Garden: Toys, TV and Children's Culture in the Age of Marketing*, London, Verso.

Kroll, B. (1995) Working with children, in Kaganas, F., King, M. and Piper, C. (eds) *Legislating for Harmony: Partnership Under the Children Act 1989*, London, Jessica Kingsley.

Kumar, V. (1993) *Poverty and Inequality in the UK: The Effects on Children*, London, National Children's Bureau.

Lakey, J. (1997) Neighbourhoods and housing, in Modood, T., Berthoud, R., Lakey, J. *et al.* (1997) *Ethnic Minorities in Britain: Diversity and Disadvantage*, London, Policy Studies Institute.

Lane, J. (1999) *Action for Race Equality in the Early Years: Understanding the Past, Thinking About the Present, Planning for the Future: A Practical Handbook for Early Years Workers*, London, National Early Years Network.

Lansdown, G. (1995) *Taking Part. Children's Participation in Decision-making*, London, Institute for Public Policy Research.

Lansdown, G. (1996) *Taking Part*, London, Institute for Public Policy Research.

Lansdown, G. and Newell, P. (eds) (1994) *UK Agenda for Children*, London, Children's Rights Office.

Lauritzen, S.O. (1997) Notions of child health: mothers' accounts of health in their young babies, *Sociology of Health and Illness*, **19**(4): 436–56.

Lavalette, M. (1999) The 'new sociology of childhood' and child labour: childhood, children's rights and 'children's voice', in Lavalette, M. (ed.) *A Thing of the Past: Child Labour in Britain in the Nineteenth and Twentieth Centuries*, Liverpool, Liverpool University Press.

Law Commission (1998) LCD Consultation Paper, February, London.

Leach, P. (1999) *The Physical Punishment of Children*, London, NSPCC.

Lealand, G. (1998) Where do snails watch television: pre-school television and New Zealand children, in Howard, S. (ed.) *Wired-up: Young People and the Electronic Media*, London, UCL Press.

Lee, N. (1999) The challenge of childhood: distributions of childhood's ambiguity in adult institutions, *Childhood*, **6**(4): 455–74.

Levy, A. and Kahan, B. (1991) *The Pindown Experience and the Protection of Children: The Report of the Staffordshire Child Care Enquiry*, Staffordshire, Staffordshire County Council.

Lewis, J. (1984) *Women in England. 1870–1950. Sexual Divisions and Social Change, 1870–1950*, Brighton, Wheatsheaf.

Liddle, A.M. (1993) Gender desire and child sex abuse: accounting for the male majority, *Theory, Culture and Society*, **10**: 103–26.

Little, M. and Mount, K. (1999) *Prevention and Early Intervention with Children in Need*, Aldershot, Ashgate.

Littlewood, R. and Lipsedge, M. (1989) *Aliens and Alienists: Ethnic Minorities and Psychiatry*, 2nd edn, London, Unwin Hyman.

Llewellyn Davies, M. (1915) *Maternity: Letters from Working Women*, Reprinted 1978, London, Virago.

Lobo, E. (1987) *Children of Immigrants to Britain: Their Health and Social Problems*, London, Allen & Unwin.

Lockyer, A. and Stone, F.H. (1998) *Juvenile Justice in Scotland: Twenty-five Years of The Welfare Approach*, Edinburgh, T & T Clark.

London Borough of Brent (1985) *A Child in Trust: Report of the Panel of Inquiry Investigating the Circumstances Surrounding the Death of Jasmine Beckford*, London, London Borough of Brent.

London Borough of Greenwich (1987) *A Child in Mind: Protection of Children in a Responsible Society: Report of the Commission of Enquiry Surrounding the Death of Kimberley Carlile*, London, London Borough of Greenwich.

Lord Chancellor's Department Consultation Paper (1998) *Procedures for the Determination of Paternity and on the Law on Parental Responsibility for Unmarried Fathers*, London, Lord Chancellor's Department.

Lowe, R. (ed.) (1992) *Education and the Second World War. Studies in Schooling and Social Change*, London, Falmer Press.

Lubelska, A. (1993) Promoting play, in Lubelska, A. (ed.) *Better Play*, London, National Children's Bureau/National Voluntary Council for Children's Play.

Lupton, D. (1994) *Medicine as Culture. Illness, Disease and the Body in Western Societies*, London, Sage.

Lyle, S., Benyon, J., Garland, J. and McClure, A. (1996) *Education Matters: African Caribbean People and Schools in Leicestershire*, Scarman Centre, University of Leicester.

Maccoby, E. (1980) *Social Development: Psychological Growth and the Parent–Child Relationship*, New York, Harcourt Brace Jovanovitch.

Macdonald, G. and Roberts, H. (1995) *What Works in the Early Years?*, Barkingside, Barnardos.

Mackay, T. (1998) Education and the disadvantaged: is there any justice? Paper presented at the British Psychological Society Annual Conference, Brighton.

MacLeod, M. (1999) Don't just do it: children's access to help and protection, in Parton, N. and Wattam, C. (eds) *Child Sexual Abuse: Responding to the Experiences of Children*, Chichester, John Wiley & Sons/NSPCC.

MacLeod, M. and Saraga, E. (1988) Challenging the orthodox: towards a feminist theory and practice, *Feminist Review*, **23**: 15–55.

MacMillan, H.L., MacMillan, J.H., Offord, D.R., Griffith, L. and MacMillan, A., (1994) Primary prevention of child physical abuse: a critical review (Part 1), *Journal of Child Psychology and Psychiatry*, **35**(5): 835–56.

Macnicol, J. (1992) Welfare, wages and the family. Child endowment in comparative perspective, 1900–50, in Cooter, R. (ed.) *In the Name of the Child, Health and Welfare 1880–1940*, London, Routledge.

Macpherson, Sir W. (1999) *The Stephen Lawrence Inquiry*, London, HMSO (http://www.official-documents.co.uk/document/cm42/4262/sli-46.htm).

McCloskey, L., Figueredo, A. and Koss, P. (1995) The effects of systemic family violence on children's mental health, *Child Development*, **66**: 1239–61.

McConahie, H. (1997) Organisation of child disability services. *Child: Care, Health and Development*, **23**(1): 3–9.

McFarlane, A.H., Bellissimo, A. and Norman, G.R. (1995) Family structure, family functioning and adolescent well-being, *Journal of Child Psychology and Psychiatry*, **36**(5): 847–64.

McGee, C. (2001) *King of the Castle: Children's and Mother's Experiences of Child Protection following Domestic Violence*, London, Jessica Kingsley (in press).

Maker, A., Kemmelmeier, M. and Peterson, C. (1998) Long-term psychological consequences in women of witnessing parental physical conflict and experiencing abuse in childhood, *Journal of Interpersonal Violence*, **13**: 574–89.

Malcolm, H. and Byrne, M. (1995) *Interchange 36: Implementing 5–14 in Primary Schools*, Edinburgh, SOEID.

Malcolm, H. and Simpson, M. (1997) *Interchange 49: Implementing 5–14. Steady Development?*, Edinburgh, SOEID.

Mama, A. (1996) *The Hidden Struggle: Statutory and Voluntary Sector Responses to Violence Against Black Women in the Home*, London, Whiting & Birch.

Marchant, R. and Martyn, M. (1999) *Make it Happen: Communication Handbook*, Brighton, Triangle.

Marchant, R., Jones, M., Julyan, A. and Giles, A. (1999) *Listening on all Channels: Consulting with Disabled Children*, Brighton, Triangle.

Marsh, P. and Fisher, M. (1992) *Good Intentions: Developing Partnership in Social Services*, York, Joseph Rowntree Foundation/Community Care.

Marshall, K. (1997) *Children's Rights in the Balance: the Participation–Protection Divide*, London, Stationery Office.

Masson, J. and Oakley, M.W. (1999) *Out of Hearing: Representing Children in Care Proceedings*, Chichester, John Wiley & Sons.

Mause, L. de (ed.) (1976) *The History of Childhood*, London, Souvenir Press.

Mayall, B. (1994) *Negotiating Health: Children at Home and Primary School*, London, Cassell.

Mayall, B. (1996) *Children, Health and the Social Order*, Buckingham, Open University Press.

Mayall, B. (2001) Children's understandings of childhood, in Alanen, L. and Mayall, B. (eds) *Conceptualizing Child–Adult Relations*, London, Falmer Press.

Mayall, B. and Foster, M.C. (1989) *Child Health Care: Living with Children, Working for Children*, Oxford, Heinemann Educational.

Mayall, B. and Storey, P. (1998) A school health service for children?, *Children and Society*, 12(2): 98–100.

Mayall, B., Bendelow, G., Barker, S., Storey, P. and Veltman, M. (1996) *Children's Health in Primary Schools*, Buckingham, Open University Press.

Mental Health Foundation (1999) *Bright Futures – Promoting Children and Young People's Mental Health*, London, The Mental Health Foundation.

Mercer, K. (1984) Black communities' experience of psychiatric services, *International Journal of Social Psychiatry*, 30(1–2): 22–7.

Meyer, P. (1996) Sexuality and power: perspectives for the less powerful, *Theory and Psychology*, 6: 93–119.

Mezey, G. and Bewley, S. (1997) Domestic violence and pregnancy, *British Journal of Obstetrics and Gynaecology*, 104: 528–31.

Mickelwright, J. and Stewart, K. (1998) *Is Child Welfare Converging in the European Union?*, Florence, UNICEF.

Middleton, L. (1996) *Making a Difference: Social Work with Disabled Children*, Birmingham, Venture Press.

Middleton, L. (1999) *Disabled Children: Challenging Social Exclusion*, Oxford, Blackwell.

Miles, R. (1994) *The Children We Deserve*, London, HarperCollins.

Millham, S., Bullock, K., Haak, M. and Hosie, K. (1986) *Lost in Care*, Aldershot, Gower.

Milner, P. and Carolin, B. (eds) (1999) *Time to Listen to Children*, London, Routledge.

Mirrlees-Black, C. (1999) *British Crime Survey 1996 Domestic Violence Findings*, London, Home Office.

Mirrlees-Black, C., Mayhew, P. and Percy, A. (1996) *The British Crime Survey, England and Wales*, Home Office Statistical Bulletin, London, Research and Statistics Directorate.

Modood, T. (1997) Employment, in Modood, T., Berthoud, R., Lakey, J. *et al.* (1997) *Ethnic Minorities in Britain: Diversity and Disadvantage*, London, Policy Studies Institute.

Modood, T., Berthoud, R., Lakey, J. *et al.* (1997) *Ethnic Minorities in Britain: Diversity and Disadvantage*, London, Policy Studies Institute.

Mooney, J. (1994) *The Hidden Figure: Domestic Violence in North London*, London, Islington Police and Crime Prevention Unit.

Moore, T. and Pepler, D. (1998) Correlates of adjustment in children at risk, in Holden, G., Geffner, R. and Jouriles, E. (eds) *Children Exposed to Marital Violence*, Washington DC, American Psychological Association.

Moorhead, J. (1999) Out of the Mouths of Babes, *Guardian*, June 2, pp. 9–10.

Morris, J. (1995) *Gone Missing? A Research and Policy Review of Disabled Children Living away from their Families*, London, Who Cares? Trust.

Morris, J. (1998) *Still Missing?*, London, Who Cares? Trust/Joseph Rowntree Foundation.

Morris, J. (1998a) *Accessing Human Rights: Disabled Children and the Children Act*, London, Barnados.

Morris, J. (1998b) *Still Missing?* Vol. 2: *Disabled Children and the Children Act*, London, Who Cares? Trust.

Morris, J. (1998c) *Don't Leave Us Out: Involving Children and Young People with Communication Impairments*, York, York Publishing Services.

Morris, J. (1999a) Disabled children, child protection systems and the Children Act 1989, *Child Abuse Review*, **8**: 91–108.

Morris, J. (1999b) *Space for Us: Finding Out what Disabled Children and Young People Think about their Placements*, London, Newham Social Services Department.

Morrison, B. (1997) *As If*, London, Granta Books.

Morton, A. (1997) *Education and the State from 1833*, London, Public Records Office.

Moules, T. and Ramsay, J. (1998) *The Textbook of Children's Nursing*, Cheltenham, Stanley Thornes.

Mullender, A. (1996) *Re-thinking Domestic Violence: The Social Work and Probation Response*, London, Routledge.

Mullender, A. and Humphreys, C. (1998) *Domestic Violence and Child Abuse: Policy and Practice Issues for Local Authorities and Other Agencies*, London, Local Government Association.

Mullender, A. and Morley, R. (1994) *Children Living with Domestic Violence: Putting Men's Abuse of Women on the Child Care Agenda*, London, Whiting & Birch.

Mullender, A., Kelly, L., Hague, G., Malos, E. and Imam, U. (2000) *Children's Needs, Coping Strategies and Understandings of Woman Abuse*, End of award report submitted to the ERSC. Award no. L129 251037, Coventry, University of Warwick (in press).

Muncie, J. (1984) *The Trouble with Kids Today*, London, Hutchinson.

Muncie, J. (1999a) *Youth and Crime: A Critical Introduction*, London, Sage.

Muncie, J. (1999b) Institutionalised intolerance: youth justice and the 1998 Crime and Disorder Act, *Critical Social Policy*, **19**(2): 147–75.

Muncie, J. and McLaughlin, E. (eds) (1996) *The Problem of Crime*, London, Sage.

Murray, S.B. (1996) 'We all love Charles': men in child care and the social construction of gender, *Gender and Society*, **10**(4): 369–85.

NFCA (National Foster Care Association) (1997) *Foster Care in Crisis: A Call to Professionalise the Forgotten Service*, London, National Foster Care Association.

NAHA (National Association of Health Authorities) (1988) *Action Not Words: A Strategy To Improve Health Services For Black and Minority Ethnic Groups*, Birmingham, NAHA.

National Children's Bureau (2000) *Stepfamilies*, Highlight No. 76, London, National Children's Bureau.

National Children's Homes (1992) *The Report of the Committee of Inquiry into Children and Young People who Sexually Abuse Other Children*, London, National Children's Homes.

National Curriculum Council (1990) *Education for Citizenship*, London, National Curriculum Council.

National Union of Teachers (1997) *Crumbling Schools, Parliamentary Briefing*, London, National Union of Teachers.

Neill, A.S. (1976) *Summerhill*, Harmondsworth, Penguin.

Newburn, T. (1996) Back to the future? Youth crime, youth justice and the rediscovery of 'authoritarian populism', in Pilcher, J. and Wagg, S. (eds) *Thatcher's Children? Politics, Childhood and Society in the 1980s and 1990s*, London, Falmer Press.

Newell, P. (2000) *Taking Children Seriously – a Proposal for a Children's Rights Commissioner*, London, Calouste Gulbenkian Foundation.

Newson, J. and Newson, E. (1978) *Seven Years Old in the Home Environment*, Harmondsworth, Penguin.

Norrie, K. McK. (1997) *Children's Hearings in Scotland*, Edinburgh, W. Green & Sons.

Noyes, J. (1999) The impact of knowing your child is critically ill: a qualitative study of mothers experiences, *Journal of Advanced Nursing*, **29**(2): 427–35.

Nussbaum, M. (1995) Human capabilities, female human beings, in Nussbaum, M. and Glover, J. (eds) (1995) *Women Culture and Development: A Study of Human Capabilities*, Oxford, Clarendon.

Nussbaum, M. and Glover, J. (eds) (1995) *Women Culture and Development: A Study of Human Capabilities*, Oxford, Clarendon.

Office for National Statistics (1999) Live births in England and Wales, *Population Trends*, No. **96**, London, Stationery Office.

Offner, A. (ed.) (1996) *In Pursuit of the Quality of Life*, Oxford, Oxford University Press.

Ogilvy, C.M., Boath, E.H., Cheyne, W.M., Jahoda, G. and Schaffer, H.R. (1990) Staff attitudes and perceptions in multi-cultural nursery schools, *Early Child Development and Care*, **64**: 1–13.

O'Halloran, K. (1999) *The Welfare of the Child – the Principle and the Law*, Aldershot, Ashgate Arena.

O'Hara, M. (1994) Child deaths in the context of domestic violence: implications for professional practice, in Mullender, A. and Morley, R. (eds) *Children Living with Domestic Violence: Putting Men's Abuse of Women on the Child Care Agenda*, London, Whiting & Birch.

O'Keefe, M. (1994) Linking marital violence, mother–child/father–child aggression, and child behavior problems, *Journal of Family Violence*, **9**: 63–78.

O'Keefe, M. (1995) Predictors of child abuse in maritally violent families, *Journal of Interpersonal Violence*, **10**: 3–25.

Oldfield, N. (1997) *The Adequacy of Foster Care Allowances*, Aldershot, Ashgate.

Olds, D.L., Henderson, C.R. and Kitzman, H. (1994) Does parental and infancy nurse home visitation have enduring effects on qualities of parental caregiving and child health at 25 and 50 months of life?, *Pediatrics*, **93**(l): 89–98.

Oliver, M. (1999) *Understanding Disability: From Theory to Practice*, London, Macmillan.

One Plus One Marriage and Partnership Research (1999) Information Pack, 2nd edn, London, One Plus One.

OPCS (Office of Population Censuses and Surveys) (1986) *Surveys of Disability in Great Britain, Reports 1–6*, London, HMSO.

Oppenheim, C. and Lister, R. (1996) The politics of child poverty 1979–1995, in Pilcher, J. and Wagg, S. (eds) *Thatcher's Children? Politics, Childhood and Society in the 1980s and 1990s*, London, Falmer Press.

Orr, F.E. (1999) The role of the paediatric nurse in promoting paediatric right to consent, *Journal of Clinical Nursing*, **8**: 291–8.

Owusu-Bempah, J. (1994a) Race, self-identity and social work, *British Journal of Social Work*; **24**: 123–36.

Owusu-Bempah, J. (1994b) Theory versus reality, *Community Care*, 1–7 December, p. 15.

Owusu-Bempah, J. (1997) Race, in Davies, M. (ed.) *The Blackwell Companion to Social Work*, Oxford, Basil Blackwell.

Owusu-Bempah, K. (1999a) Confidentiality and social work practice in African cultures, in Compton, B.R. and Gallaway, B. (eds) *Social Work Processes*, 6th edn, Pacific Grove, CA, Brooks/Cole.

Owusu-Bempah, K. (1999b) Race, culture and the child, in Tunstill, T. (ed.) *Children and the State: Whose Problem?*, London, Cassell.

Palmer, S.J. (1993) Care of sick children: a meaningful role, *Journal of Advanced Nursing*, **18**: 185–91.

Parton, N. (1985) *The Politics of Child Abuse*, Basingstoke, Macmillan.

Parton, N. (1991) *Governing the Family, Child Care, Child Protection and the State*, London, Macmillan.

Parton, N., Thorpe D. and Wattam, C. (1997) *Child Protection: Risk and the Moral Order*, London, Macmillan.

Parton, N. and Wattam, C. (1999) Impediments to implementing a child-centred approach, in Parton, N. and Wattam, C. (eds) *Child Sexual Abuse: Responding to the Experiences of Children*, Chichester, John Wiley & Sons/NSPCC.

Payne, M. (1991) *Modern Social Work Theory: a Critical Introduction*, Basingstoke, Macmillan.

Pearlman, M., Tintinalli, J. and Lorenz, R. (1990) Blunt trauma during pregnancy, *New England Journal of Medicine*, **323**: 1609–13.

Pearson, G. (1983) *Hooligan: A History of Respectable Fears*, London, Macmillan.

Pedler, M., Burgoyne, J. and Boydell, T. (1991) *The Learning Company: A Strategy for Sustainable Development*, Maidenhead, McGraw-Hill.

Penn, H. and McQuail, S. (1997) *Childcare as a gendered occupation*, Research Report No. 23, London, HMSO/DfEE.

Percy-Smith, J. (1996) Assessing community needs, in Percy-Smith, J. (ed.) *Needs Assessment in Public Policy*, Buckingham, Open University Press.

Piaget, J. (1950) *The Psychology of Intelligence*, London, Routledge & Kegan Paul.

Pinkerton, J. and Houston, S. (1996) Competence and the Children Act in O'Hagan, K. (ed.) *Competence in Social Work Practice*, London, Jessica Kingsley.

Pinkerton, J. and McLoughlin, J. (1996) Ethical dilemmas in practice – some thoughts on the Children (NI) Order, *Child Care in Practice*, **1**(4): 40–51.

Pinkerton, J., Scott, B. and O'Kane, P. (1997) *Partnership Practice with Parents and Carers: An Approach to Practitioner Self Evaluation*, Belfast, Centre for Child Care Research, Queen's University.

Pollard, D.S. (1989) Against the odds: a profile of academic achievers from the urban underclass, *Journal of Negro Education*, **58**: 297–309.

Popple, K. (1995) *Analysing Community Work, its Theory and Practice*, Buckingham, Open University Press.

Pottage, D. and Evans, M. (1994) *The Competent Workplace: The View from Within*, London, NISW.

Prewett, E. (1999) *Short Term Break, Long Term Benefit: Family Based Short Term Care for Disabled Children and Adults*, Bristol, University of Sheffield/Joseph Rowntree Foundation.

Priestley, M. (1998) Childhood disability and disabled childhoods: agendas for research, *Childhood*, **5**(2): 207–23.

Pringle, K. (1992) Child sexual abuse perpetrated by welfare personnel and the problem of men, *Critical Social Policy*, (36): 4–19.

Pringle, K. (1995) *Men, Masculinities and Social Welfare*, London, UCL Press.

Pringle, K. (1998a) *Children and Social Welfare in Europe*, Buckingham, Open University Press.

Pringle, K. (1998b) Men and childcare: policy and practice, in Popay, J., Hearn, J. and Edwards, J. (eds) *Men, Gender Divisions and Welfare*, London, Routledge.

Prout, A. (1999) Living Arrows, in *The Parenting Forum Newsletter*, Summer; see also research now emerging from the ESRC Research Programme on Children and Childhood.

Pugh, G., De'Ath, E. and Smith, C. (1994) *Confident Parents, Confident Children. Policy and Practice in Parent Education and Support*, London, National Children's Bureau.

Qvortrup, J. (1994) Childhood matters: an introduction, in Qvortrup, J., Bardy, M., Sgritta, G. and Wintersberger, H. (eds) *Childhood Matters. Social Theory, Practice and Politics*, Aldershot, Avebury.

Qvortrup, J., Bardy, M., Sgritta, G. and Wintersberger, H. (eds) (1994) *Childhood Matters: Social Theory, Practice and Politics*, European Centre Vienna, Avebury.

Reder, P., Duncan, S. and Gray, M. (1993) *Beyond Blame: Child Abuse Tragedies Revisited*, London, Routledge.

Ribbens, J. (1994) *Mothers and their Children. A Feminist Sociology of Childrearing*, London, Sage.

Richards, M. (1974) *The Integration of a Child into a Social World*, London, Cambridge University Press.

Riddington, J. (1989) *Beating the 'Odds': Violence and Women with Disabilities*, Position Paper No. 2, Vancouver, DisAbled Women's Network, Canada.

Robb, M., Doting or dangerous? Newspaper stories about men and children, unpublished research report.

Robertson, P. (1999) Expressive arts, in Bryce, T.G.K. and Humes, W. (eds) *Scottish Education*, Edinburgh, Edinburgh University Press.

Roche, J. (1999) Children: rights, participation and citizenship, *Childhood*, **6**(4): 475–93.

Rodgers, B. and Prior, J. (1998) *Divorce and Separation. The Outcomes for Children*, York, Joseph Rowntree Foundation.

Rogoff, B. (1991) The joint socialisation of development by young children and adults, in Light, P., Sheldon, S. and Woodhead, M. (eds) *Learning to Think. Child Development in a Social Context*, London, Routledge.

Rose, N. (1985) *The Psychological Complex: Psychology, Politics and Society in England 1869–1939*, London, Routledge & Kegan Paul.

Rosenbaum, M. (1993) *Children and the Environment*, London, National Children's Bureau.

Ross, S. (1996) Risk of physical abuse to children of spouse abusing parents, *Child Abuse and Neglect*, **20**(7): 589–98.

Russell, P. (1995) *Positive Choices: Services for Disabled Children Living away from Home*, London, Council for Disabled Children.

Russell, P. (1998) *Having a Say: Disabled Children and Effective Partnership in Decision Making*: Section 1: *The Report*, London, Council for Disabled Children.

Rutter, M. (1981) *Maternal Deprivation Reassessed*, 2nd edn, Harmondsworth, Penguin.

Rutter, S. and Seyman, S. (1999) *'He'll Never Join the Army': A Report on a Survey into Attitudes to People with Down's Syndrome Amongst Medical Professionals*, London, Down's Syndrome Association.

Ruxton, S. (1992) *What's he Doing at the Family Centre? The Dilemmas of Men who Care for Children*, London, NCH Action for Children.

Ruxton, S. (1994) Men – too dangerous to work with children?, *Working with Men*, **1**: 16–20.

Ruxton, S. (1996) *Children in Europe*, London, NCH Action for Children.

Ruxton, S. (2001) *Separated Children in Europe: A European Programme of Action*, International Save the Children Alliance/UNHCR (in press).

Ryan, M. (1994) *The Children Act 1989 – Putting it into Practice*, London, Macmillan.

Ryan, T. and Walker, R. (1993) *Life Story Work*, London, BAAF.

Sanderson, H. (1997) *People, Plans and Possibilities: Exploring Person-centred Planning*, Edinburgh, SHS.

Saporiti, A. (1994) A methodology for making children count, in Qvortrup, J., Bardy, M., Sgritta, G. and Wintersberger, H. (eds) *Childhood Matters. Social Theory, Practice and Politics*, Aldershot, Avebury.

Scarre, G. (ed.) (1989) *Children, Parents and Politics*, Cambridge, Cambridge University Press.

Scraton, P. (ed.) (1997) *'Childhood' in 'Crisis'?*, London, UCL Press.

Scraton, P. (1999) Threatening children: politics of hate and policies of denial in contemporary Britain, unpublished paper presented to the Organization for the Protection of Children's Rights Fourth International Conference on the Child – Children and Violence: Our Individual, Family and Collective Responsibilities.

SCRE (Scottish Council for Research in Education) (1993) *Supporting Schools Against Bullying: the Second SCRE Anti-bullying Pack*, Edinburgh, Scottish Council for Research in Education.

SED (Scottish Education Department) (1965) *Primary Education in Scotland*, the Primary Memorandum, Edinburgh, HMSO.

SED (Scottish Education Department) (1987) *Curriculum and Assessment in Scotland: A Policy for the 90s*, Edinburgh, Scottish Education Department.

SED (Scottish Education Department) (1989) *Talking about Schools: Surveys of Parents' Views on Schools Education in Scotland*, Edinburgh, HMSO.

Sellick, C. and Thoburn, J. (1996) *What Works in Family Placement?*, Barkingside, Barnardos.

Sen, A. (1993) Capability and well-being, in Sen, A. and Nussbaum, M. (eds) *The Quality of Life*, Oxford, Oxford University Press.

Sen, A. (1995) Gender, inequality and theories of justice, in Nussbaum, M. and Glover, J. (eds) *Women, Culture and Development: A Study of Human Capabilities*, Oxford, Clarendon Press.

Senge, P. (1990) *The Fifth Discipline: The Art and Practice of the Learning Organisation*, London, Century Business.

Shahar, S. (1990) *Childhood in the Middle Ages*, London, Routledge.

Shakespeare, T. and Watson, D. (1998) Theoretical perspectives on research with disabled children, in Robinson, C. and Stalker, K. (eds) *Growing up with Disability*, London, Jessica Kingsley.

Sharp, I. (1993) *Nutritional Guidelines for School Meals*, London, The Caroline Walker Trust.

Shaw, C. (1998) *Remember my Messages*, London, Who Cares? Trust.

Shaw, M. (1998) *Treatment Decisions in Young People*. Focus Information sheet, London, Royal College of Psychiatrists.

Shield, J.P.H. and Baum, J.D. (1994) Children's consent to treatment, *British Medical Journal*, **308**: 1182–3.

Shilling, C. (1993) *The Body and Social Theory*, London, Sage.

Silva, E.B. and Smart, C. (eds) (1999) *The New Family*, Sage.

Silverman, D. (1987) *Communication and Medical Practice: Social Relations in the Clinic*, London, Sage.

Skellington, R. and Morris, P. (1992) *Race in Britain Today*, London, Sage.

Smart, C. (1996) Deconstructing motherhood, in Silva, E.B. (ed.) *Good Enough Mothering? Feminist Perspectives on Lone Motherhood*, London, Routledge.

Smith, C. (2000) *Young People and Family Change – their Shout*, London, Parentline Plus.

Smith, F. (1995) *Children's Nursing in Practice: The Nottingham Model*, Oxford, Blackwell.

Smith, P. and Berridge, D. (1993) *Ethnicity and Childcare Placements*, London, National Children's Bureau.

Smith, T. (1992) Family centres, children in need and the Children Act 1989, in Gibbons, J. (ed.) *The Children Act 1989 and Family Support: Principles into Practice*, London, HMSO.

Smith, T. (1999) Neighbourhood and preventive strategies with children and families: what works?, *Children and Society*, **13**: 265–77.

Social Exclusion Unit (1998) *Truancy and Social Exclusion Report*, London, Social Exclusion Unit, website: www.cabinet.office.gov.uk/seu.

Social Policy Research Unit (1997) *Social Focus on Families*, York, University of York.

SOED (Scottish Office Education Department) (1991a) *National Guidelines: English Language 5–14*, Edinburgh, HMSO

SOED (Scottish Office Education Department) (1991b) *National Guidelines: Mathematics 5–14*, Edinburgh, HMSO.

SOED (Scottish Office Education Department) (1991c) *National Guidelines: Assessment 5–14*, Edinburgh, HMSO.

SOED (Scottish Office Education Department) (1992a) *National Guidelines: Expressive Arts 5–14*, Edinburgh, HMSO.

SOED (Scottish Office Education Department) (1992b) *National Guidelines: Religious and Moral Education 5–14*, Edinburgh, HMSO.

SOED (Scottish Office Education Department) (1992c) *National Guidelines: Reporting 5–14*, Edinburgh, HMSO.

SOED (Scottish Office Education Department) (1992d) *Using Performance Indicators in Primary School Self Evaluation*, Edinburgh, HMSO.

SOED (Scottish Office Education Department) (1993a) *National Guidelines: Environmental Studies 5–14*, Edinburgh, HMSO.

SOED (Scottish Office Education Department) (1993b) *National Guidelines: Gaelic 5–14*, Edinburgh, HMSO.

SOED (Scottish Office Education Department) (1993c) *National Guidelines: Personal and Social Development 5–14*, Edinburgh, HMSO.

SOED (Scottish Office Education Department) (1993d) *National Guidelines: The Structure and Balance of the Curriculum 5–14*, Edinburgh, HMSO.

SOEID (Scottish Office Education and Industry Department) (1996) *How Good is our School?: Self-evaluation using Performance Indicators*, Edinburgh, Scottish Office Education and Industry Department.

Stainton-Rogers, R. (1989) The social construction of childhood, in Stainton-Rogers, W., Hevey, D., Roche, J. and Ask, E. (eds) *Child Abuse and Neglect: Facing the Challenge*, 2nd edn (1992), London, Batsford.

Stanko, E., Crisp, D., Hale, C. and Lucraft, H. (1998) *Counting the Costs: Estimating the Impact of Domestic Violence in the London Borough of Hackney*, London, Crime Concern.

Stanley, L. and Wise, S. (1993) *Breaking Out Again. Feminist Ontology and Epistemology*, London, Routledge.

Stein, M., Johnstone, D., Crawshaw, M. and Bingley Miller, L. (1999) *Making Research Count*, Theorising Social Work Research, http://www.nisw.org.uk/tswr/stein.html

Stern, V. (1998) *A Sin Against the Future: Imprisoned in the World*, London, Penguin.

Stock, B. (1994) *Health and Safety in Schools*, 2nd edn, Kingston-upon-Thames, Croner Publications.

Stronach, I. (1999) On being the nation again: alternative visions for Scottish education. The 1999 SERA Lecture, presented at the Annual Conference of the Scottish Educational Research Association, Dundee.

Strong, P.M. (1979) *The Ceremonial Order of the Clinic: Parents, Doctors and Medical Bureaucracies*, London, Routledge & Kegan Paul.

Suransky, V. (1982) *The Erosion of Childhood*, Chicago, University of Chicago Press.

Sutherland, E. (1999) *Child and Family Law*, Edinburgh, T & T Clark. The Children's Hearing System at pp386–431.

Swanwick, M. (1995) Power where it belongs, *Child Health*, **2**(6): 232–6.

Tatum, C. and Tucker, S. (1998) The concealed consequences of caring, *Youth and Policy*, **N61**: 12–27.

Taylor, B. (1999) Parental autonomy and consent to treatment, *Journal of Advanced Nursing*, **29**(3): 570–6.

Taylor, M. (1995) Community work and the state: the changing context of UK practice, in Craig, G. and Mayo, M. (eds) *Community Empowerment: A Reader in Participation and Development*, London, Zed Books.

Templeton, J. (1998) Listening to looked-after children, the government's response to the Utting Report, *Childright*, No. 152.

Thoburn, J., Lewis, A. and Shemmings, D. (1995) *Paternalism or Partnership? Family Involvement in the Child Protection Process*, London, HMSO.

Thomas, M. and Pierson, J. (eds) (1995) *Dictionary of Social Work*, London, Collins Educational.

Thomas, N. (2000) *Children, Family and the State: Decision-making and Child Participation*, London, Macmillan.

Thomas, N. and O'Kane, C. (1998a) *Children and Decision Making: A Summary Report*, Swansea, University of Wales Swansea, International Centre for Childhood Studies.

Thomas, N. and O'Kane, C. (1998b) When children's wishes and feelings clash with their 'best interests', *International Journal of Children's Rights*, **6**(2): 137–54.

Thomas, N. and O'Kane, C. (1999) Children's participation in reviews and planning meetings when they are 'looked after' in middle childhood, *Child and Family Social Work*, **4**(3): 221–30.

Thomas, N., O'Kane, C. and McNeill, S. (1998) *Voices with Volume* (audiotape), Swansea, University of Wales Swansea, International Centre for Childhood Studies.

Thompson, A. (2000) Why are they being failed? *Community Care*, 4–10 May.

Thompson, K. (1998) *Moral Panics*, London, Routledge.

Thompson, R.A. (1995) *Preventing Child Maltreatment Through Social Support*, London, Sage.

Thurgood, J. (1990) Active listening – a social services' perspective, in Bannister, A., Barrett, K. and Shearer, E. (eds) *Listening to Children*, Harlow, Longman.

Tisdall, K., Lavery, R. and McCrystal, P. (1998) *Child Care Law: A Comparative Review of New Legislation in Northern Ireland and Scotland*, Belfast, Centre for Child Care Research, Queens University.

Titman, W. (1994) *Special Places, Special People: The Hidden Curriculum of School Grounds*, Godalming, World Wide Fund for Nature.

Triseliotis, J., Sellick, C. and Short, R. (1995) *Foster Care: Theory and Practice*, London, Batsford.

Tucker, S. (1999) Making the link: dual 'problematization', discourse and work with young people, *Journal of Youth Studies*, **2**(3): 283–95.

Turner, B.S. (1992) *Regulating Bodies: Essays in Medical Sociology*, London, Routledge.

Turner, B.S. (1995) *Medical Power and Social Knowledge*, 2nd edn. London, Sage.

Twelvetrees, A. (1982) *Community Work*, London, Macmillan.

Twigg, J. and Atkin, K. (1993) *Carers Perceived: Policy and Practice in Informal Care*, Buckingham, Open University Press.

UK Joint Working Party on Foster Care (1999) *UK National Standards for Foster Care*, London, National Foster Care Association.

United Nations (1989) Convention on the Rights of the Child, Geneva, UN.

Urwin, C. and Sharland, E. (1992) From bodies to minds in childcare literature: advice to parents in inter-war Britain, in Cooter, R. (ed.) *In the Name of the Child, Health and Welfare 1880–1940*, London, Routledge.

Van der Eyken, W. (ed.) (1973) *Education, the Child and Society. A Documentary History 1900–1973*, London, Penguin.

Vinson, T., Baldry, W. and Hargreaves, J. (1996) Neighbourhoods, networks and child abuse, *British Journal of Social Work*, **26**: 523–43.

Wagg, S. (1996) 'Don't try to understand them': politics, childhood and the new education market, in Pilcher, J. and Wagg, S. (eds) *Thatcher's Children? Politics, Childhood and Society in the 1980s and 1990s*, London, Falmer Press.

Ward, L. (1997) *Seen and Heard: Involving Disabled Children and Young People in Research and Development Projects*, York, York Publishing Services.

Warin, J., Soloman, Y., Lewis, C. and Langford, W. (1999) *Fathers, Work and Family Life*, London, Family Policy Studies Centre.

Warner, N. (1992) *Choosing with Care: The Report of the Committee of Inquiry into the Selection, Development and Management of Staff in Children's Homes*, London, HMSO.

Warner, Lord (1999) Speech by Chairman of the Youth Justice Board, at Parentline Plus conference on the impact of family change on children and young people, June.

Warwick, I. (1999) *Breaking the Silence*, Brighton, Pavilion.

Wattam, C. and Woodward, C. (1996) 'And do I abuse my children... no!' in *Childhood Matters: Report of the National Inquiry into the Prevention of Child Abuse*, Vol. 2, background papers, London, HMSO.

Weedon, C. (1992) *Feminist Practice and Poststructuralist Theory*, Oxford, Blackwell.

Westcott, H. and Jones, D. (1999) Annotation: The abuse of disabled children, *Journal of Child Psychology and Psychiatry*, **40**(4): 497–506.

WHO (World Health Organization) Quality of Life Group (1993) Measuring Quality of Life: the Development of the World Health Organization's Quality of Life Instrument, Geneva, World Health Organization.

Wilkinson, R.G. (1996) *Unhealthy Societies: The Afflictions of Inequality*, London, Routledge.

Williams, S.J. and Bendelow, B. (1998) Introduction: emotions in social life: mapping the terrain, in Bendelow, B. and Williams, S.J. (eds) *Emotions in Social Life: Critical Themes and Contemporary Issues*, London, Routledge.

Willow, C. (1997) *Hear! Hear! Promoting Children and Young People's Democratic Participation in Local Government*, London, Local Government Information Unit in Association with the Children's Rights Office.

Wilson, A. and Mitchell, J. (1981) *Black People and the Health Service*, London, Brent Community Health Council.

Winnicott, D.W. (1958) *Collected Papers, through Paediatrics to Psycho-analysis*, London, Tavistock.

Wolf, S. (1984) A multifactorial model of deviant sexuality, paper presented at the Third International Conference of Victimology, Lisbon.

Wolfensberger, W. (1990) A most critical issue: life or death, *Changes: An International Journal of Psychology and Psychotherapy*, **8**(1): 63–73.

Women's Aid (1998) *Women's Aid Annual 1997/98 Report*, Bristol, Women's Aid Federation of England.

Woodroffe, C. and Glickmann, M. (1993) Trends in child health, in Pugh, G. (ed.) *Thirty Years of Change for Children*, London, National Children's Bureau.

Wrench, J. and Solomos, J. (eds) (1993) *Racism and Migration in Western Europe*, Oxford, Providence.

Wright, C. (1992) *Race Relations in the Primary School*, London, David Foulton.

Wright, C. (1999) Hidden depths, *Local Government Management*, **27**: 24–5.

Wyness, M. (2000) *Contesting Childhood*, London, Falmer.

Young, J. (1971) *The Drugtakers*, London, Paladin.

Young, J. (1999) *The Exclusive Society*, London, Sage.

Index

deprivation 16–17
  and quality of life 81
Deptford Children's Health Centre 13
diet 20
disability 144, 215–23
  and challenging behaviour 222
  client relationship 219–20
  communication 222–3
  definitions 217–18
  devaluation 216
  discrimination 215
  and domestic violence 144, 150
  identity and self-esteem 221
  increased risk of abuse 221–2
  intolerance 215
  link with social disadvantage 217
  needs of disabled children 219
  part of cultural identity 221
  as positive identity 221
  protective working 221–2
  services for children 218–19
  sexuality 222
  social context 215–17
  social exclusion 215–16
  understanding 223
  working with disabled children 215–23
Disability Rights Commission 1999 180
disadvantage 25, 49–50
  cycles of disadvantage 54–5
  government initiatives aimed at 191
  link with delinquency 58
  link with disability 217
  Pakistani and Bangladeshi labour
    market 46
discrimination 68
  community development initiatives
    117
  in health care of disabled children 215
Disney 28
DSS *see* Department of Social Security
dysfunctionality 38

E
EC Childcare Network 237
education 20–1
  African-Caribbean exclusion from 21
  compulsory 12, 20
  educational provision 40
  inequalities of achievement 21
  literacy and numeracy 21
  policy 30
  primary education in Scotland 151–9
  racism in 44–5
  reforms 21
  rise of formal 27
  standards in 21

Education Act 1944 12
  change in social policy 16
Education Act 1980 195
Education Act 1993 200
Education Act 1996 89
Education (Administrative Provisions Act)
  1907 13
Education (Provision of Meals) Act 1906
  12
Education Reform Act 1988 153, 185
email 24
Employment Relations Act 1999 57
empowerment 48
  of children 93
  community development as strategy for
    112–18
  devolution of power 117
  through partnership practice 249
England and Wales Children Act 1989 30
Enlightenment 28
environment 185–92
  ecological perspective on child abuse
    185–92
  influences on parents and children
    187–90
  poverty and inequality 187–8
  social support and capital 188–9
  societal and cultural factors 189–90
Equal Opportunities Commission 180
Erikson's model of psychosocial
  development 211–12
eroticization of children 161
ethnicity 42
ethology 210
EU *see* European Union
Euronet 65–6
European Convention on Human Rights
  136
European Convention on the Status of
  Children Born out of Wedlock 137
European Network of Health Promoting
  Schools 195
European Union 65–76
  actions benefiting children 66–7
  Employment Relations Act 1999 68
  impact of policy on children 67–8
  moves towards a children's policy 72–4
  need for children's policy 69–70
  Parental Leave Directive 1996 68
  policy against violence towards
    children 66
  Pregnancy Leave Directive 1992 67
  Social Chapter 1991 67
  Social Charter 1989 67
  weaknesses of approach 68–9